Post-Yugoslav Literature and Film

Post-Yugoslav Literature and Film

Fires, Foundations, Flourishes

Gordana P. Crnković

BLOOMSBURY
NEW YORK • LONDON • NEW DELHI • SYDNEY

Bloomsbury Academic
An imprint of Bloomsbury Publishing Inc

1385 Broadway	50 Bedford Square
New York	London
NY 10018	WC1B 3DP
USA	UK

www.bloomsbury.com

Bloomsbury is a registered trade mark of Bloomsbury Publishing Plc

First published 2012 by Continuum International Publishing Group
Paperback edition first published 2014

© Gordana P. Crnković, 2012, 2014

All rights reserved. No part of this publication may be reproduced or transmitted in any form or by any means, electronic or mechanical, including photocopying, recording, or any information storage or retrieval system, without prior permission in writing from the publishers.

No responsibility for loss caused to any individual or organization acting on or refraining from action as a result of the material in this publication can be accepted by Bloomsbury or the author.

Library of Congress Cataloging-in-Publication Data
A catalog record for this book is available from the Library of Congress.

ISBN: HB: 978-1-4411-7177-1
      PB: 978-1-6289-2659-0
      ePub: 978-1-4411-7586-1
      ePDF: 978-1-4411-1303-0

Typeset by Fakenham Prepress Solutions, Fakenham, Norfolk NR21 8NN

Post-Yugoslav Literature and Film

Fires, Foundations, Flourishes

Gordana P. Crnković

BLOOMSBURY
NEW YORK • LONDON • NEW DELHI • SYDNEY

Bloomsbury Academic
An imprint of Bloomsbury Publishing Inc

1385 Broadway	50 Bedford Square
New York	London
NY 10018	WC1B 3DP
USA	UK

www.bloomsbury.com

Bloomsbury is a registered trade mark of Bloomsbury Publishing Plc

First published 2012 by Continuum International Publishing Group
Paperback edition first published 2014

© Gordana P. Crnković, 2012, 2014

All rights reserved. No part of this publication may be reproduced or transmitted in any form or by any means, electronic or mechanical, including photocopying, recording, or any information storage or retrieval system, without prior permission in writing from the publishers.

No responsibility for loss caused to any individual or organization acting on or refraining from action as a result of the material in this publication can be accepted by Bloomsbury or the author.

Library of Congress Cataloging-in-Publication Data
A catalog record for this book is available from the Library of Congress.

ISBN: HB: 978-1-4411-7177-1
PB: 978-1-6289-2659-0
ePub: 978-1-4411-7586-1
ePDF: 978-1-4411-1303-0

Typeset by Fakenham Prepress Solutions, Fakenham, Norfolk NR21 8NN

CONTENTS

Acknowledgments vii
Pronunciation Guide x
Introduction: Post-Yugoslav Literature and Film, and a Different Kind of Knowledge 1

1 Foundations I: While Falling Asleep: A Trace of the Moment in Yugoslavia 11

2 Play and the Language of Community Against Rumor and the Guns: Alenka Mirković's *91.6 MHz* 40

3 Reclaiming Charisma, Resetting the Senses: Vladimir Arsenijević's *In the Hold* 63

4 The Ethics of Listening and the Grounding of a Child: Milcho Manchevski's *Before the Rain* 79

5 Foundations II: Eternal Realms and Individual Victims in Ivo Andrić's *Ex Ponto* and *Unrest* 107

6 "The Truthful Road to Me": Short Takes on Six Bosnian Films 127

7	Under the Star of Orwell: Jurica Pavičić's *Plaster Sheep* and Ante Tomić's *Nothing Should Surprise Us*	154
8	The Museum Spills Out on the Square, the Past's Challenge to the Present: The Films of Vinko Brešan	175
9	I am You and You are Me: On Liberating Anti-Nationalism	202
10	Pleasant Distractions: The Danger of Close-ups and Maja Weiss's *The Border Guard*	223
11	Foundations III: Success vs. Logic: Miroslav Krleža's *On the Edge of Reason*	245
12	Anarchists Today: *The Lazarus Project* by Aleksandar Hemon	260

Bibliography	280
Index	291

ACKNOWLEDGMENTS

I would like to thank my teachers and professors in Zagreb, the University of Zagreb, and Stanford University for their work, talent, and commitment, and for helping me grow into the place from which I could write this book: Ana Kukić, Savka Vučković, Nevenka Kapetanović, Manojlo Mandić, Gajo Petrović, Danko Grlić, Milan Kangrga, Neven Sesardić, Goran Švob, Nadežda Čačinović, Žarko Puhovski, Zoran Kravar, Gordana Slabinac, and in particular Milivoj Solar, for his enduring inspiration to so many generations of his students. At Stanford University I would especially like to thank Herbert Lindenberger, Rene Girard, and Al Gelpi. I am also deeply grateful to my colleagues in literary and cinema studies and in other disciplines for many lively conversations and for help on this book: Sanja Bahun, Nedžad Ibrahimović, Ksenija Vidmar Horvat, Mitja Velikonja, Davor Kapetanić, Polona Petek, Andrew Wachtel, Andrea Zlatar-Violić, Neven Jovanović, Andrea Feldman, and Vjeran Pavlaković. Special thanks to the late Wayne Vucinich, for pushing me to get out there, to Seattle human rights activist Peter Lippman, and to Sabrina P. Ramet, a dearly missed University of Washington colleague, for her continued friendship and support.

Pavle Levi liberally shared his film and technical expertise with me, and Elma Tatargić, Maja Pavić, Diana Nenadić, Nicole Burgund, Damir Terešak, and Boris Matić helped me obtain film stills and research materials. My colleagues at the University of Washington, and especially Tony Geist, Gary Handwerk, Katarzyna Dziwirek, Michael Biggins, and Herb Blau, have supported me persistently and gracefully. Warmest thanks go to Galya Diment and Shosh Westen.

Sabbatical leave from the University of Washington gave me an opportunity to assemble my materials and write this book, and for that I am deeply grateful.

Very special thanks to Victor Ingrassia for helping put the stills of this book in the best shape possible, and to Marjorie Perloff for her long trust in me. I would like to thank Russell Berman in particular for his comments on this book and his generous support over the years.

My gratitude also goes to my editor Haaris Naqvi for all his work and his sure handling of this project.

A big thank you is due to my friends and family who have helped in various ways and always kept things in perspective: Davorka Horvat, Dunja Rogić, Tin Ilakovac, Azra Branković, Sanja Klima, Gloria Hubacker and Rick Angel, Hing Ng and Pete Knutson, and Vlasta and Bojan Turko; and Ljuba Bjegović, Rajka, Drago and Nina Bogdanović, our late *Zeko*—Sergej Crnković, Elena and Andrei Zvonimir Crnković, Vanja, Ivica, and Neno Horvat, and Duda and Rudi Psenicka.

And lastly, warmest *hvala!* is due to my closest family—to my late mother and father, Draga and Petar Crnković, to my sister-in-law Valerie, to my brother Čedomir for his being there for me all these years, to my husband David for his humor and strength, and to my daughters Zora and Neva for their spark and their joy.

Two chapters of this book have previously been published and are reprinted here with the kind permission of the original publishers:
Chapter 4 came out as "Milcho Manchevski's "*Before the Rain* and the Ethics of Listening", in *Slavic Review* 70(1) (Spring 2011), published by the Association for Slavic, East European, and Eurasian Studies, and is reprinted here with the permission of the publisher. Chapter 5 came out as "*Ex Ponto* and *Unrest*: Victimization and 'Eternal Art'," in Wayne S.Vucinich ed., *Ivo Andrić Revisited: the Bridge Still Stands* (IAS, UC Berkeley Press, 1995), and is reprinted here with the permission of the publisher.

A group of chapters in this book owes its existence to my previous publications that provided their starting point. I am grateful to publishers for letting me use my past publications for further work.

Chapter 3 originated from the chapter "Vladimira Arsenijevicia *Pod pokładem*. Zadziwiający bohaterowie i wyzwania serbskiej transformacji," in Halina Janaszek-Ivanickova ed., *Literatury słowiańskie po roku 1989*, tom 1 (Dom Wydawniczy Elipsa:

Warsaw, 2006), and has been reworked with the kind permission of Dom Wydawniczy Elipsa, Warsaw.

Chapters 7 and 9 originated from chapters "Contemporary Croatian Literature: Under the Star of Orwell" and "Non-Nationalist Culture, Under and Above the Ground," in Sabrina P. Ramet, Konrad Clewing, and Reneo Lukić (eds), *Croatia since Independence: War, Politics, Society, Foreign Relations* (R. Oldenbourg Verlag: München, 2008), and have been reworked with the kind permission of Südost-Institut (Regensburg) and R. Oldenbourg Verlag GmbH München.

Chapter 8 originated from "The Battle for Croatia: Three Films by Vinko Brešan," in Sabrina P. Ramet and Davorka Matić (eds), *Democratic Transition in Croatia: Value Transformation, Education & Media* (Texas A & M University Press: College Station, 2007), and has been reworked with the kind permission of Texas A & M University Press.

Chapter 10 came out as "The Border Guard's Focus and the Women's Diversions: Insights of the New Slovenian Film," in Ksenija Vidmar Horvat ed., *The Future of Intercultural Dialogue: Views from the In-Between* (University of Ljubljana: Ljubljana, 2008), and has been reworked with the kind permission of the University of Ljubljana.

PRONUNCIATION GUIDE

Here is a brief guide to aid the pronunciation of names found in this book.

c = ts, as in lots
    Svjedoci   :   Svieh-doh´-tsee

č = ch, as in church
    počeo   :   poh´-chay-oh
    Milčo Mančevski   :   Meel´-choh Man´-chev-skee

ć = tj, close to č but softer like future
    Ivo Andrić   :   Ee´-voh Ahn´-drich
    Ante Tomić   :   Ahn´-tay To´-mich
    Arsenijević   :   Ahr-se-nee´-yeh-vich

dž = j, as in just
    Sve džaba   :   Svay ja´-ba

đ = dj, close to dž but softer like verdure
    Đorđe Balašević   :   Gior´-gieh Bah-lahsh´-eh-vich
    Đurić Đuro   :   Giur´-ich-Giur´-oh

j = y, as in yellow
    Jurica Pavičić   :   Yoor´-ee-tsa Pah´-vee-chich

lj = li, like in stallion
    ljeto   :   lieh´-toh

š = sh, as in sharp
    Meša Selimović   :   May´-shah Say-leem´-o-vich
    Vinko Brešan   :   Veen´-koh Bray´-shahn
    Danilo Kiš   :   Dahn´-ee-loh Keesh

ž = zh, as in azure
    Miroslav Krleža   :   Meer´-oh-slav Kr´-leh-zha

Consonants may be grouped together in unfamiliar ways:
    Grbavica   :   Gr´-bah-veetsa
    Crnković   :   Tsrn´-koh-vich

Introduction: Post-Yugoslav Literature and Film, and a Different Kind of Knowledge

It is true: I was rather alone, but loneliness is still not a proof of not being right.[1]

MIROSLAV KRLEŽA, *ON THE EDGE OF REASON* (1938)

Works of art repeatedly question the meaning of the words "to know." Though these are, by the virtue of artistic form, reflections or questions that have nothing of the institutional authority that anoints and enforces proclamations made from the posts of academia or government, but are instead just intuitions supported or inspired only by the work itself—and potentially by that which responds to it in the reader or a viewer—their implications matter.

In her discussion of Aeschylus' tragedy *Agamemnon*, Martha Nussbaum illuminates exactly why the play's Chorus condemns King Agamemnon who sacrifices his daughter Iphigenia. If he had not sacrificed her, his fleet and all the people with it—including Iphigenia—would have perished, and thus criticism has traditionally regarded the Chorus's harsh judgment as a contradiction or a mark of "undeveloped" thinking. However, closer reading reveals that the Chorus condemns the king not because of the deed he

---

[1] Miroslav Krleža, *On the Edge of Reason*, trans. Zora Depolo (1995), 54. I have slightly altered Depolo's translation to achieve a more literal rendition of the original.

performs, but because he exhibits no proper knowledge of the fact that Iphigenia is his daughter while preparing himself to make this deed. Yes, of course, Nussbaum agrees, the Chorus is well aware that Agamemnon comprehends that Iphigenia is his daughter, and that he possesses knowledge of many facts regarding her life. But for tragic poets such as Aeschylus, passional reaction to a situation is also "itself a piece of practical recognition or perception," or, in other words, "at least a partial constituent of the character's correct understanding of his situation as a human being."[2] And because Agamemnon's emotions are so incongruous with his horrible deed, because he gets positively optimistic and cheerful in preparation for the sacrifice, rather than torn, remorseful, and desperate, "because in his emotions, his imagination and his behavior he does not acknowledge the tie ... his state is less one of knowledge than one of delusion. He doesn't *really know* that [Iphigenia] is his daughter."[3] Agamemnon's knowledge of Iphigenia being his daughter is knowledge where a "piece of true understanding is missing."[4]

A similar deficiency of the one-dimensional concept of knowledge is sensed in a number of art works through the ages. They juxtapose that which a certain, often dominant type of knowledge can grasp or do with that which is out of its reach. In Jane Austen's *Pride and Prejudice*, for instance, the narrator comments on how all Mr. Collins's quantifiable knowledge— "he could number the fields in every direction, and could tell how many trees there were in the most distant clump"—constituted "minuteness which left beauty entirely behind."[5] In the Hollywood classic *A Star is Born* (directed by George Cukor, 1954), a studio head Oliver Niles tells Matt Libby, whose job had been to follow the recently drowned star Norman Maine like a shadow day and night and manage his public relations, "You know, Libby, you missed a lot not knowing Norman Maine." Libby is shocked. "Not knowing him?! I ... I spent my life knowing him. I knew what he was gonna do before

---

[2] Martha C. Nussbaum, *The Fragility of Goodness: Luck and Ethics in Greek Tragedy and Philosophy* (2007), 45.
[3] Nussbaum (2007), 45–6. Italics in the original.
[4] Nussbaum (2007), 46.
[5] Jane Austen, *Pride and Prejudice, an annotated edition*. Ed. Patricia Meyer Spacks. Cambridge, MA: The Belknap Press of Harvard University Press (2010), 197.

he did it. I knew him backwards." Unperturbed, Niles replies: "You didn't know him at all. He was quite a guy." Being privy to the fact that Maine's death was actually suicide, disguised as a drowning accident, in order to free Vicki Lester, a woman he loved, from his destructive impulses, viewers understand why Niles says so. He would be able to imagine Maine doing this, because he knew him. Libby would not be able to imagine this or really grasp much of Maine because, ultimately, although he knew so many things about him, he "didn't know him at all."

And the same sense of the inadequacy of the dominant concept of knowledge is present in a response which Rora, a Bosnian now residing in Chicago, gives to Brik, his fellow Sarajevan also living in Chicago, as the two go about their seemingly absurd trip through Moldova and Ukraine in Aleksandar Hemon's 2008 novel *The Lazarus Project*:

> Even if you knew what you want to know, you would still know nothing. You ask questions, you want to know more, but no matter how much more I tell you, you will never know anything. That's the problem.[6]

In Athens of the fifth and fourth centuries B.C.E., Nussbaum reminds us, "the tragic poets were widely regarded as major sources of ethical insight. The philosophers [were] competitors, not simply ... colleagues in a related department. And they competed in form as well as in content."[7] Pursuing insight about "the good human life,"[8] philosophers starting with Plato went about giving primacy to the intellect over all other human capacities including emotion, a primacy tied to the privileging of rational or literal language over poetic language, and of philosophy and, later, science over literature and all the arts. We live in a world largely marked by this hierarchy and division, which is nowadays mostly taken as "the way things are," so habituated into the texture of our thinking and living that it is all but imperceptible. Or, as Ludwig Wittgenstein put it, "people nowadays think that scientists exist to instruct them,

---

[6] Aleksandar Hemon, *The Lazarus Project* (2008), 210.
[7] Nussbaum, (2007), xv.
[8] Nussbaum, (2007), xv.

poets, musicians, etc. to give them pleasure. The idea *that these have something to teach them*—that does not occur to them."⁹

The poets of ancient Greece did not see themselves, and were certainly not seen by the community, as only entertainers, leaving all the "serious" things and even love or joy to the others. They were also not seen as trying to get to the same goal of conceptual knowledge as philosophers do, but only using different means to do so, art instead of philosophy, thus instrumentalizing their art into a tool of getting what really matters, the pure notions of the pure truth. And they were not after some kind of socialist realism *avant* the age, where correct opinions are to be "vaccinated" into public with the help of a pleasant form; they were not after the didacticism that to this day is confused with the emancipatory potential of art. Instead, the literary form was itself the goal, as was the response elicited by it, that "passional reaction" that is itself at least "a partial constituent" of the "correct understanding" which could not be achieved otherwise. Such a passional response on the part of ourselves—as spectators of a play, readers of literature or, later, cinema audiences—is "supposed to provide us with, and to help to constitute, just this sort of learning."¹⁰

"To grasp either a love or a tragedy by intellect is not sufficient for having real human knowledge of it,"¹¹ Nussbaum reminds. One could chime in that grasping a myriad of things by intellect alone "is not sufficient for having real human knowledge of it." There are different kinds of knowledge and different kinds of understanding, and we need them all. Art conveys its own knowledge in its own ways specific to its being, and can inspire a particular kind of learning on the part of its audiences. It works across the ages too, so that, say, a few thousand years old *Gilgamesh*, or the less ancient *Odyssey*, or the few hundred years old *Pieta* of Michelangelo, or the decades old *Citizen Kane* can still profoundly affect us, even more so if we have some training in communicating with them. Similarly to the ways in which works of art function across the ages, they work across space, travelling horizontally among different places. One can grow through contact with these works

---

⁹Ludwig Wittgenstein, *Culture and Value* (1984), 36e. Italics in the original.
¹⁰Nussbaum (2007), 46.
¹¹Nussbaum (2007), 45.

coming from various places, and perhaps experience, see, and do things differently.

Post-Yugoslav literature and film have much ingenuity and humor, and wisdom of such "real human knowledge," to offer to the world. They have been made in the wake of the violence in the Former Yugoslavia during the 1990s, the worst in Europe since World War Two, and in the environment of the lightening-speed transition from a multi-ethnic, partly atheist and partly multi-religious space of idiosyncratic socialism into a region of severe crisis, wars, population exodus, and then Western-style democracy and often unbridled capitalism. Related to each other by emerging from an environment of such changes, the post-Yugoslav literary works and films have much to tell to the world, especially about things that bring wars—the often subtle elements that destroy communities and minds, and participate in the hollowing and worsening of the world, eventually facilitating the onset of wars—as well as on those things that revive and nourish the world, and make up the textures of peace.

Nine chapters of this book focus on recent post-Yugoslav works and their articulations of "fires" and "flourishes." These are complemented with three "foundations" chapters elucidating some of the heritage of the past literature, cinema, or intellectual landscapes. The purpose of these foundations sections is to give some temporal context to the more recent works that were made in an artistic and intellectual environment largely affected and shaped by those earlier works and moments. The first of such chapters outlines a few aspects of one moment of Yugoslavia in the 1960s and touches on Dušan Makavejev's film *Man is Not a Bird* and Meša Selimović's novel *Death and the Dervish*. The second is dedicated to Ivo Andrić's early twentieth-century works *Ex Ponto* and *Unrest*, their response to World War One, and the difference of this response to the war to the one that can be implied from his later well-known novels; and the third discusses the dynamics between logic and success in Miroslav Krleža's novel *On the Edge of Reason*.

The book discusses some of the outstanding literature and film made in the post-Yugoslav region in the last 20 or so years, after the dissolution of the country and the establishment of the successor states, as they are sometimes called, which include Bosnia and Herzegovina, Croatia, Kosovo, Macedonia, Montenegro,

Serbia, and Slovenia. The book is not a survey of literature and film from this region, and is not done according to the national or country "quota," with representatives from each country or an equal number of works from each of the Yugoslav successor states. Instead, the book engages with literary and cinema works that seem to me both exquisite in themselves and standing as a model of a score of other works from the region grappling with the same realms.

A few disclaimers and clarifications may be in order here. First, in opposition to the currently rather strong ethnography-influenced trend in the humanities that negates the specific distinctiveness and autonomy of literature and other arts by regarding them as being primarily manifestations of various power discourses of the period, which they reproduce or subvert and so on, this book—as is probably evident from the whole previous exposition—claims the separation of arts from such discourses, and foregrounds radical potential of arts, in this case select post-Yugoslav literature and cinema, to change and enrich the global realms of sensitivities, concepts, and politics. The book does this by spelling out the exploratory activity of specific works. If we let them, these works can create some new "neural pathways," so to speak, in our collective brain.

Second, *Post-Yugoslav Literature and Film: Fires, Foundations, Flourishes* hopes to be a champion of these works, and to bring these outstanding literary and cinema creations into a wider and different view. Most are available in English translation or on English-subtitled DVD editions, but have so far been seen mainly as either literal responses to their specific historical and political contexts, or else within the critical framework of their relationship to the so-called Western discourses of the Balkans. Third, I do not propose that national denominations are unimportant, or that works discussed in this book are more "post-Yugoslav" than they are Bosnian, Slovenian, Macedonian, and so on. They are both, and in many cases they have a number of other denominations as well. What interested me in this project, however, is the artistic and conceptual realm that they create when they are brought together and allowed to relate to each other simply by being put together. Fourth, this book wishes to be of use to scholars and critics of the region's literature and cinema, but also "reader friendly" to those within and without academia who may have an interest in this particular subject, this region, or in world literature and cinema in general. I have thus avoided the theoretical jargon often used as a kind of shorthand speech in humanities disciplines, and tried to offer a transparent and hopefully pleasant reading. Individual chapters are inspired and led by the novels and films in question, not by the pre-existing theoretical concepts or by current debates within the experts' circles, though philosophy, literary criticism, and history are included in a dialogue.

The chapters are stylistically varied, relating to different matters in different manners. The chapter on Milcho Manchevski's film *Before the Rain*, for example, is more philosophical in kind, focusing on one issue in depth; that on Bosnian films is more essayistic and touching on a plethora of topics; that on Jurica Pavičić's *Plaster Sheep* and Ante Tomić's *Nothing Should Surprise Us* is concerned with providing some basic historical information that is directly invoked in these novels. Given a choice to engage with select works at greater depth, this book focuses on only a selection of the excellent works from the region; there are many more.

A Few Words About the Place

For people outside of the region, and not somehow related to it, it is one of those peripheral places that drift in and out of sight and do not have a steady place in the mind, in contrast to the way the omnipresent USA, China, or "Europe" do. Some may remember it as the site of the worst violence in Europe since World War Two. In the early 1990s, the dissolution of Yugoslavia and the wars in Slovenia, Croatia, and—the one mostly remembered—in Bosnia and Herzegovina, put the region on the forefront of the world's news, to be slowly drifting towards the back pages as the violence wore on and new flashpoints in other places occurred, such that the violence in Kosovo and the NATO bombing of Serbia at the close of the decade were perceived with already weary eyes. In a more connected and ever-faster world, all the events and their individual victims and perpetrators, their helpful allies and deterring foes, quickly become ever-smaller and more transient, like a being who stays behind us forever anchored in its space and time, while we are carried away in a fast vehicle through a rapidly changing landscape.

We do not drive this thing called history, as Paul Klee (according to Walter Benjamin) saw in his *Angelus Novus*—a painting of an angel carried backwards by a gale of wind, unable to stop himself and leaving ruins in his trail. And we are overwhelmed with the speed of movement and our unwitting participation in the many destructions the movement brings, in the sights around us and the imperative to survive and go on. We can even try to see things of the past, but inevitably they become smaller and smaller in our rear-view mirror, swallowed by the new environments in which we need to live.

Those with longer memories or better information might remember the country that was there before, from 1918 to 1991, bearing a few different names and most recently called the Socialist Federative Republic of Yugoslavia (*Socijalistička Federativna Republika Jugoslavija*). In its post-World War Two period this country may have drawn the attention of some with its so-called third path—not Western capitalism or Soviet-bloc socialism, but something else—and with its ideas and practices of workers' "self-management," or of the Non-Aligned Movement which Yugoslavia founded in the early 1960s along with India and Egypt. Some people may even know about the quite remarkable art scene in Yugoslavia, alive and ambitious beyond the confines of professional success, of museums or theaters. It was cosmopolitan, curious, and open. John Cage, one of the major names of the American post-war avant-garde, writes how in the mid-1970s, when a festival in a western European country "ridiculed" his piece *Canfield*, "Beograd's Festival gave *Canfield* first prize."[12]

The same country that was at times perceived as being on the exciting forefront of different thinking and practice, or at least as being the most liberal and progressive of the East European countries, was transformed quite suddenly—by many of those who were making policy decisions regarding Yugoslavia—into the "Balkan backwaters," once the violence and aggression began in 1991. The sentiment was propagated by parts of the media and academia that knew how to listen to the unspoken demands of power. Though it was rather clear from early on that the violence in the former Yugoslavia was not the case of two or three or more

---

[12] John Cage, *Empty Words*. Middletown, CT: Wesleyan University Press (1979), 86.

bloodthirsty ethnic groups unleashing their primordial violent urges in an orgy of mutual destruction, but instead a well-planned aggression with clear territorial, military, and economic objectives, it was more convenient and sometimes profitable, and it justified the outsiders' own policies, to blame the aggression and loss of lives on the innate wildness of the inhabitants of this "uncivilized" region.

In a cartoon from a prestigious international paper, a well-dressed gentleman with an "EC" (European Community) badge and a benevolent but stern face is surrounded by three vicious dogs who chase each other circling him. The gentleman is pointing at a table with a "negotiations" sign on it and with three cushions labeled "Croatia," "Serbia," and "Slovenia" around it, as he is unsuccessfully commanding: "Sit! Sit!"[13] The main problem seems to be the state of the gentleman's coat and trousers, which are being torn at the ends by the snapping dogs. The transformation of people living in post-Yugoslavia's regions into rabid dogs is paralleled with their being turned into "village idiots," as they were referred to in another article where the writer handsomely exhibited his wittiness and his good sense of what the powers-that-be might want him to say to make their course of action seem appropriate.[14] A few of the chief catches today facing The Hague's International Criminal Tribunal for the former Yugoslavia were comfortably speaking on the major TV networks and meeting with the ever-patient international negotiators in the 1990s, just at the time when they were going about their war crimes. They were always seen in their fine suits, and they looked quite like that worried gentleman from the cartoon.

But there were also, of course, many individuals in academia, the media, government institutions and various organizations, and countless so-called "ordinary citizens," who did their best to help and eventually succeeded in altering the world's perceptions and practices regarding this violence. Reporters on the ground were

---

[13] KAL [Kevin "Kal" Kallaugher] 91 CW Syndicate, "Opinion," *International Herald Tribune*, September 7–8, 1991, p. 8.
[14] Paul Reid, "An old feud in the new Europe: In Yugoslavia, the latest in a series of tribal clashes that go back a millennium," *Boston Globe*, October 7, 1991, p. 11. The full quote: "This is clearly not what the architects of 'Europe 1992' intended. The planners of the global village failed to account for the village idiot."

intentionally targeted by those who profited from the perpetuation of lies and stereotypes, and a number of journalists lost their lives trying to report on what was actually going on, or simply attempting to communicate a faithful image of the region's people rather than portraying them as "dogs" or "village idiots." From their side comes another image: a photo of a young woman in a parka, in a bombed-out library where shelves full of books stand naked under an open sky.[15] The woman has a book in her hands and is looking into it, or perhaps reading its words. Is she deciding which book to save and which to leave, as it's unlikely she can save them all before it rains or the shelling starts again? Or is she trying to remind herself of those words and worlds that these books make, which may have to live from now on only in her? Or perhaps she is simply taking a break from the still so incomprehensible destruction, letting her mind go to some other place?

One wonders: which books would make sense to this woman? What would she read? And what books would she write in the years after, and what films may she make, old enough to have lived in the before, and young enough to start again?

---

[15] Photograph by Christof Birbaumer, Associated Press, *New York Times International*, October 26, 1991, p. Y 5. The photograph appears on the cover of this book.

1

Foundations I
While Falling Asleep: A Trace of the Moment in Yugoslavia

> That rediscovered, recovered part of me, which was more than a memory, was beautified and returned from unreachable distances by time, which joined me with it. Thus, it had a two-fold existence, as a part of my present personality, and as a memory. As the present, and as a beginning.
>
> MEŠA SELIMOVIĆ, *DEATH AND THE DERVISH*[1]

Falling Asleep

Imagine Danica, a young woman in Zagreb, Yugoslavia, on 23 October 1967. We don't know much about her, but we do know that she works as a recently graduated chemical engineer in a successful factory, is single, and happens to be interested in the arts. She pricks her finger on one of the old spinning wheels left in an

---

[1] Meša Selimović, *Death and the Dervish* (1996), 250. The original title, *Derviš i smrt*, translates as *Dervish and Death*.

attic many years ago by a village grandmother, gently falls asleep, and goes on sleeping for 43 years. She wakes up in October 2010. What images and thoughts would she have while falling asleep, what would she find upon waking up, and what sense might she make of it all?

1967. Last night Danica saw the short film *Scusa signora*, an experimental film made by *Kinoklub Zagreb* in which the cameraman filmed her too—we see only the legs of passers by walking Zagreb streets, hers are the ones that appear right at the beginning, bordered by her diaphanous gray skirt. She smiles as she remembers how her friend could not recognize her. Then a fleeting memory of another fine pair of legs in that strange film; what was it called again? *Man is Not a Bird*, yes, it's just a few years old, and she saw it in Belgrade while visiting her dear friend; it had that vivacious Belgrade blonde in the main role, Milena Dravić, who just appeared in Zvonimir Berković's *Rondo*. And then she remembers, for no apparent reason, the fast-moving *Ersatz*, an animated film by Dušan Vukotić (Figure 1.1). "It's so interesting, how they do it!"[2] The film had won an Oscar for the best animated short, the first ever non-American film to do so. That was a fine laurel wreath for Vukotić and the entire Zagreb School of Animated Film. And the Americans bestowed it on him and she dreamily feels a touch of regret that she did not get her act together in time, a few years ago, to go with a few of her friends to Ljubljana, which is really so close, to see Louis Armstrong in the new Tivoli Hall that is supposed to be so impressive.

And then Hassan appears in her mind, from the novel *Death and the Dervish* that came out last year, in 1966. It is fortunate that this is a novel and not a film; she finished reading it for the second time the other day. Hassan, who you have to fall in love with the way dervish did; with "his light, limpid smile, which blossomed all on its own," and his "serenity that surrounded him like a light"; Hassan, who "resembled a deer, a tree in bloom, a brisk wind."[3]

---

[2] Dušan Vukotić's *Ersatz* (*Surogat* (Zagreb: Zagreb Film, 1961)), is sometimes translated into English as *Substitute*. Along with other classic works of the Zagreb School of Animated Films, it is available on DVD: *The Best of Zagreb Film: Be Careful What You Wish For and the Classic Collection* (Zagreb Film; Compilation: Rembrandt Films; Chatsworth, CA: Distributed by Image Entertainment, 2000).
[3] Selimović, *Death and the Dervish* (1996), 124–5.

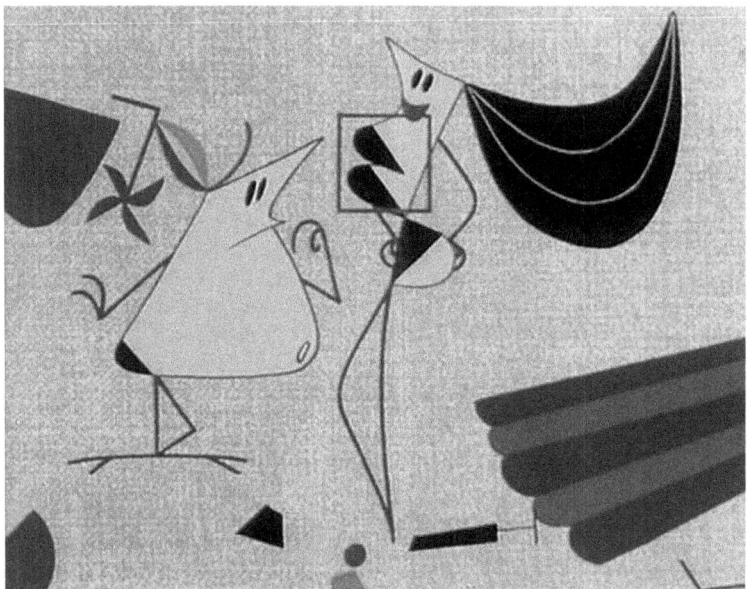

Fig 1.1 *Ersatz* (1961)

And his enigmatic advice: "Live as beautifully as you can, but so that you are not ashamed."[4]

"Live as beautifully as you can ... and the beauty of life ...," and its intensity, more than anything else, she ponders while falling asleep. The meetings of the Workers' Council, making more sense on some days than others, her factory with its smell and bustle, its increasing production and possibly a new market, and those workers who laugh and have kind faces and trust her, and who do not talk much except when there's a glitch and the machines could be stopped and they come to her and say: "Dear engineer Danica, just tell us what to do and we'll do it right away!"[5]

---

[4]Meša Selimović, *Derviš i smrt* [*Dervish and Death*] (1970), 134. This phrase translated by Gordana P. Crnković.

[5]Danica's thoughts before falling asleep are based on personal interviews, as well as on memoires and scholarly literature on the Former Yugoslavia. It seems that the scholarship of the time (1960s and 1970s) has a different take on, and more of a "close-up" look into, the then Yugoslav situation than does later work on Yugoslavia; therefore a number of volumes from that period were used to construct

"Just tell us what to do ..." But it can be so wretched, and she can never tell them about the loneliness of the laboratory where things don't go as they should, and a woman hears the clicking of

this personal yet historical "stream of consciousness." Among those are Dennison Rusinow's *The Yugoslav Experiment: 1948–1974* (1977), George W. Hoffman and Fred Warner Neal's *Yugoslavia and the New Communism* (1962), Fred Singleton's *Twentieth Century Yugoslavia* (1976), and Wayne S. Vucinich ed., *Contemporary Yugoslavia: Twenty Years of Socialist Experiment* (1969). With regard to gender issues, a newer volume contributes less represented information and insight: Sabrina P. Ramet ed., *Gender Politics in Western Balkans: Women, Society, and Politics in Yugoslavia and the Yugoslav Successor States* (1998). Regarding gender politics, the following quote may be illuminating:
Socialist Yugoslavia undertook a relatively unusual experiment during the forty-six years of its existence (1945–1991)—to eliminate the sources of social, economic, and gender inequality while laying the foundation for a society in which women and men could enjoy complete equality in politics, in education and careers, and in family life. Although the aspiration was shared with other communist countries, Yugoslavia gave its experiment a unique twist by linking its program with institutional changes to be realized through self-management organs and a complicated delegate system. The socialist system represented an improvement where gender equality was concerned over the pre-existing system associated with the interwar Kingdom of Yugoslavia, but it did not fulfill its promises. (Available online at http://www.psupress.org/books/titles/0-271-01801-1.html/; accessed 31 October 2011.)

A more elaborate summary of the findings of this volume regarding "what Ramet calls the 'Tito era'" is offered in Branka Magaš's "Afterword":
The Communist Party granted women the same legal rights as men, opened all levels of education to them, adopted a highly liberal policy in regard to abortion and contraception (helped by exclusion of the Churches from political life), and made women major beneficiaries of an advanced welfare system. However, [Ramet] writes, the Party's belief that social change would of itself transform values and attitudes prevented it from tackling the persistence of traditional patriarchal attitudes in people's minds ... Consequently, and despite the evident and impressive progress women made during the Tito era, the end result was disappointing ... Could it be, as Ramet remarks at one point, that the same could have been achieved under some other system? If "some other system" means capitalism developing in Yugoslav conditions, then the answer must be no. However, as she points out, capitalism neither achieves nor does it promise to achieve gender equality or social justice. Socialism, by contrast, does make these claims; so its failure to fulfill them is far more serious. Its failure is all the more instructive in that it demonstrates how only a frontal assault on each and every bastion of patriarchy will deliver progress toward gender equality. (Branka Magaš, "Afterword," in Sabrina P. Ramet ed., *Gender Politics in Western Balkans: Women, Society, and Politics in Yugoslavia and the Yugoslav Successor States* (1998), 279.)

the seconds, ever louder, in her heartbeat—production may stop if she does not find that magic formula. And the incompetent workers who can never lose their jobs, her colleague's brother who drinks four days of every week and then comes in on the fifth day and there is nothing you can do to make him change or leave. And it chips away, she can hear the underground gnawing on all these optimistic new laws making it all but impossible to lose a job, misused and abused laws; and perhaps made to be so. Why do they always show and talk to a worker at the machine, for the television, with all the factory noise around so that you can hardly hear what he is saying anyway, and they never show them, the engineers, who sweat so much to make it all happen? And whenever the factory brags about the engineers' discoveries, they always say "our team," and never want to name names, even internally, who actually did what, or did not do a thing; and now the lab technicians are asking for white coats, or rather demanding them with that loud self-righteousness, so that they get the equality that is due to them and look the same as the engineers; and they will probably get the white coats, the way things go—but would they ever be able to do the engineers' work? They could not begin to. But such a simple question is so hard to ask today.[6]

And yet, still, all the ties with so many people in the factory, and even in the tram where, every morning, they all laugh and say "here we are at the customs again!" on that corner of Branimirova and Držićeva streets where the traffic light takes an eternity to change from red to green; the ties with friends and with neighbors too, their windows and doors open and fluid with each other in the mingling of voices and laughter and sometimes yelling and eggs and flour, and always children. Growing old together, welcoming children, worrying about the old and the sick. And coffees after work on a fine afternoon like this one. The air is sweet, and the sun dances arabesques on the tablecloth of an outdoor café. The light passes through the murmuring leaves of the tree above the table where she sits with her friend.

---

[6] "Workers' Councils were taking the easy way out when belts had to be tightened by sacking a handful of needed engineers and technicians instead of a hundred surplus unskilled workers and by cutting research and development or scholarship funds, economically dysfunctional and sometimes socially unjust measures which only State directives or budgetary interventions could prevent." Rusinow (1977), 179.

But those who are treacherous are here too; and those who do not care as long as it is good for them, and those she does not know, and then there are always those who don't want it to work or are just not getting it and are draining your life from day to day. She knows but would not focus on them, because there are others who push and find the solutions day in and day out, like her good friend Victoria D., her *Vikica*, a German Yugoslav who practically adopted her and taught her so much, who tells the director, in front of the whole assembly, that he makes no sense, and tells her, Danica, "Are they [the ones in charge] still learning? And when do you think they'll have learned?" And things too, all of them, things that go their own stubborn ways and not the ways they were supposed to, and you have to be fixing it and adjusting it and changing everything all the time. So many changes and so much to do. Maybe it really cannot work? But why not, if it is done well? Sometimes she is very tired, and her friends tell her she is silly when she declares, as if she would know, that the old-fashioned Western-style democracy would be a better way to go. One can want more, but one may not be able to have it, not here and not now—things and people are not changing fast enough. Or else—they change in ways in which they should not, and do not change in ways that would make them better.

But also, always, the constant presence of people who died, knowing they probably would, in that horrible war, so that she, Danica, may survive and live. They were and are her guardians, and are silent but seeing, all around her. And the sense of those who are children or yet to be born and live in this city, in this autumn. She remembers Hassan again—"live as beautifully as you can, but so that you are not ashamed." Beauty of life, yes, hers is to live and also build that beauty and not be ashamed, live in a way that would not make her ashamed. She will have a good sleep now, wake refreshed, and then she will go at it again tomorrow.

Danica managed to overcome her shyness and wrote last winter to the author of *Death and the Dervish*, Meša Selimović in Sarajevo. She still remembers every word of her letter:

> Respected and dear Mr. Selimović,
> After I read your *Dervish*, I remained under the impression that this prose of yours has in itself more lyricism than

many, many collections of poems! That is wonderful, comrade Selimović! I congratulate you on your great achievement with all my heart, and I greet you warmly and friendly.

D.P.
Zagreb, February 1967.[7]

If Danica had been able to see what another great writer, Zagreb's Miroslav Krleža, wrote that same year, 1967, in his diary, she could have seen a note about his schooling at the Ludoviceum Military Academy in Budapest in 1912, when so much of what was now the materialized past had still been the uncertain future. "We spread apart like crab's children to all sides of the compass ... from higher grades one heard that someone had brought in to the boys a strange word, 'revolution,' and another one even stranger, 'socialism' ... some will be tortured by the thought of whether the Mother of God is indeed 'Immaculata,' and others will give it all in the whirlpool of the People's unity."[8] But Danica does not know about this diary, and so she wants to read an "avant-garde" novel that her friend from the university told her about. It came out a few years ago but she hasn't gotten to it yet, apparently it's a kind of new writing and it's very interesting. The writer lives in Belgrade, the Montenegrin–Hungarian–Jewish young Yugoslav

---

[7]The translation of an actual letter sent from Zagreb in February 1967 to Meša Selimović, and signed by a woman whose name starts with the initials used in this text, D. P. Translated by Gordana P. Crnković. Razija Lagumdžija ed., *Kritičari o Meši Selimoviću, sa autobiografijom* [*Critics on Meša Selimović, with Autobiography*] (1973), 276. I diverged a little from the literal translation to better convey the spirit of the letter (i.e., by not using "comrade" twice; the word mostly connotes membership in the Communist Party in the English language, whereas the original word used in this letter, *drug* or *drugarica* (fem.), is an old word that primarily denotes a person someone socializes with in a positive manner [the verb *družiti se* means to socialize with], and is often friends with. The word was also used as a standard form of address in the Yugoslav era.)
[8]Miroslav Krleža, *Dnevnik* (1977), as cited in Enes Čengić, *Krleža* (1982), 92. Čengić notes this passage with only "*Diary* 1967," without giving a full bibliographical citation. Regarding Krleža, the year 1967 is also marked by his signing of the important March 1967 "Declaration about the name and position of the Croatian literary language" [*Deklaracija o nazivu i položaju hrvatskog književnog jezika*].

man, a mixture of a sort like she is; his name is Danilo Kiš, and the novel's title is *Garden, Ashes*.

Unknown to the woman, a young man, originally from a village called Bunić in Lika and now for years with family in Vinkovci, a town in the fertile Pannonian Basin of Slavonia in eastern Croatia, has come back from his home town to Zagreb this same fall of 1967, bringing along home-made sausages, *ajvar*, and brandy, to enroll in the second year of his acting studies at the Academy of Dramatic Art in Zagreb. The 21-year-old actor's name is Rade Šerbedžija, and he, as opposed to Danica, will not be sleeping for the next 43 years.

Man is Not a Bird

The woman falls asleep, and while she sleeps, let us reflect on a few of the books and films that have just appeared in her mind. Dušan Makavejev's film *Man is Not a Bird* (*Čovek nije tica*, 1965) takes place in the eastern Serbian town of Bor and its copper processing plant (this region has rich copper reserves and long mining tradition).[9] (Figure 1.2) The film is an exhilarating aesthetic achievement that functions on a number of levels other than the ones of the connections with and references to the immediate historical context. Yet, the film also strongly engages and deals with that context, and points at aspects that are relevant for the social environment of its setting. This environment, the 1960s, can be broadly described as "a dynamic period in Yugoslavia's social and political life, characterized by developments in the theory and practice of its project of socialist self-management"—developments that Danica was wrestling with day in and day out.[10] Related to the other progressive moves in the economic, political and social

---

[9] Dušan Makavejev is one of the few best known Yugoslav-era directors; much has been written on him, including the book by Lorraine Mortimer, *Terror and Joy: The Films of Dušan Makavejev* (2009). For introductory readings on Yugoslav film that include extended discussions of Makavejev's work, consult Daniel Goulding's classic *Liberated Cinema: The Yugoslav Experience (1945–2001)* (2002), and a newer volume by Pavle Levi, *Disintegration in Frames: Aesthetics and Ideology in Yugoslav and Post-Yugoslav Film* (2007).
[10] Levi (2007), 16.

Fig 1.2 Rudinski with a technician, *Man is Not a Bird* (1965)

sphere, "New Film 'claimed for itself the right to serve as a critic of all existing conditions' and 'to be a conscience ... of the land.'"[11] As Pavle Levi points out, "although often strongly critical of the concrete social, political, and cultural manifestations of Yugoslav socialism, the views of these filmmakers were for the most part not opposed to socialist ideas as such. They were, however, opposed to ideological dogmatism and reification."[12]

Makavejev's *Man is Not a Bird* exposes in a humorous and playful manner the discrepancy between the official ideology of the socialist Yugoslav state and the real situation on the ground. According to a simplified version of the ideology at the time, workers are in charge in the "workers' country," have a high level of class consciousness, and are, on top of it all, genuinely interested in so-called high European culture such as German classical music, which in this particular case is Beethoven's *Ode to Joy*. (In his report written in advance of the performance of the *Ode to Joy* in the plant, a journalist uses the phrase "delighted workers' faces" to describe the audience.) The real state of things as depicted by the film, however, shows that workers, all men in this case, may work extremely hard (such as the character Barbulović) but are

---

[11] Goulding (2002), 66. As quoted in Levi (2007), 16.
[12] Levi (2007), 16.

not in charge of the more complex decisions regarding their work. It also seems obvious that they should not be simply fully "in charge," given that the task of running the intricate plant within a complex environment is not something they know how to do. They are strictly patriarchal, as seen in Barbulović's attitude towards his wife. Regarding cultural affairs, the workers distinctly prefer the more participatory and familiar popular culture, such as fairs with acrobats and other marvels, to the "high culture" they are unaccustomed to, and the local bar's noisy brawls and its buxom woman singer to the strangeness of Beethoven's *Ninth* performed by Belgrade musicians in their factory, during which performance one cannot even move the seats, let alone say something or sing along. One of the most hilarious scenes of *Man is Not a Bird* is when the Belgrade musicians get lost in the plant. The train of the soprano soloist's evening dress catches fire from sparks flying from the infernally loud machines; the musicians turn to the workers and are desperately trying to be heard over the pounding of the plant: "We're from Philharmonics ... Beethoven ... Ninth Symphony," with one worker, not being able to catch anything but the very few last words, yelling back: "We don't make these things!"

Man Is Not a Bird involves a love story between a middle-aged man who came to the plant to direct the assembly of a new processing turbine, the highly qualified and dedicated engineer from Slovenia, Jan Rudinski (Janez Vrhovec; "Rudinski" connotes the word *ruda*, a mineral), and Rajka, a local girl played by Milena Dravić. (Figure 1.3) They are of different ethnicities, and this will also be the case in Makavejev's next film, *Love Affair, or the Case of the Missing Switchboard Operator (Ljubavni slučaj ili tragedija službenice PTT,1967)*, in which an attractive woman postal employee of Hungarian ethnicity has a relationship with a Muslim man in Belgrade,[13] and in the director's most well-known

---

[13] In the former Yugoslavia, the term "Muslim" could mean either ethnicity or religious affiliation. When it referred to ethnicity, it was written with upper case (*Musliman*) and denoted South Slavs whose families converted to Islam in the past, who felt ethnically neither Croat nor Serb and who grew up in Muslim culture, but were not necessarily Muslim believers. Muslim written with lower case (*musliman*) meant a religious denomination. This distinction, and the official affirmation of Muslim ethnicity that it brought, was not officially established until late 1960s, after this Makavejev film was made.

Fig 1.3 Rudinski and Rajka, *Man is Not a Bird* (1965)

film, *WR: Mysteries of the Organism* (*WR: Misterije Organizma*, 1971), in which Belgrade's Milena (again played by Milena Dravić) gets together with Russian ice skater Vladimir Ilyich (Ivica Vidović).

The important difference between the two lovers in *Man Is Not a Bird* is not that of ethnicity, or of the disparity of age or education, but of something else. The two eventually fall apart over their attitude towards the tension between individual life and its desires, wishes, and fulfillment, on one hand, and a commitment to one's community on the other. Rajka is a barber who works because she has to; she is young in a young country, not very well educated but lively and smart, and limited to getting the most of life mainly from her playful sexual encounters rather than from a broader field of possibilities that would include work, a variety of social and intimate relationships, and politics, among other things. Rudinski's outlook and practice is different, characterized by his great commitment to his work, his coworkers, and the broader society. The film shows the gradual creation of a tight-knit community of the workplace consisting of highly trained mechanics and the engineer Rudinski, mutually increasingly appreciative of and loyal to each other, as well as the commitment this engineer feels not only towards the mechanics he works with daily, this workplace and this particular project (which is incidentally very important because it will enable valuable exports), but also towards the wider community of his society and that society's future. As he accepts a symbolic award, a medal—given that the plant's director was not successful in persuading the higher-ups in approving a monetary rather than symbolic award—Rudinski gives a brief, unpolished speech: "Thank you, comrades. We were doing our job. It's a human being's character ... to build as best as one can ... one's own happiness, and our future, and ... Thank you!"

Writing about Yugoslavia of the period, Fred Singleton asked: "Is there in Yugoslavia today a new class of non-acquisitive, socialist-minded men and women, instinctively working for the good of the commonwealth and inspired by the principles of socialist humanism in their everyday relations with their fellow men?"[14] With all its display of contemporary social problems, many of them based on a refusal or hesitancy to accurately state the facts on the ground, which would facilitate a productive dealing with them (refusal based on the fear that such an accurate description would give ammunition to the enemies of the socialist project in general, or on the intention to cover up individual ineptness, corruption, or else a structural impossibility to do something, or on other reasons), *Man is Not a Bird* also presents a true socialist person. Not desiring personal enrichment or power, Rudinski genuinely cares about others and is building "our future" that for him makes much of the texture of his "own happiness." He is a real communist the way one is ideally meant to be, but he does end up betraying his own intimate contentment by eventually putting the good of all ahead of his own. Gentle and kind, he rarely laughs out loud, and visually appears at the opposite pole from those chuckling workers who steal copper wire from the plant and act for their own personal advantage to the detriment of others.

Death and the Dervish

Another work that flashed through young Danica's mind while she was falling asleep is a remarkable novel by Meša Selimović that came out in Sarajevo in 1966, *Death and the Dervish*. (The original title, *Derviš i smrt*, translates as *Dervish and Death*; I am using the

---

[14] Singleton (1976), 312.

reverse order of words as it stands in the title of the English translation.) In chapter six, the first-person narrator and main character, dervish Ahmed Nurrudin, has a seemingly abstract discussion with a man named Hassan, that quickly turns very specific. Prompted by something Hassan said, the dervish asks:

> "But how should we live? Without order, without purpose, without any conscious goals that we try to accomplish?"
> "I don't know. It would be good if we could determine a purpose and goals for ourselves, if we could create rules for all of life's circumstances, if we could establish our imaginary order. It's easy to invent general principles, looking over men's heads into the sky and eternity. But try to apply them to the lives of real people, whom you know and maybe love, without harming them. You'll hardly succeed."
> "Doesn't the Koran determine all relations between people? We can apply the essence of its prescriptions [*suštinu propisa*] to each individual case."
> "Do you think so? Then solve this riddle for me. [...]"[15]

Hassan goes on to describe the "not uncommon and not unusual" case of the love triangle or "adultery," or more specifically, the case of a woman, her husband, and her lover, all living together as employees in Hassan's household. The discussion continues:

> "The Koran tells us: an adulteress is to be stoned. But you must admit, that's rather old-fashioned. So what should I do? Tell her husband? Threaten her? Get rid of the youth? None of that would help. ... So there you have it, find whatever rule you like, solve this for me, set up your order! But without destroying them. Because then you've done nothing."
> "You're talking about consequences and not about causes, about the impotence of principles when something happens, and not about the sin of people who don't adhere to them."
> "Life is larger than any principle. Morality is an idea [*zamisao*; the concept of something not or not yet there], but life

---

[15] Selimović, *Death and the Dervish* (1996), 121–2. I have replaced the word "spirit" (of principles) from Rakić and Dickey's translation with the word "essence."

is that which happens. How can we fit it into this idea without damaging it? More lives have been ruined in attempts to prevent sin than because of sin itself."
"Should we live in sin then?"
"No. But prohibiting it doesn't help at all. It creates hypocrites and spiritual cripples."
"So what should we do?"
"I don't know."
He laughed, as if that made him glad.[16]

If life and real people are of supreme value, as they are for the humanist Hassan, then prescriptions such as these of specific rules of behavior achieve nothing because they destroy that life. Prescriptions destroy life because they are too limited, too general, and too fixed. They are too limited to deal with "life [that is] larger than any principle." They are too general: invented by "looking over men's heads into the sky and eternity," general principles do not correspond to "all of life's circumstances," and thus cannot be rules for these circumstances. And they are also too fixed: the principles as ideas are simply too static and unmoving for the life "which happens" and is as a movement and change in time. In other words, the problem with the *Quran* is not merely that it is "old fashioned" in this particular case of a wife's adultery, but rather the more general fact of its being a collection of prescriptions which are too limited, general, and fixed when put next to life which is larger, always specific, and always moving. Thus, they cannot be simply "applied to each individual case" of that life's happening, the way the dervish puts it, without destroying that case itself, the people and their lives. The point relates not only to the *Quran*: a simple deductive application of *any* system of ideas "onto life" destroys or would destroy life and people because of the conflation of levels, so to speak, which takes lives to the level of prescriptions embodied in words, words that are by definition *ideas*: a "woman" is any woman at any time, an "adulteress" is any adulteress. A word cannot utter or contain a specific woman, a specific adulteress. Such conflation of levels cripples the material "what happens" (unique, changing) by cutting it down—limiting it,

---

[16] Selimović, *Death and the Dervish* (1996), 122–3.

emptying it of its specificity, stopping or petrifying it—to the level of limited, general, and fixed ideas and sameness.

As opposed to such submission of real and specific temporality of material developments to eternity, this premise of the "heaven" ("sky," "eternity") of dematerialized ideas being superior to the earth of the material "what happens," Hassan advances the supremacy of temporality over eternity, and of living people over general principles. It is them, not the principles, who should not be harmed or destroyed: "find whatever rule you like, solve this for me, set up your order! But without destroying them [the people involved]. Because then you've done nothing." By harming or destroying people and their lives through the application of prescriptions onto them, one has done no good; instead, one has done nothing. (This "doing nothing" can be seen in a weak sense, as achieving nothing or maintaining the *status quo*. But it seems that "doing nothing," when connected with "destroying people," could be seen in a stronger sense, as the advancement of the cause of nothingness or death through an activity that turns real people into nothing in order to bring the rule of the idea into being.) Instead of yearning to approach the state of unchangeable and general prescriptions, of cutting down one's life so that it fits into those categories, one should, it seems, put those prescriptions aside and try to figure out how to live differently this life "which happens" and which is "larger than any principle." The hold of eternity (prescriptions, ideas, words as prescriptions) on the temporality of what actually "happens" is put aside with Hassan's simple "I don't know," meaning "I don't know" what to do in general terms. There are no general principles that could be applied to all of life's circumstances.

If temporality is released from eternity, two things happen: first, eternity is shown as actually not eternal because it does not really apply to specific cases as they are born by time. In addition, some temporal decrees, those of their specific time, are seen as simply having been hypostasized into non-temporal and eternal, which they are not. As Hassan puts it, such decrees are not eternal but merely "old-fashioned." Second, temporal reality can proceed on its own, not crippled by a fixed realm it has to imitate, not defined by that which is already said and known (words as prescriptions), but going into the realms of genuine future, not imitating the given past but developing its own present and future which has never been around and has thus never been said before. The release from the *Quran*'s words, read and used as general prescriptions to be "applied" to specific lives, is a release of real temporality with its genuine future potential from the perpetuity of eternal repetition, a release of non-crippled and non-hypocritical lives and practices from the pre-given petrified rules. And it is also a release of the not-yet-uttered from the already spoken. In short, not knowing what to do in some more general sense, or not having "general" principles, is seen as positive: Hassan repeats twice his "I don't know," the second time accompanying the statement with joyful laughter, "as if that made him glad."

As the novel later reveals, Hassan's refusal of general rules, his "I don't know" (how to live in general), is complemented by his knowledge of how to live in any specific situation, or rather by a particular sensitivity of a situation, rather than knowledge, that makes him act, or refrain from acting, in ways that do not make him "ashamed."

In relation to Yugoslavia of the early 1960s, *Death and the Dervish* may be seen as, among other things, dealing on a more general level with some of the same problems the country faced, and finding its own solutions. Moving away not only from a specific ideology but more broadly from any more general and less temporal system of knowledge or belief as a basis for action, the novel foregrounds a need for pragmatic, goal-oriented, and temporally sensitive practices. The practice itself is emptied of any more specific definition, and is named circuitously and only negatively as "behaving so that you are not ashamed of yourself."

The novel includes several tales from Hassan about the application of well-intended ideas to material realities, with results completely different from the ones anticipated, tales that directly question the very idealism of a possible practice that applies pre-existing ideas to the material reality. In one such story, Hassan remembers how he once met and befriended a wealthy widow on one of his journeys, whom he later inspired into doing charitable deeds for her village, such as giving money to the poor villagers and building a school. But the good intentions ended in a complete fiasco, with the now richer village men using the extra money for alcohol and consequently getting more abusive towards their wives and families, and with the children not learning much on account of an uncommitted teacher and the opposition of the village parents to the removal of child laborers from the fields. This parable about the good ideas not necessarily leading to analogously good material realities, which tend to burst out with a life of their own, can be read as a direct commentary on some of Yugoslav socialism's functioning and its inherent idealism, where good ideas may be applied to society with genuinely good intentions, but can lead to unexpected and often undesirable results. The emphasis of this specific parable is not on questioning the motives and goals of those who were implementing various aspects of socialism; rather, the parable looks into the unpredictable functioning of idealism itself.

Death and the Dervish also takes as one of its themes the importance of fear in politics. Looking back at the Yugoslavia of the 1960s through the texture of the novel's "solutions," it seems that the country, at least for a while and in some of its aspects, chose the course of moving in directions similar to those indicated in the novel. The need to remove fear from politics was addressed by the removal from power in July 1966 of Aleksandar Ranković, head of the Yugoslav secret police, and by the restructuring of this department, as well as by the overall liberalization of the country in the second half of the decade. This allowed the thriving of, among other things, the *Praxis* collective and philosophy, the wide-spread artistic neo-avant-garde peaking in the late 1960s, the public and rather open-ended debates among Marxist and Christian philosophers, the students' and workers' protests, and roughly lasted until the beginning of the 1970s.[17] The need for a more pragmatic and less ideological practice was also recognized in the market-oriented reforms of 1965, ushering in the era of so-called "market socialism" which accompanied the political system of "socialist democracy."

Some of the most original non-dogmatic behavior was exhibited in the international arena, with Yugoslavia's founding, together with India and Egypt, of the non-alignment movement. Instead of accepting the previously established "fact" of the finality of

---

[17] For more on the fascinating neo-avant-garde of the period, see Dubravka Đurić and Miško Šuvaković (eds), *Impossible Histories: Historic Avant-gardes, Neo-Avant-Gardes, and Post-Avant-Gardes in Yugoslavia, 1918–1991* (2003).

the division of the world between two blocs, Yugoslavia utilized the untapped potentials of that moment in history and pursued the creation of a new political factor and model, a nonalignment movement. Even though "the Yugoslavs [after 1957] continued to press within the Communist world for acceptance of their ideas of independence and national approaches to socialism, which came to be called *polycentrism* [and] opposed practices of monolithic leadership, of hegemony (by either Russia or China) over world Communism,"[18] and worked according to Tito's speech delivered right after the 1956 Soviet invasion of Hungary, in which he stated that "Yugoslavia must not be withdrawn into itself ... must work in every direction ... by contacts and conversations,"[19] they put increasing energy and thought into the non-alignment movement. This movement "may be defined as a grouping of countries of many different political systems, loosely linked together by moral ties, to use their joint efforts to promote the solution of world problems by peaceful means."[20] There were two conferences of the non-aligned countries in the early 1960s; the first took place in Belgrade in September 1961, with 23 countries in attendance; the second was held in Cairo in October 1964, with 47 countries as well as 11 observer countries attending. In his opening speech of the first conference, Tito set down the principles of non-alignment as "active peaceful coexistence between various social systems," and called for the "final eradication of colonialism."[21] He called the conference to "devote special attention to the question of economic cooperation among non-aligned countries,"[22] and had as his speech's "highlight ... the subject of disarmament and the need for banning nuclear weapons and their tests."[23]

---

[18] Phyllis Auty, "Yugoslavia's International Relations (1945–1965)," (1969), 181.
[19] Auty (1969), 180.
[20] Auty (1969), 190.
[21] Auty (1969), 191–2.
[22] Auty (1969), 192.
[23] Auty (1969), 192.

A Socialist Experiment

A little less than two years before young Danica from Zagreb fell asleep, a conference took place on December 4 and 5, 1965, at Stanford University in the USA, concerned with the same region that we speak of today, except that the "region" was then called, of course, "contemporary Yugoslavia." Organized by history professor Wayne Vucinich, the conference gathered eminent scholars from American universities, and focused on the country's history and current economy and politics, dealing especially with the concepts and practices of Yugoslavia's "socialist democracy" and "market socialism." In his contribution, "The Yugoslav Variation on Marx," M. George Zaninovich wrote:

> The Yugoslav theorist also acknowledges that a socialist society is replete with contradictions which, however, must continually move toward constructive resolution. ... new contradictions will emerge and reemerge within a socialist system ... Since the Yugoslavs begin with the premise that the concrete material interest of the working man provides the basic stimulus to activity, they also recognize the need for a competitive market economy and some level of interest-conflict to achieve socioeconomic progress. ...
> The Yugoslav theorist also points out that contradictions found in socialist society reflect a multidimensional aspect. In addition to that between personal and collective interests, contradiction exists between man-the-producer and man-the-consumer, federal state controls and regional self-government, distribution according to work and according to need, skilled and unskilled types of work, the demand for privilege and the pressures for leveling. It is significant that none of these contradictions are viewed as being absolute or unresolvable, while it is also acknowledged that new contradictions will unavoidably and continually appear. ... The upshot of the Yugoslav position is that both society and theory are viewed as dynamic and adoptive, a position based on conviction that it is unwise to be irrevocably wed to any specific set of principles.
> The overriding abstract goal of Yugoslav socialism is to overcome man's alienation ... This requires that two forms of

alienation be directly assaulted—the one economic, the other political. ... the economic form of alienation can be reduced by the gradual elimination of both private and state property, to be achieved by establishing social ownership of the means of production. And, secondly, the return of effective political power to the working citizenry by extending mass participation in direct socialist democracy serves to attenuate political alienation. ... The basic Yugoslav commitment might best be defined as involving indefinite experimentation with sociopolitical forms, with the view of eliminating dysfunctional contradictions and reducing the intensity of the experience of alienation.[24]

Waking Up

Danica knew nothing about the Stanford conference, or, most likely, about many of the concepts about which George Zaninovich wrote. Yet she lived and worked in an environment in which the "indefinite experimentation with socio-political forms" was taking place, the environment that was also characterized by the strong presence of traditional communal bonds that strengthened the "normalcy" of the rather egalitarian views on society. The vast disparities of wealth were seen as ethically bad, and the maxim "from each according to her or his ability, to each according to his or her needs" still sounded like an acceptable goal, as liable as it was to be interpreted, used and abused in many different ways, and as mitigated as it was by both the attempts to reward those who contributed more and the resistance to such attempts.

Given the above improvisatory sketch of a few aspects contained in one moment of the late 1960s, we can better imagine just how shocked and surprised our Danica was when she finally woke up in 2010. There is a weird mixture of times around her, as if some things moved ahead and some went backwards. Technology has obviously advanced. But the system now in place is capitalism, which was supposed to have been overcome years ago as an obsolete one. The countries she knew— Czechoslovakia,

---

[24] M. George Zaninovich, "The Yugoslav Variation on Marx", (1969), 295–6.

USSR, DDR—are gone, the two blocs are gone, and gone also is Yugoslavia; the Socialist Republic of Croatia, one of the six states of the Socialist Federative Republic of Yugoslavia, has now become its own country, Croatia, ditto the other formerly Yugoslav states and the formerly autonomous province of Kosovo. A war took place in her country during the time she slept, in the 1990s, and its traces remain everywhere.[25] No one mentions socialism in public; it is a bad word now, and "democracy and free market," said like that, in one breath, are the order of the day, replacing the former slogans of "self-management" or "brotherhood and unity." Competition, the market, success, rich, poor, globalization, elections, strikes, banks, and unemployment ("that one again!"); debates not on how to do it our way or the way that works or may best work for us, but on how it's done "in the world" and should therefore be done by us; desire, real or manufactured or imposed or unsure, of becoming a part of that world, a part of that elusive Europe above all. Mimesis.

Connecting Pathways

The political elites and national governments customarily assert the new states' difference and separation from the other Yugoslav Successor States and from the Yugoslav past. Yet, one of the first things that becomes apparent to Danica is that much of the prominent artwork—from all new post-Yugoslav countries—creates connecting pathways and energizing links with the artistic and intellectual, living legacies of a once common and now divided space. The prologue of the Macedonian film *Before the Rain* (*Pred doždot*, 1994), for instance, is a sentence from *Death and the Dervish*: "I am waiting, we are waiting, my blood aches from waiting." But whereas the novel begins with the main character,

---

[25] A large number of volumes discuss the causes and aspects of the so-called Wars of the Yugoslav Succession. On this, see Sabrina P. Ramet's *Thinking About Yugoslavia: Scholarly Debates About the Yugoslav Breakup and the Wars in Bosnia and Kosovo* (2005), among Ramet's many books on Yugoslavia before the break-up and in the wars, and on the newly independent states. Also see V. P. Gagnon Jr., *The Myth of Ethnic War* (2004) and Josip Glaurdić, *The Hour of Europe: Western Powers and the Breakup of Yugoslavia* (2011).

dervish Ahmed Nurrudin, betraying a man who hides in his *tekke*, *Before the Rain*'s Macedonian monk Kiril does not reveal the Albanian girl Zamira, hiding in his monastery, to those who pursue her, and the different opening of the film indicates the possibility of a different action in a similar violently charged situation. *Before the Rain*'s implied dialogue with *Dervish and Death* makes the sphere of the film vastly more complex and interesting for those who know Selimović's novel.

The actor reading this prologue to the film, who also plays the main role of war photographer Aleksandar Kirkov, is that young student Rade Šerbedžija, a Croatian man of Serb ethnic origin, who was coming from his city of Vinkovci to study in Zagreb in 1967, and who, while Danica was sleeping, became one of the most prominent actors of Yugoslavia and, especially, of his home state of Croatia. His life story seems symbolic of those artists who were committed to be working on both national and supra-national levels (Croatian and Yugoslav in his case); its recalling may show how this orientation fared in recent times. During the Yugoslav period, Šerbedžija played in Croatian national classics, as in the television series' adaptation of the classic nineteenth-century novel *In the Registrar's Office* (*U registraturi*) by Ante Kovačić. But he was also one of the main promoters of the Yugoslav theater *KPGT* (the first letters of the word meaning "theater" in four languages of Yugoslavia, Croatian—*kazalište*, Serbian—*pozorište*, Slovenian—*gledališče*, and Macedonian—*teater*), that was initiated by Belgrade's theater director Ljubiša Ristić, and that created one of the most fascinating theater productions of the 1980s, Dušan Jovanović's *The Liberation of Skopje* (*Oslobođenje Skopja*). The actor also played main roles in numerous Yugoslav-era films, was for years the most beloved Hamlet of the *Dubrovnik Summer Festival*, and put together and performed his own monologue based on the texts by Miroslav Krleža. He participated in Sarajevo's anti-war protests of April 1992 that ended with the gathered people being shot at in one of the actions that marked the official beginning of the war in Bosnia and Herzegovina. Šerbedžija stayed in the besieged Sarajevo for some days and then left for Belgrade to be with his wife, theater director Lenka Udovički, as she was giving birth to their child. He appeared on Croatian state television in the winter of 1993–4, in a call-in show where he was treated like an enemy of the state on account of his misrepresented recent actions and his Serbian ethnic background. Smoking one cigarette after another, he tried to talk sense and communicate with the audience, while selected callers—presented as "the people"— phoned in to abuse him. He moved to Slovenia where his loyal colleagues helped him obtain Slovenian citizenship that allowed him to travel, whereupon, after a few more changes of residence, he relocated to London where he was a year-long guest of British acting legend and human rights activist, Vanessa Redgrave. (The name given to Šerbedžija's and Udovički's second daughter, born in Redgrave's apartment, is Vanessa-Vanja.) In London Šerbedžija met Macedonian-American director Milcho Manchevski, who cast him in *Before the Rain*, which jump-started the actor's subsequent career in Hollywood. He moved to Los Angeles with his family, and worked there for years. He also founded, in the year 2000, the summer theater *Ulysses* on the island of Brijuni (formerly Brioni) off the coast of Croatia, which has become one of the most prominent theater sites in the region. He has most recently relocated with his family back to Croatia, to the city of Rijeka, to live there as well as found and direct the interdisciplinary program "Acting, Media, Culture" at the University of Rijeka. In the last two decades, Šerbedžija appeared in numerous international productions but also in Bosnian, Serbian, Macedonian and Croatian films, linking all these films with his presence.[26]

A number of literary and cinematic works from the Yugoslav Successor States create direct or indirect ties with the common Yugoslav history and with the realms of other Yugoslav Successor States. The Slovenian film *The Border Guard* (*Varuh meje*, directed by Maja Weiss, 2002), for example, has a character who says, looking across the river Kolpa/Kupa into Croatia, "this really makes no sense; before we fished together ... and now ...," leaving unsaid what this now is, and how it actually relates to that "before." Warned against the wild Croats, the three Slovenian girls cross the border

---

[26] The information about Šerbedžija is assembled from newspapers and his autobiography. See Rade Šerbedžija, *Do posljednjeg daha: Autobiografski zapisi i refleksije* [*To the Last Breath: Autobiographical Notes and Reflections*] (2004). *Do posljednjeg daha* is also a Croatian translation of the title of Jean-Luc Godard's film *Breathless* (*À bout de souffle*, 1960), and Šerbedžija's autobiography plays with that connotation as well.

and form the single positive relationship of the film with a retired Croatian actor. Another Slovenian film, the very popular *Cheese and Jam* (*Kajmak in marmelada*, 2003), written, directed, and starring Branko Đurić Đuro, not only has a multi-ethnic (reminiscent of old Yugoslav) relationship at its center, with him being a Bosnian emigrant and her a Slovenian local, but also inscribes, with the appearance of the main actor Đurić Đuro, the memory of the *Top List of Surrealists* (*Top lista nadrealista*), Sarajevo's 1980s hit radio and TV series, whose special brand of surrealism and Monty Python-like political commentary was endorsed and loved throughout the Former Yugoslavia. Established Croatian writer of the younger generation, Zagreb's Zoran Ferić, dedicates his story "The Island on Kupa" ("*Otok na Kupi*") to Serbian author Milorad Pavić, "with trepidation," and Croatian writer Ante Tomić models the main character of his novel *Nothing Should Surprise Us* (*Ništa nas ne smije iznenaditi*, 2003), Ljuba Vrapče from Belgrade, after the character from Serbian writer Dragoslav Mihailović's novel *When the Pumpkins Blossomed* (*Kad su cvetale tikve*, 1968). Tomić's novel, set in the late Yugoslav era (1980s), features characters from Montenegro, Slovenia, Bosnia and Herzegovina, and revolves around an unlikely friendship between a doctor from Croatia's coastal city of Split, Siniša, and a young hoodlum, Ljuba Vrapče, from Belgrade, Serbia. Another very well liked Croatian novel revolves around multi-ethnic relations among people from now separate countries: Renato Baretić's *The Eighth Representative* (*Osmi povjerenik*, 2003) spins a tale of a young Croatian politician sent to a deserted island, where he forges an unlikely friendship with an odd Bosnian couple. Mirjana Karanović, an actress greatly popular in the region, formerly Belgrade-based and now residing in Sarajevo, plays a Croatian mother in Vinko Brešan's *Witnesses* (*Svjedoci*, 2003, a Croatian film), a Bosnian-Serbian mother in Ahmed Imamović's *Go West* (2005) and a Bosnian-Bosniak mother in Jasmila Žbanić's *Grbavica* (2006; both Bosnian films).

Retrieving Words from the Past

But there are other and more direct examples of bringing back, retrieving and reactivating this Yugoslav intellectual and artistic past in the present, in the form of reprinting or publishing for the very first time not only the artistic works, but also the most "literal-level" words of those who were the active threads of that Yugoslav reality, the words of their interviews or even their previously unpublished notes. These include the 2001 reprinting of Predrag Matvejević's *Conversations with Krleža* (*Razgovori s Krležom*, 1969), and the first printing of Miroslav Krleža's conversations with Belgrade's Miloš Jevtić, recorded or assembled from Krleža's writings for Radio Belgrade and printed in Zagreb under the title *To the Much Respected Gentlemen Ants* (*Mnogopoštovanoj gospodi mravima*, 2009). Krleža, 1893–1981, is one of the most important and influential Yugoslav and Croatian writers and intellectuals, commonly seen as the greatest Croatian writer of the modern era. His 1938 novel *On the Edge of Reason* (*Na rubu pameti*) will be discussed here in Chapter 11.

Given that there is so much talk, in these times, in the Yugoslav Successor States about "joining Europe" and "becoming part of Europe," let us quickly remember the stance of writers such as Miroslav Krleža, Ivo Andrić, and Danilo Kiš regarding Europe. Cosmopolitan and polyglot, these writers have lived in and experienced "Europe" first-hand, from Krleža's many travels and residencies abroad—including the one in the USSR in the 1920s, recorded in his *A Trip to Russia* (*Izlet u Rusiju*, 1926), Andrić's diplomatic service in European capitals, to Kiš's later life in France, with his first stay there recorded in his *Trip to Paris* (*Izlet u Pariz*, 1960). More importantly, they studied this Europe and its history, and knew the works of European culture—its literature and art—deeply and thoroughly.[27] This intimate knowledge allowed

---

[27] Young Ivo Andrić, for instance, "was an avid reader, and his breadth of literary interest was enormous. He read Greek and Latin classics in addition to the major works of many European authors, including Carlyle, Cervantes, Chernyshevsky, Conrad, Flaubert, Goethe, Heine, Hugo, Ibsen, James, Kafka, Leopardi, Mann, Masaryk, Maupassant, Montaigne, Nietzsche, Pascal, Rilke, and Scott. Andrić liked Polish literature and claimed to owe a great deal to Polish poets and novelists. He held several South Slavic writers in high esteem, particularly Vuk St. Karadžić and Petar Petrović Njegoš of the older generation, and the more contemporary Petar Kočić and Aleksa Šantić. Andrić favored the Slovene poets Fran Levstik, Josip Murn, and Oton Župančič, and translated some of their works. The literary creations of several Scandinavian writers appealed to him, and he translated Strindberg. He was also influenced by Franz Kafka, whose work may have inspired Andrić's more mature prose. Probably no author left as strong a philosophical impact on young

a discerning, non-generalizing, and critical attitude, the one of an intellectual equal, instead of the inferior attitude of a pupil having to learn, or desiring a mimetic approximation of the "European" ideal, that is often felt in the post-Yugoslav cultural space. Consider, for instance, Danilo Kiš's reflection on French literature, from the 3 March 1965 interview with Milan Vlajčić in the magazine *Mladost*:

MV: You spent a lot of time in France and had a chance to see how the translations of our distinguished writers fare with the French literary critics. Which of our [i.e., Yugoslav] values get a real response?

DK: We have a better writer from all of the contemporary French writers, including Sartre: that is Krleža. His book *A Banquet in Blitva* was unnoticed in Paris. His other books will fare the same in France and in the West. And Krleža is a greater writer and greater philosopher than Sartre. A French bourgeois is not interested in our artistic values but in our tourist attractions. I am convinced that our literature today, and especially our poetry, is above the French, and particularly this unread, unrecognized *Karleja*, who cannot be found in the [writers'] dictionary because he is transcribed as *Kerleja*. But what do we care? We still learn at his side.[28]

So what are some of the things that one could learn today from Miroslav Krleža or, as Kiš puts it, "at his side"? Let us look at a few fragments from these new editions of conversations with Krleža. Here, for example, is Krleža answering questions on various topics.

Andrić as Søren Kierkegaard. Andrić also attached great importance to a number of distinguished American authors, especially Walt Whitman. At one time Andrić was interested in Chinese and Japanese authors, whom he read in French and German translations." (Wayne S. Vucinich, "Introduction: Ivo Andrić and His Times," in Wayne S. Vucinich ed., *Ivo Andrić Revisited: The Bridge Still Stands* (1996), 2–3.

Andrić's university studies took place at the University of Zagreb, University of Vienna, and Jagiellonian University in Cracow, Poland.

[28] Danilo Kiš, *Varia*, ed. Mirjana Miočinović (1995), 492–3. Translated by Gordana P. Crnković. Krleža becomes more visible in the French literary scene a few years after Kiš's interview.

On socialism:

Socialism means a peaceful life under warm roofs and not feeding fires across the whole world. Socialism means hospitals, and not the creation of mass hunger and sickness. Socialism means a cult of good books and beautiful arts, and not a betrayal of ethics and manslaughter. Socialism means the human morality amongst peoples and countries, and not the cult of lie, death, and political murder ... Socialism is nothing else but a preventive, prophylactic action that decreases all kinds of Suffering, thus Pain, thus Evil. Accordingly, socialism is exactly "only that," the fight against earthly evils by earthly means, and not any "idea from above."[29]

On technology:

In that regard the results are usually merciless caricatures of hopes and expectations. Here is one contemporary example: landing on the Moon ... I will add, without intention to undermine the technical success of the endeavor, that during this first flight one of them (the astronauts) celebrates mass like a Protestant priest, which means he believes in and prays to god, and the other, when he saw the Moon up close with his own eyes, could think only of naming one crater with the name of his wife. A touchingly sentimental gesture! They thus carried to the Moon their own earthly views of the world ...

In connection to that, I would remind you of one excerpt from [Krleža's book of essays] *Ten Bloody Years* (*Deset krvavih godina*, 1937):

"In accordance with Divine Command, the ranks and orders of the Triple-United Kingdom undertook with their deepest servility the expedition to the Moon, landed on the coast of Plato's Sea, waiting in unison and obedience the further Divine orders and always ready to sacrifice lives in their loyalty, not only for the invasion of Luna, but also of the

---

[29] Miroslav Krleža, *Mnogopoštovanoj gospodi mravima (razgovarao Miloš Jevtić)* [*To Much Esteemed Gentlemen Ants (Conversations with Miloš Jevtić)*] (2009), 87–8. Translated by Gordana P. Crnković.

other planets, within the realm, and if necessary outside of the frame of our solar system." With this I wanted to say that if one goes on with such low logic, we should not be surprised if one day comes the news that the astronaut forces of Bloc A or Bloc B landed on the coast of the Sea of Silence and exchanged rocket fire from posts at the craters Copernicus and Aristotle.[30]

On science and art:

A scientific consciousness rose up above the problems of various human worries and sicknesses ... but it is utterly helpless before politics ... [A human being] has command over a whole range of destructive forces, but cannot yet figure out how to protect himself and future generations from the cobalt bomb. Curing measles and diarrhea and pneumonia with the injection of viruses, a human being, on the other hand, menaces his survival with much more refined "antibiotic" inventions, losing his way so much that one could assert, without exaggeration, that the mind has become the greatest danger for human life ...

Science actually dreams, and that, if one sees it right, is not such a stupid thought. Science often sleeps with a dead dream devoid of ideas. It snores at the university departments and that thunder resounds through all the halls of the world.

Art makes its way through the centuries under the unclear, unintelligible, and often nervously aggressive dictates of so-called scientific truths. Scientific hypothesis changes on a whim through the ages ... scientific formulae follow rhythmically the game of blind and destructive forces, the forces regarding which poetry had its own melancholic picture a long time ago.[31]

On history or, as Predrag Matvejević puts it, on Krleža's take on history that is much closer to Nietzsche than to Marx, where the "class struggle" is only a "superficial episode whereas the negation of that which is human is a veritable tragedy," Krleža said:

---

[30] Predrag Matvejević, *Razgovori s Krležom* [*Conversations with Krleža*], (2001), 77–8. Translated by Gordana P. Crnković.
[31] Krleža (2009), 71–2.

It is true: history detached itself from everything that is human. But what is here a human being? In what measure is he a constant? A human being, of the Old Testament type? The Helenist of the fourth century who fears for his life day and night because he secretly reads Sophocles and Euripides? Around him scream hermits, ascetics, future metaphysical career-makers. Saints. Before illiterate masses they burn books, temples, libraries, kill women and children, make history. These are the "super humans" who will in the name of their morally-intellectual consciousness control history for the next two millennia. And the Hellenistic decadents will dissolve into the air like laments from Boethius to the present day. The lyrical resignation of the lonely mind in a long night. That too is history. And those saints were the engines of progress.[32]

Recalling these few fragments by Krleža shows one of the many ways in which Yugoslav-era heritage is present and reactivated today. In addition to people's experiences and memories of the past, their ties of family, friendship, or work, and to what they hear from their elders or find themselves in books, museums, concert halls, or the material realities that surround them and would not go away, it is the Yugoslav intellectual legacy—as a realm of art and ideas—that is not solely a matter of the past but also a matter of the present that starts living the moment one looks at it, reads it, thinks about it or enters into a dialogue with it. Alongside all the other elements of an individual artist's make up, this productive realm, whose elements Danica may recognize—though seeing them in a different context and related to in different ways—will nourish in a number of different ways post-Yugoslav literature and film, either literally or more obliquely. One should be at least somewhat aware of that realm before proceeding to examine a few of the most captivating post-Yugoslav art works.

---

[32] Matvejević (2001), 125.

2

Play and the Language of Community Against Rumor and the Guns

Alenka Mirković's *91.6 MHz*

Words are deeds.

LUDWIG WITTGENSTEIN, *PHILOSOPHICAL INVESTIGATIONS*[1]

Vukovar, once characterized by an ethnically diverse population, is a baroque town in eastern Croatia close to the Serbian border. It was attacked and besieged by the Yugoslav People's Army and Serbian paramilitary units for some three months until it was overrun in November 1991. Many of its citizens were killed, with many others wounded or forced into exile. When the siege was over, the city was so utterly destroyed that it was compared to Stalingrad and Dresden.

A Silent Archive

A lifelong resident of the city of Vukovar, Alenka Mirković—a lively and intelligent college graduate with many interests and a

---

[1] Ludwig Wittgenstein, *Philosophical Investigations*, I, #546, as quoted in Wittgenstein (1984), 46e.

wide network of friends and acquaintances—worked in 1991 as an elementary schoolteacher and newly employed reporter for Radio Vukovar, under the leadership of program director Siniša Glavašević. Mirković is not a professional writer but rather a technician, as she describes herself, and her book, *91.6 MHz: With The Voice Against the Guns* (*91.6 MHz: Glasom protiv topova*, 1997) is a non-fictional narrative shaped as a novel. Literary scholar Andrea Zlatar unequivocally calls it "a novel," adding that "real persons and events are shaped into characters and a chronologically structured plot," and that "the story begins with episodes from the war's 'prelude' from 1990 and ends with an escape from the surrounded city, in the night before the city's fall."[2] Indeed, with an abundance of individualized dialogues and engaging characters, a disciplined first-person narrative, relentless suspense regarding the progression of the plot (despite our being aware of the tragic ending in advance), and an absorbing narrator's voice, *91.6 MHz* reads more like a novel than a memoire.

Mirković's book, however, has an emphatically referential goal—to convey as accurately as possible the author's own personal experience of the siege of the Croatian city of Vukovar, in as direct a way as possible, formatting the text in a basic chronological manner, one chapter per month. The writing is simple and transparent, and in a number of places it recalls an oral mode of narration. The text feels as if Mirković recounts this past in front of a live audience: the pace is brisk, and the vocabulary and syntax those of animated speech. The well-known formulaic devices often present in speech (e.g., "a smile froze on my face and my stomach twisted")[3] do not "estrange" the language and make it an object of reflection, but on the contrary create a text that largely feels familiar, like a recorded though elaborate speech. People are described with a few words, and then solely through their actions and speech, and dialogues are so personalized and vivid that one wonders whether Mirković actually had her tape-recorder on at all

---

[2] Andrea Zlatar, *Tekst, tijelo, trauma* [*Text, Body, Trauma*] (2004), 166.
[3] Alenka Mirković, *91.6 MHz: Glasom protiv topova* [*91.6 MHz: With the Voice Against the Guns*] (1997), 90. All translations from this book are by Gordana P. Crnković. Further citations from the book will be marked by the page number in the main text.

times, to be able to reproduce these exchanges in such an authentic manner.

The book presents an abundance of raw material related to what took place on the ground level of an individual experience, what people around Mirković said or did, what the author herself experienced, with a precision of details, but without spelling out any broader generalizations made on the basis of these primary materials. Mirković's text thus exhibits some generic paradigms of a traditional chronicle, such as noting events in chronological order without offering or constructing the causal explanations of a historian. Mirković's own reaction to events is reduced to brief commentaries but almost never brings up any overarching generalizations about what is happening around her. The materials chronicled thus have a unique feel of breathing freely, not being subsumed under this or that concept. The text does not have a quality of either highly formed literary artefact or an ambitious and explicatory historical narrative, but rather creates the space of a silent archive unwittingly assembled and roughly organized, a space in which a reader can wander among its as yet unlabeled materials and see what they themselves may reveal.

Among other things, the book details the successive stages of the breaking down of a number of harmonious inter-ethnic circles that Mirković was familiar with. The narrative recounts the advent of aggressive nationalism, but the text does not offer or speculate much on any definitive reasons as to why things happened the way they did, why and how they went from one stage to another. What we get instead is a series of perfectly clear snap-shots of distinct moments of time, all seen from Mirković's own individual perspective, which by themselves do not reveal the underlying logic by which one moment leads to another. In the beginning stage, for example, "an inseparable gang of four—four male physical education teachers" from the school where Mirković used to work, two Serbs and two Croats, had for years "organized a soccer game, [cooking and eating of] *fish-paprikash* and playing of *bela* [a popular card game] until the late night hours" every Friday. (61) Or Mirković remembers how "in Vukovar itself everything still looked the same" even as tensions grew in the rest of the country, and how "we went on functioning like a community, we worked together, went out and had fun together, went to each other's weddings and celebrations." (14) We get a sketch of Mirković's own special and affectionate relationship with Nada, an older school colleague who happens to be a Serb living in Borovo Selo:

> Little by little, we became friends, and when she heard that I had recently lost my second parent as well she decided to "adopt me" because she had two sons, and wanted a daughter as well. Soon we jokingly called each other mom and daughter. (36)

Some time later, after the May 1991 killing of Croatian policemen in Borovo Selo, a predominantly Serb village close to Vukovar, the four teachers keep up their "seemingly normal communication but there are no more parties on Fridays," and Nada withdraws from the school's common room for teachers, and spends the breaks between classes on her own. The conversations between Alenka and Nada reveal that not only the two women's takes on the situation, but also their most basic understanding of what is actually happening, who is involved and how, and who is doing what to whom, start an increasing and radical divergence to the point where communication becomes impossible. For instance, when Alenka believes "*chetniks*" (Serb paramilitary units) entered the area because "at least ten people I know saw them there," Nada is genuinely convinced that this is an invention and there are "only our people [local villagers] and the Army." Eventually, the previous "mother and daughter" do not only see and understand things in diametrically opposite ways, but Nada's reactions also convince Mirković that Nada, her "second mother ... does not care at all about people who die right in front of her nose from bullets and grenades, people like Slavica [another school colleague] and her family, people like me." (83)

Right or wrong, the conviction that Nada, her "second mother," would "chirp how nothing special is going on" even if Alenka herself were in grave danger leads to Mirković's internal collapse, her first attempt to leave the city ("Within half-an-hour I was at the bus station;" Mirković later decides to stay (83)), and her own seemingly complete detachment from her erstwhile good friend.

Two people who have genuinely liked each other have at the end of this brief period become indifferent to the other's destiny, and the "gang of four" drops out of the narrative altogether. What happened? And how could that which happened between Alenka and Nada happen elsewhere?

Everyday Life and the Community's Self-Understanding

Before this separation and alienation took place, the Vukovar of Mirković's memoire is remembered as a site of socializing based not on one's ethnicity but rather on one's own individual "matching" with other people. As Bojan Glavašević, the son of Siniša Glavašević, put it some years after the city's fall: "My peers and friends in Vukovar, people I know, did not grow up thinking they were Croats, Serbs, Hungarians, or Ruthenians. Some thirty different national minorities lived in the city and no one thought this was important."[4] Alenka is at this stage genuinely connected with Siniša B., a Croat, Svetlana, a Serb, with many people coming from so-called "mixed families" (parents or partners of different ethnicities), and also, though not so closely, with Siniša Glavašević. Individual identities take clear precedence over group ones, which themselves include professional affiliation (teachers), or local and regional attachments aside from, and sometimes rather than, national affiliations. People considered themselves citizens of Vukovar or neighboring villages, and inhabitants of the region of Slavonia, and this local or regional affiliation included all of them and excluded members of their different respective nations and minorities who lived in other regions. Tired of the pre-election tensions, the four physical education teachers joked that they would found the "Party of Fat Slavonians," whose greeting would be "Heil Liter!" (21), and Mirković also mentions other instances of people's reactions in which "Slavonians in them won over the great Croats." (26)

---

[4] Slavica Lukić and Boris Oreškić, "DjecaVukovara" ["The Children of Vukovar"], *Globus* (Zagreb), 25 November 2005, p. 44. Siniša Glavašević was executed after the fall of Vukovar by the occupying forces.

This first stage is characterized by people of varying ethnic backgrounds working and living together in neighborhoods and apartment houses, and by many instances of their shared communal life, such as the first swim in the Vuka in May accompanied by a festive barbeque, celebrations of Catholic Christmas (enjoyed not only by believers but also by many young people for whom this was a unique opportunity to "stay out from early afternoon until the wee hours of the dawn"), of many Serbian Orthodox *Slava* holidays (celebrations related to an individual family's patron saint held on that saint's day), and of *kirbaji* (*kirbaj* or *kirvaj*, from German *Kirchweih*, a church festivity), elaborate weddings, celebrations of traditional festivities coming from different ethnic traditions, or simply the numerous impromptu gatherings of friends in cafés, squares, or homes. Much joy and pleasure is derived from the intense activity and the endless creative possibilities of social interaction. In this society that had largely bypassed developed capitalism, having transitioned into modernity by changing from a mostly rural traditional society into an industrialized and socialist one, festivities still held much of their traditional characteristic of not being just an empty time mostly dedicated to resting from work. They had a lot of their own spiritual and social content, and were most importantly marked by joy in and the creativity of socializing with people who one was with so much that they became an extended community with its various levels of closeness.[5]

Work was important, and people mentioned in the memoire worked hard in their schools, factories, fields, and other varied places of employment. Mirković tells matter-of-factly about all that the teachers and administration of her own grammar school did to maintain regular teaching, the safety of the children, and emotional and social support for the families in increasingly difficult and eventually dangerous circumstances. Yet, society is not "monomaniacal" in the sense of privileging work, or, indeed, anything else

---

[5] As Zlatko Janković of the Kopenhagen University puts it for the whole region, "it is precisely this everyday life, in all its variety, that was the most important part of the lives of the Yugoslavs. And although this was a 'lived reality' of the Yugoslavs—in a much larger degree than the inter-ethnic relations—the last twenty years [i.e., 1991 to the present] put that everyday life in the background ..." Personal email to the author, 8 April 2011.

like a nuclear family, political engagement, or consumerism, over many other aspects of one's life. These other aspects include friends and friendships, extended family, one's special relation with one's town, hearty *Slavonian* food, sports (a reader who knows a bit more about regional sport arrangements can imply from one piece of information in the memoire that Mirković herself was an exceptional tennis player, something she does not mention herself), books (Mirković's relationship with Siniša Glavašević who "loved to read" the way she did was largely based on their mutual delving into books), and, most of all, *zezanje,* or fooling around, are all very important parts of one's life.

Everyday life in Vukovar is thus largely marked by its being rich and varied, and by its many different social relationships. It is also marked by an individual's idiosyncratic self-creation: many people from Mirković's memoire come across like fictional characters on account of their captivating distinctiveness, fullness, and completeness; they are at ease with themselves. They are also characterized by steady integrity: after the start of the siege, Mirković notes that she "was glad, and not" when she found out that her brother left Vukovar with his family as things got dangerous; after a few days, when she meets him in the city and realizes that he had returned immediately after having taken his family to a safe place, she closes the scene with the same words—"I was glad, and not." The same clean, quick, and sure decisions were repeated around the city in the last months of 1991, where people did not seem to go through angst-ridden dramas on what is probably their most important decision ever—whether to stay to defend one's city and risk dying, or leave and save one's life. When one of the city's defenders decides in a moment to help Mirković, whom he has just encountered and will not see again, by giving her something that he himself needs, she "felt warmth, endless gratitude, and sadness: my god, what people die here!" (313) Mirković herself listens to her body that tells her what she herself cannot conceptualize; every time she decided to leave, as the situation grew more desperate and "Death frenetically mowed around Vukovar ... sparing no one," (282) her stomach started hurting so badly that she changed her mind, at which point she immediately felt better. Trusting her instincts, Mirković made an improbable escape at the last moment, just before the fall of the city which, in the night and from the corn fields where she found herself, looked "like all the devils were raging in it, the incandescent point in the distance that was falling apart under rumbling and shooting." (315)

Getting back to the characteristics of everyday life before the war, one of the most important aspects still to be mentioned is this life's playfulness, about which more will be said later. It suffices now to mention that this playfulness is generously remembered and often recreated in detail. Before their mutual alienation, Nada is much appreciated on account of her talent for constant joking and playful flirting, Siniša Glavašević is first noted as someone who simply has the great talent of being around children who love him, a school colleague Slavica is really "seen" and truly communicated with for the first time when she uncovers her own great comedy potential, as she and Mirković spend long hours working on the students' final comments in the highest of spirits because Slavica has just then decided to "tell all those jokes" that she knew. The spirit of playfulness permeates Mirković's own behavior and speech at the time, as well as her *a posteriori* text. The chapters of *91.6 MHz* are divided into many smaller units of narration, and a part that reports a tragic event is often followed by one that recalls this joking spirit. After lying in the mud and hearing an enemy tank so close that she "thought how the tank was going to cross over us," (320) Mirković gets up and takes a cigarette from a friend:

> In a little forest ahead of us we stopped to compose ourselves, Toni took out cigarettes. *Marlboro*, man! He offered me a cigarette saying:
> "Just watch so that your tip is not seen ..."
> "Come on ...," I said half-seriously. "I too started smoking in high school ..." We tried to smile. This was one of the dearest memories of every younger person from Vukovar. The generations started to smoke in Vukovar high school's yard, and the first lesson was to hide the tip of your cigarette in your fist so that passing professors would not notice it. (321)

Johannes Huizinga's classic definition of play as something disinterested and free comes to mind here.[6] But as opposed to his

---

[6] "Here, then, we have the first main characteristic of play: that it is free, is in fact freedom. ... As regards its formal characteristics, all students lay stress on the

assertion that play has its own well defined space and time outside the earnest space and time of everyday life, play in Mirković's memoire spills out and infuses much of everyday life before the siege, and even, quite unbelievably, the relations during the siege.[7] This playfulness and humor saturate Mirković's language as well.

The one activity that emphatically does not seem to be taking place within the varied communities of pre-war Vukovar, however, is the production of communal meaning or self-understanding, or of some shared understanding of what these communities are about. People do not really seem to be discussing matters of common importance. People are socializing by doing things together: there is a clear primacy of doing over talking, or, more precisely, of work or leisure-time-related socializing, often coupled with playful non-referential "poetic" talk—jokes, puns, improvised dramatic or humorous dialogues mixed with some stenographic referential speech—over the more politically engaged speech concerning the larger community. The established communities of Vukovar, in short, are not communities marked by their "communicative rationality," that is, communities that consistently make and remake their own community-wide meanings.[8] Rather, the communal self-understanding seems to have been established at some unidentified moment in the past, appears shared by all, and includes a belief that "[l]ife in small environments the likes of Vukovar presupposed that the storms of big, historical, destiny-changing events would usually mostly have spent themselves rather well by the time they reached them." (9) Mirković writes that she was "sure that the majority of people in Vukovar, like [herself], thought that the dissolution of Yugoslavia would affect their own life very little." (9–10)

---

disinterestedness of play." Johan Huizinga, *Homo Ludens: A Study of the Play Element in Culture* (1955), 8 and 9.
[7] "This is the third main characteristic of play: its secludedness, its limitedness." Huizinga (1955), 9.
[8] I am referring here to a community marked by what Jürgen Habermas calls "communicative rationality," a term that stands for some rationality shared by all the members of community, and developed through their own interpersonal conversations, as opposed to rationality that comes into the community from the centers of the production of meaning external to the community itself.

91.6 MHz shows everyday community existence largely as un-conceptualized and non-verbal, in the sense that there is no conceptualizing of or talking about the main aspects and values of one's community or of one's vision of one's community. There is no activity in which community creates and re-creates its own self-understanding. However, when the established reality all of a sudden changes drastically, and one is at a loss to understand and say it, this lack of community's understanding of itself becomes fatal. Those who have helped bring about the violence have their prepared narratives, slogans, and new truths. The un-uttered past and present "loses out" before these highly produced and enforced narratives. In other words, the descriptions of the community or of the individual's life that might not have been accepted before, in times of peace, become much stronger now when both material realities and accepted or conventional concepts are in crisis and undergoing rapid change, and when people have no prepared words to tell what is happening to them now or what, indeed, was taking place before. The enforced "spoken non-reality" may win over the unspoken, "tongue-tied" reality, and words may get the upper hand over the facts.[9]

---

[9]Writing some years after the events, Mirković herself pays great attention to not allowing her language be affected with such spoken non-realities, as opposed to its saying only the remembered realities. Yet, her text also includes a few non-factual generalizations that seem to simply infiltrate language like a virus and become invisible. For example, early on in the book she writes that "Vukovar Serbs quickly accepted the game of their people from the other side of Danube and started loudly exclaiming how they were deprived of their rights." (18) Perhaps a qualifying "some" (as in "some Vukovar Serbs") disappeared in the editing process, or perhaps it was simply assumed, but the way it stands, the sentence generalizes from some Serb people who asserted non-factual claims to all of the Vukovar Serbs. Many citizens of Vukovar who were ethnic Serbs put themselves on the side of their city and not the side of the city's attackers. "By the end of August, only 15,000 of the town's original population of 50,000 were still there. Those who were left retained the ethnic mixture that had characterized the town before the war. Serbs and Croats suffered alike in the bombardment that followed." Laura Silber and Allan Little, *Yugoslavia: Death of a Nation* (1996), 176.

Kruno Kardov writes about how these Vukovar Serbs, who shared everything with their co-citizens, got ostracized and invisible after the war, and that "the memories of a great number of Serbs who stayed in the city, living with Croats for three months in basements or city shelters, were not represented in official versions." Kruno Kardov, "Remember Vukovar: Memory, Sense of Place, and the National

Mirković's memoire offers a unique insight into the important individual differences towards the reception and creation of such an "invasive" language of crisis. The main division emerging in her book is that between two main types of speech channeling and production, one that I will call the language of *Fama* (rumor personified), and the other that attempts to build the language of community. *91.6 MHz* focuses on differences in the individual processing (receiving, transmitting, creating) of the language of crisis. On one hand, some people try to build the language of community in its present turmoil, by attempting to contrive a previously non-existent, different kind of communal behavior, a communicative interaction which could produce some badly needed new shared meanings. Mirković's own apartment, for example, becomes a private space that allows passionate debates among her friends' clashing opinions:

> My living room would become a real debating club ... and I was proud of the reputation I had among friends, that one may say whatever one thinks in my house. It cost me time, nerves and stomach, but I thought that friendship was more important than politics ... (15)

It Fama per Urbes: Rumor Traverses the City

> *In those days Rumor took an evil joy*
> *At filling country-sides with whispers, whispers*
> *Gossip of what was done and never done.*
>
> Vergil, *Aeneid*

But some of these same people meeting in Alenka's apartment were increasingly sounding like the media they were following. Thus, one of the friends who often "debated" in Mirković's home gradually started to sound pretty much like "Serbian TV [meaning Belgrade state television]," (15) and another was often quoting assertions that he would have heard on Croatian state television (Zagreb TV).

Tradition in Croatia," in Sabrina P. Ramet and Davorka Matić (eds), *Democratic Transition in Croatia: Value Transformation, Education & Media* (2007), 70.

In addition to sounding like various media outlets, the language practice of some individuals is also increasingly characterized by the spreading of unfounded gossip.

> ... [Mirković's friend S.] came to my place for a cup of coffee, politely inquired about my job on the radio and then suddenly asked what kind of a man is "that Siniša Glavašević." I tried to describe him in a few sentences, mostly in superlatives, to which she reacted a bit skeptically:
> —I don't know ... he may be fine, but I heard all kinds of things about his father ...
> I got silent guessing what all she could have "heard" and from whom, hoping that she would shut up too, but then, from the sofa on which she was lying, the icy voice of my aunt was heard:
> —And what is it you heard about Perica?
> —Well I heard ... even how he killed some neighboring Serbs during the [Second World] war ...
> She didn't even manage to finish when my aunt sat up and started in an agitated manner:
> —Come on, don't talk nonsense, pray who said that to you? Perica was a child at the time ... Whom was he killing? Nonsense, by God ... She paused for a moment, and then, already snarling, she went on: Now ... everyone slaughtered someone ... you all only talk that without any sense [*bez veze*], just to talk ... just to make trouble, that's it!
> I listened in astonishment to this outburst of anger, and [S.] tried to get herself out of it:
> —Well, I don't know ... that's what I heard ...
> —So why are you talking when you don't know? If you have nothing else to say you didn't have to take that up either ... my aunt interrupted her angrily. (88)

In addition to spreading implausible rumors about locals, some people actively start to create texts about themselves on the basis of the given victimization parameters:

> I remember a man from one of those news stories [seen on Belgrade TV], a Serbian man from Bobota, who was saying, almost in tears, how it is hard for him to live in "ustasha territory" because they do not let him get a job, how he has nothing to live

off, how his children are mistreated in school because they are Serbs ... By sheer accident I knew the man—by his estate. He had an unbelievably large house at the very entrance of the village Bobota, a two story, two-apartment one, with a huge yard full of machinery, a few garages ... And by a sheer accident I knew that in Bobota, for years now, all the teaching is done in the Serbian language, and children in the third grade learn—Latin letters.

I could not understand how and why someone can lie so much ... Regardless of the facts ... regardless of the probability that those lies could cause a great evil, they insistently and scrupulously kept lying ... (19)

Some people started spreading nationalist "master-narratives" they heard from the media, as well as spreading or even creating fictional stories about themselves as victims and others as victimizers. A propensity of oral communities for something called "homeostatic adjustment," that is, a situation in which "any speaker or oral performer is vulnerable to the pressures and predispositions of the audience,"[10] could also have exacerbated this process of the spread of potentially deadly stories and rumors in the increasingly ethnically homogenized circles. With more aggressive nationalist speakers gaining the upper hand in a conversational situation, other speakers ("performers") might become "subject to the possibly intrusive behavior or even threatening pressures of the recipients,"[11] and speak in a more nationalist way themselves or become silent altogether. The sociable, playful and largely oral culture of Vukovar can thus also become an environment of increasingly separated groups where there is "suspicion ... toward non-conforming individuals" who do not fit into the newly loudly asserted nationalist molds of speech.[12]

Some people were breaking their erstwhile community into adversarial ethnic sides by transmitting received gossip or by creating their own victimization narratives. Yet, the increasing

---

[10] Russell Berman, *Fiction Sets You Free: Literature, Liberty, and Western Culture* (2007), 88.
[11] Berman (2007), 89.
[12] Berman (2007), 89.

ethnic separation of some portion of Vukovar's people was also due to progressively different realities into which now separating "sides" were pushed, the realities that they knew were factual but which for the now "other" side seemed like paranoid stories and pure fiction. For instance, Mirković obviously believed that she could be sure in her saying that the Croatian Serb peasant from Bobota was lying. However, she may at least theoretically have been wrong here because the fact that the situation she describes was factual even a short while ago, when she last knew it to be so, was not proof that things did not change in the most recent period of the last month or even the last one or two weeks. Mirković knows that Serbian paramilitary forces were indeed present in the area because of the accounts of a number of trustworthy people who simply "saw them," while her Serb friend Nada is most likely genuinely convinced that this is a "fictional story." The photographs of the fall of Vukovar, showing people in *"chetnik"* uniforms leading the prisoners, alongside all the other information we have at this point about the involvement of Šešelj's *"chetniks"* in this region, confirms Mirković's assertion. However, Mirković herself does not seem to know that a radical HDZ [*Hrvatska demokratska zajednica*, Croatian Democratic Union party] official, Gojko Šušak, actually went from Zagreb to Slavonia and shot a few rockets into Borovo Selo as early as April 1991.[13] The image of the rockets was shown on Belgrade TV and strengthened by its own real factuality the alleged factuality of many other claims made by the Milošević regime, of the Croatian victimization of the Serbs living in Croatia, allegations and "news items" that were themselves fully fabricated. Mirković also seems as if she, like many other people in Croatia, did not know that a number of Serb civilians had indeed disappeared and were disappearing in the Vukovar region in the period before mass violence broke out. As journalist Slavica Lukić reported years after the publication of *91.6 MHz*, "the mining of the houses, the break ins ... the disappearances and liquidation of the [Serb] civilians in the area of Vukovar and Borovo Naselje became frequent after May 2, 1991 ... [those Serb civilians that

---

[13] Laura Silber and Allan Little, *Yugoslavia: Death of a Nation* (1996), 140.

were killed] ... before the beginning of the armed battles in Vukovar ... numbered more than fifty."[14]

What was happening here was a planned provocation and acceleration of hostilities, initiated by the regime of Slobodan Milošević but at some point accepted and adopted by Croatian nationalist hard-liners, with the goal of initiating war and bringing with it territorial and material gains, and political power. The Serbian hard-liners' provocation at the beginning of April 1991 with the first casualties of war at Plitvice Lakes was followed by Croatian hard-liners' provocation in Slavonia near Vukovar, undertaken by "radical HDZ activists" who ...

> ... did what they could to provoke conflict. In the middle of April, a group of highly-placed HDZ members, led by Gojko Šušak, an extreme nationalist who was one of President Tuđman's closest advisors and whose personal fortune, from an Ottawa pizza company, had helped fund Tuđman's 1990 election campaign ... From outside the village [Borovo Selo, a Serb-populated village near Vukovar], Šušak and his companions fired three shoulder-launched Ambrust missiles into the village. ... One rocket hit a house; another landed in a potato field and failed to explode. It was later exhibited on Belgrade TV as evidence of Croat aggression.[15]

The hard-liners from outside the region, and some from within the region, intimidated, oppressed, and often "cleansed" and even liquidated moderates from their own political parties or "their own" ethnic groups. Indeed, these moderate people were the main enemy precisely because they could create an alternative voice and thus alternative action for the national groups that the hard-liners aimed to control, or could potentially diffuse the newly enforced formation of ethnic groups as mutually adversarial.[16]

---

[14] Slavica Lukić, "Crna knjiga Domovinskog rata" ["The Black Book of the Homeland War"], *Globus* (Zagreb), 10 August 2005, p. 27.
[15] Silber and Little (1996), 140.
[16] Thus "the regional police chief Josip Reihl-Kir [who was] of mixed German and Slovene descent [and] considered himself Croatian ... was a moderate who had worked tirelessly, on both sides of the rapidly-forming front lines, to remove barricades and restore mutual trust." Silber and Little (1996), 140. "Kir

The media outside Yugoslavia also sometimes transmitted fictional stories, with tragic consequences. Reuters' Belgrade office, for instance, reported one such invented story, alleging that 41 Serb children were killed by the retreating Croatian forces at the time of the fall of the city. The news agency retracted the story 24 hours later, "[b]ut the damage had been done."[17] According to Alan Little and Laura Silber, the story, which "turned out to be nonsense," was based on "a claim made by an unnamed JNA colonel to a Belgrade photographer."[18] Reuters reported it like a fact, and "[t]he news spread like wild-fire across the Serb-populated areas of Croatia and neighboring Bosnia."[19] In this case, the news agency participated in the dissemination of fictional words that were helping to bring about factual deaths, just as Mirković's gossiping friend may have

---

was murdered by HDZ extremists on July 1." Ibid., 144. V. P. Gagnon Jr. writes that "the violence and terror did not end with the expulsion of the non-Serbs. Indeed, even after Krajina [a part of Croatian territory occupied by Serb forces in 1991–5] was cleansed, the violence mounted, as moderate Serbs in the region who criticised the Belgrade-allied Krajina leadership were harassed, threatened, and even killed. Consistently ... extremists in the ruling political parties used terror and violence against those Serbs who called for a more moderate policy that reflected the values and priorities of the Serb population in Croatia prior to the war." V. P. Gagnon, *The Myth of Ethnic War: Serbia and Croatia in the 1990s* (2004), 5.

The "purposefully provoked conflicts" by the Milošević regime "were publically characterized by Belgrade in its communications with the outside world as 'ethnic conflicts'" (Ibid., 100). "These Serbian moves gave Croat hard-liners an excuse to step up their repressive actions against the Serbs in areas where the ruling HDZ controlled the local government. In turn, these actions were pointed to by Belgrade's allies as proof of the threat to Serbs" (Ibid., 100–1).

[17] Silber and Little (1996), 181. Silber and Little write: "On the day Vukovar had fallen, Reuters' Belgrade bureau had reported that Croatian National Guardsman had slaughtered forty-one Serb children in revenge as they fled the city. The news spread like wild-fire across the Serb-populated areas of Croatia and neighboring Bosnia. Western news organizations, anxious for some 'balance' to include in their accounts of what otherwise seemed an impossibly one-sided sequence of events, also gave the claim undue prominence. The story turned out to be nonsense. The claim had been made by an unnamed JNA [Yugoslav People's Army] Colonel to a Belgrade photographer. Reuters issued an unqualified retraction twenty-four hours later. But the damage had been done." Ibid.
[18] Silber and Little (1996), 181.
[19] Silber and Little (1996), 181.

helped the abduction and execution of Siniša Glavašević's father with her stories about him. Bits of factual reality such as acts of violence against one's own ethnic group (themselves often provoked by the hard-liners who wanted war) were blown out of proportion by the respective state media and supplemented with a massive production of fictional reports, and a viewer or listener who may actually have known that one element of all of this was indeed factual might tend to believe that other alleged things were factual too. As the *Aeneid* put it, *Fama* (Rumor) fills "country-sides with ... gossip of what was done, and never done." Increasingly living in different communicational (media and everyday oral communication) and experiential environments, some—but not all—of the people in Mirković's circle of friends and acquaintances, who had until recently shared much, found themselves seeing and experiencing different things, and thinking and saying incompatible words. They got pushed apart, and their good relations got compromised and sometimes broken, making the dense living communities of Vukovar weaker and exposed to centrifugal forces that were tearing them into mutually antagonistic "sides."

"You Just Fool Around ..."

Rumor divided the space with fabrications, fear-mongering, misrepresentations, amplifications, and grotesque renderings. It was often orally transmitted, and forcefully promoted by the official state media. Fighting it, Radio Vukovar, at 91. 6 MHz, created a different and much-needed voice in this hall of echoes and distorting mirrors. Siniša Glavašević, the 31-year-old program director, envisioned local radio as a contact site where people themselves could call in and talk to each other in real time, but not in person. They were thus able to say and hear mutually discordant things they could not say or hear in face-to-face contact, and therefore hopefully create some measure of referential and at least partially agreed upon language relating to the increasingly volatile situation in which they found themselves.

I heard Siniša's voice ... He asked people to calm down, to call the phone lines of the radio and try to talk to one another directly on air, try to mollify the situation. It was a futile job. While in Borovo Naselje people fought with arms, on the waves of Radio Vukovar the war of words raged ... One hard word brought about a second, and then a third ... From time to time someone called who begged people to collect themselves and calm down because we would all be destroyed otherwise ...

I understood what Siniša wanted. It was better that people quarreled and took their violence out on air than on the street. And though it was hard to even only listen to all that, he doggedly tried to channel that anger ... to be a voice of reason in a situation that got out of control. (81)

Later on, when isolated incidents became a real siege of the city, Radio Vukovar served the people by providing information about shelters and food supplies, by broadcasting private messages to citizens deprived of phone lines, and by trying to keep their spirits up. Radio Vukovar also became a voice through which the city tried to relate the situation in the city to the international audience, as well as to the broader Croatian audiences outside Vukovar, and it encountered major problems in both of these endeavors. This voice, in short, is itself increasingly weakened and isolated: Mirković remembers how at one point "they started cutting down our reports." (279) "They" referred to Radio Zagreb, the Croatia's central station broadcasting around the country, which increasingly redacted reports about the situation in the city coming to them from Radio Vukovar, especially ones about the increasingly helpless situation and the likelihood of the city's being overrun and totally destroyed unless help is sent. In the end, "all the Croatian media outlets—with the sole exception of Zagreb's 'Radio 101' [a main oppositional radio station]—refused to broadcast in November 1991 the last message from besieged Vukovar, better known as Vukovar's indictment."[20] The city never got the needed military reinforcements and was largely destroyed and overtaken in November 1991.

---

[20] Lukić and Oreškić, "Djeca Vukovara," p. 45.

What kept Radio Vukovar going day after day was not only deep ethical commitment, loyalty to their city and their work (Alenka remembers how this was "the most important thing she had ever done"), and personal courage, but also joking or *zafrkancija*. This is not an easily translatable term but it roughly means playing and making fun, an emphasis on the absurd, funny or silly aspects of a situation, or seeing things in a humorous light that are not at all funny. In this case, *zafrkancija* was a determined "clowning around" in the midst of horror. As Mirković simply states: "This fooling around was the most important thing for us. It was the therapy that freed us from fear, frustrations, that relaxed us and that, in short, helped us stay normal." [158] The sheer volume of the text dedicated to recounting all the instances of such fooling around is telling, as almost everything becomes welcome material for this playing.

> ... Siniša and Josip would get into their usual "program" with which they raised our spirits. One evening they went about inventing new nicknames for us.
> "All the people have some war names, only we don't have them," Josip said.
> "All right then, let's call Branko 'Kitty' ...," said Siniša, and we all started laughing like crazy. This was a joke on behalf of Zvjezdana who, as soon as the shelling started and she did not have her husband in front of her eyes, would start yelling: "Kitty, come down here, what are you doing up there anyhow?" Siniša found this very entertaining and when the shelling commenced he too would yell in falsetto, imitating Zvjezdana, "Hey Kitty!", and we would all giggle joyously. The funniest thing in all of this was that Branko, the oldest man of our news desk, so large, dark, and always deadly serious, was the last person in the world to wear the nick-name "Kitty." (212)

Zafrkancija creates a fissure between a situation and the language accompanying this situation, most startling in the disjunction between a dangerous situation and the accompanying language. As he is about to give her a car ride through the heavily shelled city, Siniša asks Alenka, "you aren't really afraid, are you?" and then starts the car with a loudest possible "Yeee-haaa!"; while shrapnel hits the door of their make-shift studio he yells: "Who is it?" (168)

When Mirković asks one of the city defenders about the news of her aunt's apartment building, he asks, "Is it that last building ... with four floors?", and after Mirković's confirming that that is the one he just curtly says, "Well, it's got only a ground floor now." (200)

Alenka's aunt accepts the previously refused offer to move to Alenka's (safer) apartment, and comes unannounced to her, simply saying at the door: "Here. As you can see, I changed my mind." She sees that Mirković is totally packed.

> "And what are you up to?"
> "Well, I got ready to go to Germany. By bus," I said, grinning.
> "So when's your bus leaving?"
> "It left at 8 AM ..." I said and shrugged. We looked at each other and began to laugh. "As you can see, I changed my mind too ..." (87)

When Mirković herself gets an official draft notice from a man named Zdravko, she "almost started to laugh."

> "I will not sign this to you, no, no, no ..." I said looking into Zdravko's eyes and trying to keep my face straight.
> "Listen, kid ... by now you could have made your decision. There's no going back ...," Zdravko said sternly.
> "Well, I know that, but look, Zdravko, it says right here that I'll get two pairs of socks, two pairs of underwear ... until I get that there's nothing doing with this draft ...," I said, started to laugh, took the pencil and signed my draft paper.
> "F*** ... you ... and your ... you only fool around ...," mumbled Zdravko while going away.
> I put the little paper in my purse and thought ironically: "Here, I became a soldier. And that in Vukovar. A lucky girl, that's what I am ..." (247)

Most often, joking around is simply and only speech, something that can be done anywhere and at any time, and creates a separation between the people and the reality that engulfs them, a realm of freedom where they detach their joy and lives from this reality. One of the sons of Gordana, the radio station's honorary "aunt," "drove his mother crazy by saying that 'this war is not much, really, and he can't figure out why she gets so excited,'" and her younger, "gorgeous" son, would ask her in a mock-serious tone, upon examining the underwear she prepared for him before he would return to a battlefield: "All right now, mom, but why did you give me this colorful underwear? ... What am I going to do now if the *chetniks* catch me? Imagine they take my pants down, and here I am in the panties with little toffies painted all over them!" (153)

"The association of play with death is one of the oldest themes in literature," writes Christopher Clausen, and adds:

> Play, useless activity engaged in for its own sake ... is the *only* activity other than religious ritual (which has much in common with play) that has traditionally seemed an appropriate response to the fact of death. ... [T]he playful state of mind seems to accomplish something that work—activity carried on for useful reward—can never approach.[21]

Surrounded by death and dying, the young people working at Radio Vukovar keep their and their city's spirits going by means of irreverent playfulness. Under daily fire and in constant danger, witnessing and experiencing horrors, and on the ruins of the previous community, a new one is built. The community of the local radio station attempts to create as well as it can the language of referentiality and reason, and is itself kept going and strengthened by the language of playfulness and joking, indirectly reminding everyone of what it is they are actually trying to save. As Mirković puts it, "playing around [*zafrkancija*] allowed us to stay normal." Staying normal means not hating those who besieged the city, not abusing them when they are caught, not losing basic humanity on account of strategic goals. For instance, Mirković opposes the idea of reading on the air the private letters which the wife of a killed Yugoslav People's Army soldier sent to her husband, who was in her view "at military exercises" far too long. Staying normal also means retaining a discerning perception of events and people, including soldiers of the attacking army who are caught and then imprisoned. Mirković is intrigued by Nebojša, a young man from Kragujevac (Serbia):

---

[21] Clausen (1986), 26.

Nebojša tried to avoid getting drafted any way he could. The first time they came for him to his house. He managed to run away and hid with friends and acquaintances. The second time they caught him at the University and sent him to the front. He escaped but they caught him and sent him back to the front. He tried to be a good soldier but could not do it. When he got wounded in his leg, he decided to surrender. With his gun raised above his head he limped across the empty space to the first units of the Croatian defense. I asked him how come he decided to do that. Their propaganda kept repeating that *ustashas* killed their prisoners, so he would, according to that logic, have more chance if he stayed with his own side ...

"Do you know ... how it feels when the grenades are falling around you all day long?"

"I do," I said, somewhat amused by his honesty.

"Listen, I only wanted to study, work with the student-service, and earn some money for books and vacations. I did not want to come here ...." he said quietly and decisively.

He was the only one [of the captured enemy soldiers she met] that I believed to. (294)

At the end, as she was about to leave Vukovar, Mirković recalls how Nebojša "stood in front of me, gave me his hand, and said quietly: 'Good luck! Watch out for yourselves!'" (311)

Fiction Beyond the Book

Mirković's memoire—or novel—implies not only that "words are deeds," as Wittgenstein put it, but also that words may easily be stronger than realities or "deeds" on the ground in crisis situations. *91.6 MHz* provides an account of the ways in which fictional words cause actions and a chain of events that brings catastrophic consequences. If one is not limited to making words that relate to the accessible facts, if one takes the liberty to make purely fictional words, like writers do, but does not call them fiction but instead a truthful naming of things, one can make words that are able to prevail over the realities on the ground long enough to achieve a desired effect. Words can be stronger than material facts because they can be made out of nothing, made to fit their intended function and reception, and can spread speedily. On the other hand, even the most transparent material realms are immobile and very hard to "get to," and often accessible only through highly contested networks of representation or communication.

3

Reclaiming Charisma, Resetting the Senses
Vladimir Arsenijević's *In the Hold*

> ... *Vanja bent double and fell headlong from the high railings so that I almost yelled out in fear, but he landed neatly on his feet, in a spectacular imitation fall. Once again at the level of my eyes, he hopped about a bit, and then smiled. "Ooph!" he said in a satisfied tone, shaking his head. A few waxed locks of hair fell over his forehead, to meet up with his carefree smile.*[1]

The Foam and Liquefaction

A novel *In the Hold* (*U potpalublju*, 1994) is set in Belgrade at the beginning of the Wars of Yugoslav Succession, during the months of October through December of 1991. The story revolves around a nameless narrator, a young man living with his pregnant wife

---

[1] Vladimir Arsenijević, *In the Hold* (1996), 86. All further citations from this book will be noted by a page number in the main text. I have altered or added to this translation in a few places in order to achieve a more literal rendition of the original text.

Anđela (recently retired from a brief but successful drug-dealing career), who leads a seemingly ordinary day-to-day life of going to work, and then takes a protracted leave of absence during which he prepares for the baby, visits family and friends, spends time with his wife, smokes pot and writes. All of these mundane activities become different and strange, affected as they are by the war—the siege and destruction of Vukovar, called "liberation" on Belgrade TV, take place in exactly this period—and the changed atmosphere in the city. The Milošević regime had initiated wars in Slovenia and Croatia, with the violence in Bosnia and Herzegovina yet to come. The strangeness of the city is caused by the fact that, on one hand, it actually looks much the same as before, because even though the war is largely triggered by the government that resides in this city, it is taking place somewhere else and "in a way, that was all TV. The real world never did offer the protection of a definite conclusion." (24) On the other hand, there are profound changes in the social and visual landscape of the city, where, for instance, individuals suddenly appear without limbs, such as Dejan whose empty right sleeve "whipped the passers-by who tried to avoid its lash" (49), or else disappear completely.

"Perhaps we were in the hold, perhaps we would never get out of it, but that night it didn't matter. We laughed, both of us, heartily, but I know that we were asleep." (95) This fragment, bringing back for the first and only time the space and the concept of the title, appears only at the very end of the novel. The metaphor works on several levels. For one, the city of Belgrade itself, and the world in which the narrator finds himself, seem to be transformed into a ship navigating strange territories and a ship over which one has no control. The narrator and the people around him, immobilized within this hold, are all taken for a ride: they are in the hold, not on the bridge, and all they can do is observe and note the changed seascape their ship—the city—is navigating. A familiar environment has become strange and sickly: "If I remember rightly, the October evenings of 1991 year were sort of flaky, and greenish-yellow, like sick mucus. For days a strange cloud floated over Molerova Street, I'm certain of that at least." (6) The imprisoning hold of one's environment is emphasized and echoed in the hold of one's own body. The narrator feels that "it seemed ... silly that I should have to accept that body as *mine*, when, despite all, I floated inside, like an embryo in amniotic fluid," (7) the wife Anđela was "arranging her body as though it didn't actually belong to her," (95) and the narrator's as yet unborn child is in "the hold" as well. Aside from the quick, uncontrolled movement, new vistas which appear before one's eyes, and individual immobility, the metaphor of being "in the hold" also articulates the "liquefaction" of the usually solid environment: the ship does not sail through solid but through a fluid medium. The liquefaction of the environment, a dissolution of the firm logic, sense, values, or, in a way, goodness, started before October 1991 and is already experienced in the late 1980s, the time which the narrator recalls as the one of many individual and often grotesque deaths from drugs, AIDS, or unexpected suicides, all chronicled in the "APPENDIX 1, a Compilation of Deaths: 1989, 1990, 1991." (99) Yet, the decisive moment of the liquefaction of firm forms—of the world, of oneself, one's senses, abilities, and logic—happened with the crushing of the March 1991 Belgrade peace protests:

> Even now I am not able to tell what happened to us, but I am fairly sure that some fate fulfilled itself, which everyone forgot about in the meantime. Well, that happens too. For something yelled, and in an instant it had created a torrent, and swept us away. It was a biblical experience. Intermittently, in that whirlpool like a turbulent river, a head would rise to the surface, a helpless limb would stretch up to aim a feeble kick at the swollen buttocks of the sky, sodden eyes snatched at views which were ever more distant from one day to the next, hands flew out like strange beings to seize things that had never been there in any case. As time went on, there were fewer of us in that whirlpool, and we were all ranting, in agitated voices, about the foam through which one sank, which offered no support, through which one was buffeted grotesquely, which did not nourish, which could not quench one's thirst, which was no use for anything, which had no color, or taste, or smell, which was false and deceitful, and undermined all precious, logical things ... (28–9)

What happened to the opposition, to one "whole multitude of Us," in short, was a forceful dissolution of rational, defined, and formed practice and bodies (political, verbal, private, collective), a dissolution of graspable and speakable forms into ungraspable and unspeakable formlessness, a process that can better be grasped by metaphor than by literal description. In other words, whatever took place was totally beyond one's abilities of perception, comprehension, and reaction. "Even now I am not able to tell what happened." (29) What went on evaded all available concepts and logical assumptions. It thus became shapeless—the formlessness itself, the *foam*. "[S]omething yelled, and in an instant it had created a torrent, and swept us away." (28) On the literal level, this "whirlpool" was made by the regime's skillful Machiavellian combination of specific political actions with the speeding up and multiplication of various bits and pieces of falsification, disinformation, lies, and the most fantastic couplings of public pronouncements saying one thing with covert actions that did something completely different and were suspected only after their unexpected, shocking results were felt. The opposition held the upper hand in April 1991, the students mounted a successful campaign against the regime, the regime faltered, and yet "by July [the opposition was] effectively silenced and marginalized."[2]

---

[2] V. P. Gagnon, *The Myth of Ethnic War: Serbia and Croatia in the 1990s* (2004), 109. Gagnon gives a detailed step-by-step account of how Milošević and his allies dismantled the opposition, showing that, while in April "in terms of public rhetoric and actions, Serbia's conservatives seemed to be heeding the protesters and adopting their moderate demands... [b]ehind the scenes... Milošević was gearing up his strategy to demobilize the opposition." (Ibid., 103) This strategy included a secret meeting with Croatian President Tuđman in late March, secret talks in Moscow in Spring 1991 between Defense Minister Kadijević and Soviet Defense Minister Yazov (a leader of the coup attempt in the USSR a few months later), where a transaction was arranged whereupon a huge stock of weapons would be given to the Yugoslav army, the increasing provocation of conflict in Croatia, the labeling of the opposition as "enemies of Serbia" who collaborated with international forces that were bent on destroying the Serbs, the media escalation of a negative portrayal of Croatia, the alliance between Milošević's party and the neo-fascist Serbian Radical Party, the further escalation of the conflict in Croatia in the summer by the Yugoslav Army and the Serbian paramilitary forces, when not only Croats but also Serbs who did not go along were "terrorized and silenced." (Ibid., 106) Milošević's regime wanted and got the war, and now "[o]ne of the main effects of the war was that it greatly helped Milošević in his domestic crisis, effectively demobilizing the opposition ... Whereas [the opposition] seemed poised to overthrow the SPS [Socialist Party of Serbia, Milošević's party] in April, by July they had been effectively silenced and marginalized." (Ibid., 107 and 109).

Slobodan Milošević ran for election as a peace-maker yet he was starting wars and denying having anything to do with them; there was no war and yet thousands of young men in Serbia, and especially in the city of Belgrade, were sleeping in a different place every night to avoid being drafted into this non-existent war; preparations for war in Croatia were going on but Milošević nevertheless held secret talks with Croatian president Franjo Tuđman.

These new events were orchestrated by and understandable to their perpetrators, but were literally ungraspable to those who were subjected to them and had no ability of seeing and accurately comprehending all that was being done by the other side. The regime's superbly executed devastation of the peace movement with "a blitzkrieg of continuous low blows" (28), and the multi-faceted and multi-centered driving of the country towards war, altogether overwhelmed one's ability to adequately perceive, comprehend, or react to it with anything approaching a torrent's own force. That what happened lost any recognizable and nameable form, any form at all, and became a formless foam that would "corrode, merge, swallow" everything.

"The foam through which one sank" dissolves not just any specific particular position, replacing, say, a claim that something is a war of aggression with the claim that it is, on the contrary, a battle of self-defense. Instead, this foam dissolves all the basic logical modes of thinking, the modes of cause and effect, of argument or proof. One "sank" through it and it "offered no support": one could not get "support" from this foam, that is, get something firm and solid that one could build an argument against, because nothing is being said in the first place, nothing substantial asserted which can be leaned on while one is repudiating it. Students were saying "we want peace" and the regime was responding with "I am peace" while sending tanks against them.[3]

---

[3] On Saturday, 9 March 1991, "Milošević sent tanks into his own capital ... The city stank of tear gas. A seventeen-year-old student ... lay in a pool of blood." The regime went against the opposition with "hundreds of policemen ... dogs, horses, and armored vehicles." (Laura Silber and Allan Little, *Yugoslavia, Death of a Nation* (1995), 119.) And yet that same evening in a televised speech, Milošević stated that "[p]eace was jeopardized ... I am thus asking ... that all citizens of Serbia contribute to peace." (Ibid., 122) Belgrade Television itself "was firmly in Milošević's grip ... the ideal tool for stirring up hatred against 'the enemies of the Serbian people'—first

One could not deal with such foam by rational or logical means because this colorless, odorless, and tasteless foam "undermined all precious, logical things." (29)

The foam dissolves everything one has; it destroys the possibility of directed movement or action, and it throws one's body any which way, thus also destroying the fixed coordinates of up and down, front and back, or left and right. "A head would rise to the surface, a helpless limb would stretch up to aim a feeble kick at the swollen buttocks of the sky, sodden eyes snatched at views which were ever more distant from one day to the next, hands flew out like strange beings to seize things that had never been there in any case." Seeing mirages and opposing phantoms, one looks in one direction and thinks in one way, and then something happens which was not seen and could not even have been imagined. Beyond the realm of the imaginable, that which was to happen was fully in the realm of the invisible and non-existent, of nothingness; and yet it happened. By destroying the firm shapes of the world, the voracious foam dissolves and destroys one's senses and practice. If only material objects can confirm human senses and relation to the material world (so that only music can awake one's musicality, as Marx put it), then the loss of the objects, their total unyieldingness, will result in the loss of one's senses, one's body and one's ability to relate to one's environment. A limb is now trying to "kick the sky" which is intangible anyway, the views grow ever more distant for the sodden eyes which seem to retain some memory of closer, clearer views, the hands are trying to seize things that are not there and had never been there in any case—thus, hands themselves become "strange beings." The torrent of foam disintegrates all logic and differentiation, corrodes and swallows language and its cognitive and narrative abilities; it destroys "all our stories."[4]

Kosovo's Albanians, then the Slovenes, the Croats, and finally the opposition in Serbia itself." (Ibid., 120) One of the main demands of the students who "on Sunday night ... broke through the police cordons and headed for the city center" was "the dismissal of Dušan Mitević, the head of Belgrade Television." (Ibid., 122) And "over the next week, tens of thousands of Belgrade's liberal elite made their last stand." (Ibid.)

[4]Formlessness has been explored in philosophy (e.g., Aristotle, Kant, Georges Bataille and his *informe*), mostly as a state of things that cannot be conceptualized

That which had been recognizable and defined became fluid: turned into something unrecognizable and strange.

> In this seething maw of a city ... people's lives were falling apart under the prevailing pressure. They had appeared happy and secure, and then people they were fond of started to abandon them, they discovered that their wives were cheating on them with their best friends, their husbands started beating them with signet rings for some reason ... (77–8)

In this liquid environment, "the crust of ... faith" of Anđela's brother Lazar "turned out to be painfully thin" (19), and allowed Lazar to morph smoothly from a seemingly dedicated follower of Hare Krishna into the willing recipient of a military draft notice (who will, without "major problems, replace his mixture of teas with brandy, his chick peas with roast pork from a Slavonian sow blown apart by a grenade" (19)), and soon after, to transform again into a "body, with its seven bullet holes" that "arrived in an unusual coffin, accompanied by an escort in regulation brown." (54) The contour of Lazar's body had dissolved to reveal the simple mechanism that moved it, in which a hidden "Commander" controlled the helpless "Executor." "Just underneath it there hid a Commander, who said, in Lazar's name: 'Well, I actually don't know... There is something in this. Maybe I'll accept [the draft].'" (19)

In the liquid environment, people became fluid too, and turn into something unrecognizable and strange to themselves. Dejan,

---

or even intuitively apprehended. Recent art history has also prominently used this notion; see Yve-Alain Bois and Rosalind E. Krauss, *Formless: A User's Guide* (1997). Arsenijević's foam metaphor itself has a strong visual quality. Another interesting example of the exploration of formlessness can be found in the work of a Russian philosopher, Leonid Lipavsky. Branislav Jakovljević writes how "formlessness is at the center of [Lipavsky's] 'Water Tractatus' and 'Investigation of Horror' ... Lipavsky's interest in the formless is clearly related to his philosophical concern with the questions of ... time and fear. ... Lipavsky relates formless to the absence of distinction, to non-separation, and ... to non-individualization. ... The formless ... inhabits the very boundary between the animate and inanimate. Lacking definition, it could be either living or dead. It is the region of indecisiveness in which the animate absorbs the inanimate, and death invades life." Branislav Jakovljević, *Daniil Kharms: Writing and the Event* (2009), 106–7.

just back from the front where he lost an arm, sinks "into a long, disconnected lament about the fact that ... his mouth was full of a pseudo-march with oaths of a Rabelaisian nature which he had learned at the front ... Whatever he did ... that march kept coming back to torment him." (51) Fluid people have changed perceptions too, and see only the previously unsuspected fluidity of the world around them: Dejan "looked at the people in the streets and saw nothing but units at ease, wild companies of armed citizens, fingernails and teeth. And they all looked suspicious to him." (51) Or else people—once solid, multi-dimensional creatures—suddenly melt into two-dimensional, brief and formulaic texts, those of the "blue obituary notices stuck crookedly on telegraph pools," (28) or of the postcards from abroad that all look "as if written by the same person," texts that are then themselves quickly dissolving into nothingness.

> The majority of our friends were far away, beyond the borders of the country...
> From time to time a postcard would reach us from Budapest, Prague, Copenhagen, Casablanca, Athens, Amsterdam, London, from all those splendid places, and they were genuinely welcome, those postcards; but still it was hard to resist the impression that they had all been written by the same person. Their other sides were filled with meager scrawls, and somehow even the words resembled one another, regardless of the local conditions: "I can't get work," "I'm earning a bit," "it's hard", "but I'm OK", "I'm coping", etc. etc. (26–7)

The liquid environment with its unpredictable, fantastic features makes one feel one is dreaming while being awake, or that one is somehow not fully awake: the novel opens and closes with descriptions of the mind in between sleep and wakefulness. In the beginning of the novel, in October 1991, the narrator is lying in bed with eyes closed, not moving a muscle, "acting for a non-existent audience the idyll of a post-prandial sleeper" (5), while actually being "perfectly wide awake" and, in fact, "disintegrating in indecisiveness." (5) In the end the narrator and his wife Anđela are caught in the gray zone between night and day, sleep and wakefulness: it is the end of December 1991, and the two of them "laughed, both of us, heartily, but I know that we were asleep." (95)

Not fully awake, seeped in the fantasy of dreams, the mind is open to sudden visionary insights:

> In the glare of a sudden and all-pervasive vision that split the ordinary street scene before my eyes, I caught sight of all of us, running, while the ground beneath our feet was breaking up and opening with a terrible cracking sound, and out of those depths came the unbearable stench of the centuries which, in our inertia, we had omitted to use in a dignified way, a great, slimy pulsating monster was mocking us from in there, unconcerned about the horror which we were conjuring up with our irresolute movements, and our desire not to be. In the course of this carnal bacchanalia, which lasted for one second, the chosen victims had vanished randomly in the depths of that well of flesh. There were many of them. All those who had not managed to find a shelter, all those who had been caught unawares, they were all whisked away, like kites snatched from our hands by the November gales. (48)

The ship travels through time, from day to day, and one cannot control its voyage; yet one can still move within the hold. In-between sleep and wakefulness, tiredness and guilt (the mind is "stuck in the crevice whose two sides are made by Tiredness and Guilt" (6)),[5] the novel's body reads like a phantasmagoric journey through the dense, enchanted, unknown landscape of the first three months of the war.

Figures in the Hold

In the Hold is divided into three chapters that format the journey of a ship through time—"October 1991," "November 1991," "December 1991"—and these chapters proceed through parts that are commonly titled after people, who become signposts in the misty

---

[5]This is my translation of the original part of this sentence, "*zaglavljen u procepu čije dve strane čine Umor i Krivica ...*" Vladimir Arsenijević, *U potpalublju* (1998), 9. Hawkesworth's translation here reads: "wedged in the gap between weariness and guilt ..." (6)

hold. "Why Anđela's courage scares me?", "My drug-dealer wife," "How I fell in love with Dejan all over again," "A relative, and my total nosedive, from which I would emerge in one piece, endowed with a unique moral," "About my mother and father," "With Vanja on All Kinds of Things, Including Dejan." These smallest units of the novel's structure focus on the narrator's experience of these people. The encounters with them, especially with the most prominent characters—wife Anđela, friends Dejan and Vanja—are always marked by their sheer impact. They wake up the narrator ("Anđela did not come to 'wake' me until just before dinner" (8)) or rather, they push him out of the in-between state by, for example, Anđela's making him "staggered" or "astounded." (40 and 43) The announcement of Dejan's improbable entrepreneurial idea prompts the narrator to "[shout] with pure delight" (77), Vanja's "private jargon" leaves him "amazed" (87), and Vanja's decision to join the Croatian Army or the Croatian "*paras*" (paramilitary troops) causes a profound shock. The connection among the three characters emphasizes their shared, intriguing natures: Anđela "has always had a thing for [Dejan]" (90), and is "offended" at the narrator's exaltation over him, as if acknowledging a hidden commonality and thus an implied rivalry between Dejan and herself ("'Listen, if Dejan's so fantastic, why don't you live together?'" (79)). As the narrator walked the streets "preoccupied with thoughts of Dejan," it is Vanja who "at once jumped down after me and called, exactly as I had, then, to Dejan: 'Hey!'" (85) And "[t]hat constant leaping out of the train of his [Vanja's] own thoughts made him resemble the Dejan of our last meeting, except that Vanja's ramblings were more ragged, more aggressive and longer." (88) The connection between the two young men echoes their past tie in the rock group GSG 9, where Vanja "sang ... purely out of loyalty and love for Dejan" (86), at the time when the narrator "had met Vanja through Dejan." (86)

Though different in many ways, the three characters share a few important aspects. First, they are largely "non-porous" with regard to their surroundings. Indeed, the only time Anđela is clearly affected by her environment is at the time of the fall of Vukovar:

> Dubrovnik, shelled and in the news in October, had been replaced by mind-blowing Vukovar vignettes. Anđela wept,

leaning her chin on the arm of the sofa, as she watched splinters of the devastated settlements on the Danube and Vuka in the background of the rustic-featured, wartime TV reporter's saccharine outpourings. Winding across our screens, columns of numb figures, who had just emerged from their cellars after a hundred days, stared blankly, gray-haired children smiled shyly at us, showing their broken teeth, the body of a man leaning his head against the wall of something that might once have been his home, an undignified heap of plaster piled on his head, a soldier burned to the bone, the black mass, still hot, smoking hideously; we saw also a young woman with half a head, refugees freezing in sports halls, the corpses of people and animals strewn through the streets of a shattered town where some men were driving around in jeeps, their job done. (44)

In general, though, Anđela, Dejan, and Vanja are non-porous and also non-derivative—though not to the same extent. In other words, an environment of any kind, not just the contemporary political one of Belgrade or Serbia, does not seem to penetrate them or make them "harmonize" with it. They can also not be derived, constructed from, or understood by any recognizable system of belief or behavior. These characters are not, for instance, definable by their work or career, their beliefs, by anything they do, or even by being a somewhat predictable political opposition (though Anđela delivers a fiery impromptu anti-war speech in the late stages of pregnancy). The three are also not ethical in any of the more conventional or at least recognizable sense of the word: Anđela is characterized by a complete absence of any pangs of conscience on account of her trade. The first substantial description of her in "My drug-dealer wife" indicates that she was serenely untouched by any possible ethical issues related to her work. Complementing Anđela's tranquil drug-dealing is the catalogue of inventive tortures she used for years on her younger brother Lazar, whom she also, incomprehensibly to the narrator, claims to have deeply loved all that time. Anđela also does not seem to mind even the most basic mental "conventions" of self-preservation: she does not worry as she is becoming addicted to drugs in the company of her drug-dealing ex-boyfriend, and she is as immune to any outside influence when she decides to abruptly stop any association with drugs and stay clean for the intended pregnancy. As former customers literally "besieged" the flat she shared with the narrator, she "didn't take the slightest notice of them, nor of the fact that, without her regular income, we were more and more frequently penniless." (37) And Vanja's joyful playfulness—scaring the narrator with his "spectacular imitation fall" (86) from a high railing—and his "carefree smile" (86) are so incongruous with the environment and mood of Fall 1991 Belgrade that they appear surreal.

The three characters also share a radical inner inconsistency and thus absence of predictability. Anđela and the narrator went to Rome for their honey-moon, where Anđela was thoroughly and persistently indifferent to and disappointed with the city, and yet she later calmly declares: "I've been thinking ... In fact, we had a great time in Rome, didn't we?" (9) Dejan astonishes with his unexpected and unbelievable business project radiating strength and determination, and then again with his sudden suicide. Vanja, after spending "at least half of his powers of reason" (88) some years ago to avoid military service, and then, against all consistency with himself as he was in the past, "doing everything in his power to jump onto that bandwagon [of being conscripted]" (88–9) in the recent times and being repeatedly refused, shocks the narrator again with the revelation that he has now decided to join the Croatian forces:

> "So, I think, what," he said finally, "that's like, brains, get, brains, man, what, I'm going to Croatia, why not, I can tell you that the Croatian Army and the paras there pay more."
> "Good God!" I blurted out, shocked. I couldn't believe that such a pronouncement could be serious. But it was. (89)

Anđela, Dejan and Vanja also gain a peculiar kind of charisma: they exert a heightened impact on the narrator and are experienced as "auratic" figures. In his essay "Art in the Age of Mechanical Reproduction," Walter Benjamin posits that "aura" which had earlier belonged to religious objects—aura being the special authority and presence of the real object that profoundly affects a beholder and makes her/him respond to this object and its claims—has been transferred to the art objects, and was then in the modern age appropriated by charismatic political leaders, who create themselves and their performance as the auratic presence to which the recipient surrenders.[6]

After witnessing an utterly improbable and extravagant undertaking by Dejan, the narrator "shouted with pure delight" (77) and saw how Dejan "had risen up" (78) from the "seething maw of a city" (77), "[t]ransformed into a charismatic figure." (78) Dejan, whom the narrator had already "fallen in love" with before (in "How I fell in love with Dejan all over again"), becomes an object of adoration:

> I want to stress that I had never prostrated myself before this Dejan. But since our November meeting I had begun to adore him, and I accepted the T-shirts simply as gratification that my private outpourings of infinite trust and love had not been misplaced. All that was left me was to admire him with adolescent tenacity ... (79)

The narrative dismantles many customary placeholders of aura and enacts with them a move of opposite direction to the one that makes charismatic characters. Spectacular places such as the city of Rome, for instance, leave one "indifferent ... or else ... secretly disappointed," gods are non-existent and religion irrelevant ("I smiled at the absolute impotence of the Heavens" (58)), a customary respect towards European literary classics is dispensable: "Anyway, who cared about Rabelais?" (10) The community rituals, deprived of meaning and comfort, become grotesque. At Lazar's burial, "the funeral official with thick glasses ... [t]aking a ritual step backwards ... waved energetically like a traffic policeman, then bumped into a rubber plant and toppled onto the marble floor, his behind slapping loudly against it. 'Ouch!' he cried, on top of everything." (55) Sometimes, this dismantling of aura is done in the spirit of so-called "grotesque realism," a procedure itself attributable to Rabelais.[7] Grotesque realism brings

---

[6] Walter Benjamin, "The Work of Art in the Age of Mechanical Reproduction," in Walter Benjamin, *Illuminations* (1969).

[7] "The essential principle of grotesque realism is degradation, that is, the lowering of all that is high, spiritual, ideal, abstract; it is a transfer to the material level, to the sphere of earth and body in their indissoluble unity." Mikhail Bakhtin, *Rabelais and His World* (1984), 19–20. Rabelais is mentioned a few times in the novel in ways

down the elated or spiritual to the level of bodily and earthly, lowers the tragic into comic and grotesque; a somber funeral ritual becomes a slapstick comedy, the heroic "death in action" of Ivan, an acquaintance, becomes a grotesque incident that happens while Ivan is peacefully "having a morning pee, wondering sleepily what to do with the 200 jars of pickles he had stolen from his Hungarian host." (24)

The narrator and the narrative take charisma away from the assorted habitual places and put it into a few chosen characters; the narrator transforms these close people into the auratic centers that help him move within the hold. Non-porous and unpredictable, admired people in Arsenijević's novel are like innovative artistic creations, like original texts that inspire with their liveliness and their own freedom.

"[O]ne page of Montaigne, a single Verlaine poem, or one sentence by Proust ... are free and therefore they are liberating," Witold Gombrowicz wrote.[8] Similarly to such literary creations that are free themselves and are thus liberating, charismatic characters in Arsenijević's novel are precious because they create themselves as intriguing unpredictable texts full of enchanting surprising aspects. Serenely self-created, Vanja even has his own language, and the narrator finds himself "[a]mazed, as ever, by [Vanja's] private jargon, which progressed with the years, leaving ever less space for the meaningful parts of the sentence, and elaborating only a torrent of indistinct phrases." (87) Vanja conveys to the narrator crucial news about their mutual friend Dejan in his own inimitable way too:

> And then he did something strange. Putting his hands together in an attitude of prayer, he took on what could have resembled an expression of beatitude, and then he began flapping his arms, like an angel's wings. "Dejan," he reinforced his pantomime, in a quiet voice.
> "Dejan what? Dejan what?" I shouted so that Vanja lurched to one side and fell off the railings again ...

---

that themselves invite interpretation; e.g., Anđela refuses his book, Dejan cannot escape from a song related to him.

[8] Witold Gombrowicz, *Diary* (1988), 18.

But then he tapped me lightly on the shoulder, came right up to me and the overpowering stench of the glue hypnotized me. Vanja calmly kissed me on the cheek. "He killed himself, man," he whispered, as though confiding a secret. (90–1)

While Vanja increasingly went about creating his "private jargon," Dejan is eventually unable to get rid of the world and the language that invaded him. "[H]is mouth was full of a pseudo-march with oaths of a Rabelaisian nature which he had learned at the front ... He would wake up in the middle of the night with the song on his lips." (51) This song proved unconquerable. The other two charismatic characters remain at the end of the novel, Anđela, "who didn't take the slightest notice" (37) of her environment and of the elements that tried to get her off of her own ways of doing things, and Vanja, also not harmonizing with his surroundings in any way, and comfortably creating his own private space in the middle of the public one. Vanja was "sitting on the high railings in Kondina Street ... and he led me back to those railings and welcomed me there ... with such warm gestures, that he might have been leading me into the place where he lived (which was probably not far from the truth)." (85) Vanja's reshaping of a public space as a private one may show the way out: in Arsenijević's next novel, *Anđela*, he will become the surreal voice of opposition in his nightly radio shows.

By creating themselves in freedom, these strange characters embody the improbable or impossible. In their absurd, incomprehensible ways ("But why on earth did you do it all?", the "staggered" narrator asks his wife Anđela [40]), they have the glow of a miracle about them. Detaching themselves so radically from all given contexts—political and historical, ethical and logical—they show that it is possible to detach and create oneself in freedom. With his inexplicably "carefree smile" (86) and his natural, unforced playfulness in the middle of the "seething maw of a city" (77), Vanja shows that one can be absurd, non-derived from one's environment or systems, free to make oneself in freedom. It seems as if the novel implies that, if one's thoughts, motivations, or actions can be "figured out," they can also always be predicted, plotted, and destroyed by those with superior resources. The one way against the system that calculates one better than one can do it oneself is to be incalculable, absurd, inconsistent, unpredictable, new in every moment. Vanja, who spent half his reason to get out of the army, and then did all he could to get in, and then decided to join the enemy army, cannot be calculated and predicted, and—perhaps—could not be as easily destroyed as the narrator and his whole rational, transparent, honest peace movement was destroyed. This kind of creativity and innovation, usually associated only with art, may create the way out of the impasse.

In order to recognize and help activate the artistic potential of people themselves, their actions, and their politics, one has to first, so to speak, "re-auraticize" these people. The aura which can be given to and acknowledged on close people, and which they can well deserve (the narrator adored Dejan, but Dejan also proved that this "trust and love" were warranted), is often worn thin by the presence, enforced and self-chosen, of the "wider world" with its charismatic spectacles and global dimensions, where everything that we or our loved and important people do gets diminished and made small and impotent, or is known in advance and dismissible. *In the Hold* proposes a move in the opposite direction: one is to experience close people the way a sheltered young child experiences and sees her brother when she takes his head into her hands, and looks, and sees the world. It will help such people grow firmly and absurdly into their newness and their artistic energy, which may in turn build some yet-unimaginable shapes that will open up the hold.

4

The Ethics of Listening and the Grounding of a Child
Milcho Manchevski's *Before the Rain*

With a shriek birds flee across the black sky, people are silent, my blood aches from waiting.

MEŠA SELIMOVIĆ, *DEATH AND THE DERVISH*

From Seeing to Listening

A genuine artistic achievement and a "hugely successful movie" with both international audiences and critics at the time of its release, *Before the Rain* (*Pred doždot*, 1994), scripted and directed by Macedonian-American Milcho Manchevski, won the Golden Lion at the Venice Film Festival and was nominated for the Academy Award as best foreign film. It is one of a very few films—if indeed still not the only one—that art cinema audiences may associate with the term Macedonian cinema, and it has engendered considerable and sustained critical interest.[1]

---

[1] *Before the Rain* is described as a "hugely successful movie" in Péter Krasztev's article "Who Will Take the Blame? How to Make an Audience Grateful for a Family Massacre" (2000; 27), available online at http://www.kinoeye.org/03/10/

The film opens with the above citation from Meša Selimović's *Death and the Dervish* that appears on screen and is simultaneously read in voice-over by actor Rade Šerbedžija. In the novel, this passage marks the end of the chapter in which the dervish triggered a set of events which may or may not bring about the desired resolution.[2] Things will indeed happen afterwards but they will be both intended and unintended and they will, as often happens, get out of control. The point in time marked by this quote chosen by Manchevski takes place after a certain course of action is set but before it actually happens, when it is still possible to change direction, do things differently, and avoid catastrophic consequences.

Set in the early 1990s, *Before the Rain* concerns war photographer Aleksandar Kirkov (Rade Šerbedžija), who, after resigning from his job in London following an assignment in war-ravaged Bosnia and Herzegovina, returns to his native Macedonian village, now torn by ethnic division, saves an Albanian girl, Zamira (Labina Mitevska), from Macedonian village men (who accuse her of murdering one of their number), and is consequently shot to death. Zamira hides in an Orthodox monastery where Kiril (Grégoire Colin), a young Macedonian monk, helps her until she is discovered by the other monks. They leave the monastery and are captured by a group of Albanian villagers. Zamira is shot and killed by her brother Ali.

The narrative twist lies in the radical disjunction between this real-time story and the *sujet*, or the way this story is actually shaped by the film's own temporal enfolding. The film's first segment, titled "Words," revolves around Zamira's hiding in the monastery and ends with her death; the second part, "Faces," depicts Aleks's

---

celluloidtinderbox.pdf/ (accessed 28 October 2011). Regarding this film's role in the visibility of Macedonian cinema, Dina Iordanova wrote: "Macedonia, a country whose entire film production consists of about 50 feature titles, came onto the spotlight with the celebrated film by Milčo Mančevski *Pred doždot* (*Before the Rain*, 1994)" (Dina Iordanova, "Introduction" to A. J. Horton ed., *The Celluloid Tinderbox* (2000), 12).

[2] Meša Selimović, *Death and the Dervish* (1996), 376. Manchevski uses a somewhat different translation, quoted here, which is closer to Selimović's original.

London encounter with his British lover Anne (Katrin Cartlidge), and Anne's later meeting with her husband in a restaurant where an unrelated shooting spree leaves him dead; and the final part, "Pictures," begins with Aleksandar's return to his Macedonian village and ends with his dying under an open sky as the first drops of rain begin to fall—the same rain that the fleeing Zamira will use to wash her face as she approaches the monastery. The end thus precedes the beginning and the beginning is the end in this circular structure.[3]

I would propose that the focus of our new experience of *Before the Rain* be removed from the role of seeing itself—as paradoxical as this may seem in a discussion of a film and given the fact that the "ways of seeing" are also additionally and repeatedly emphasized by the film's thematic and formal features. After all, the central character, Pulitzer prize-winning war photographer Aleksandar Kirkov, is a professional "viewer" himself, and the film reflects on the ways in which people see, try to see, think they see, or are made to see something, and on the ways in which visual objects—including photographs, films, and medieval frescoes—relate to the violence, the ways in which the distant viewers may "process" the violence coming to them via its visual encapsulation, and on different levels of politics, from private to international, related to all this visual activity. Criticism of the film has also largely focused on the viewing, watching, or gaze present in or allegedly constructed by the film, some of it discussed as intersecting with the Western perception of, and "gaze" at, the violence in the 1990s in the former Yugoslavia, connected with the broader Western discourses on the Balkans and related politics.[4]

---

[3] *Before the Rain* is available in The Criterion Collection edition (2008). For a more detailed summary, see Erik Tängerstad, "Before the Rain—After the War?" (2000), pp. 175–81.
[4] While some of the critics perceive the film as, in Slavoj Žižek's phrasing, offering "to the Western liberal gaze ... precisely what this gaze wants to see in the Balkan war—the spectacle of timeless, incomprehensible, mythical cycle of passions, in contrast to decadent and anemic Western life," Victor A. Friedman gives a welcome corrective, commenting on the viewers "seeing grim outcomes where no fatalism was meant," as Dina Iordanova sums up Friedman's interpretation, who himself asserts that this seeing of grim outcomes was "not a failure of the film but of the [viewer's] gaze." Slavoj Žižek, "Multiculturalism, or the Cultural Logic of Multinational Capitalism" (1995): 38; Victor A. Friedman, "Fable as History: The

And yet, as with all other aesthetic achievements that are relevant and inspirational to wide audiences and different times because they are not primarily, most importantly, or sometimes not at all about the literal place and time in which their stories may be set, *Before the Rain* goes beyond the early 1990s Balkan setting of its story to articulate and make apparent realms and dynamics that are present and active on a much larger scale. In order to become aware of one of these realms, I would suggest that we put aside the various issues of seeing to be able to sense the more subtle presence of listening in this film. After all, in contradistinction to the central character who is a viewer par excellence, the film also revolves around another character who is often overlooked in critical accounts of the film, and who is not a viewer but rather a listener—though a listener in a broader sense than merely auditory—the young monk Kiril. The film as a whole not only functions as a visual event but also creates a space, social environment, ethics, and politics of deep listening. In other words, I would suggest that *Before the Rain* be approached not primarily as a visual but rather as an aural event, though aural in a more philosophical sense denoting an attitude characterized by an openness and receptiveness to—or by "listening to" and "hearing"—whatever comes to a person, as opposed to an attitude characterized by the forceful application of pre-established categories (or "discourses") onto that something.

Macedonian Context" (2000), p. 143, cited in Dina Iordanova, *Cinema of Flames: Balkan Film, Culture and the Media* (2001), 84.

Conceptually centered around the tropes of seeing, watching, being watched, and the demands of the eye or gaze, and often related to some aspects of postcolonial criticism, much of the criticism of the film is connected with issues of Western discourses on the Balkans. However, while one can read a film set in a specific space and time as creating a specific representation of that space and time, and thus participating in the creation of a discourse about them, to do so is a result of a chosen interpretive approach and not of the film itself, or of cinema in general. Such a critical approach often negates or diminishes a film's essential nonliteral or aesthetic dimension that functions outside the sphere of immediate and recognizable political and cultural concerns. For more on this, see the "Introduction" in Gordana P. Crnković, *Imagined Dialogues: Eastern European Literature in Conversation with American and English Literature* (2000). Also see Russell A. Berman, *Fiction Sets You Free: Literature, Liberty, and Western Culture* (2007). Milcho Manchevski addresses this issue in some of his interviews; see, for instance, Keith Brown, "An Interview with Milcho Manchevski" (2008), pp. 12–15.

Articulating the fundamental quality of hearing, Martin Heidegger writes: "We wrongly think that the activation of the body's audio equipment is hearing proper. But then hearing in the sense of hearkening and heeding is supposed to be a transposition of hearing proper into the realm of spiritual."[5] And this from Hans-Georg Gadamer: "Openness exists ... not only for the person to whom one listens, but rather anyone who listens is fundamentally open. Without this kind of openness to one another there is no genuine human relationship. Belonging together always also means being able to listen to one another."[6]

Such proper listening and the related proper hearing seem to be rarely achieved in *Before the Rain*: the forceful application of rigid, pre-given private or social notions onto another person or group precludes the possibility of actually listening to and hearing that other person or group. Anne's mother and husband seem unable to hear anything she is trying to tell them; the Albanian youngster Ali does not listen to his grandfather Zekir when he asks him to uphold the traditional customs of community hospitality and kiss the hand of the visiting Aleksandar; and Zekir himself does not hear his captured granddaughter Zamira when she says that Kiril loves her. Macedonians do not hear each other, Albanians do not hear each other, Macedonians do not hear Albanians and vice versa, and this ubiquitous lack of listening and hearing imbues the film and shapes its tragic outcomes: Aleksandar is killed by his own cousin Zdrave who does not hear him, Zamira by her own brother who does not hear her.

And yet, *Before the Rain* also articulates several poignant instances of proper listening and related proper hearing that are particularly noticeable given the pervasive inability or unwillingness to listen. These instances profoundly affect a "listening" person and often result in radical ethical and political acts. The most intriguing example of proper listening, the center of the whole first part of the film, is Kiril's genuine listening to Zamira, listening that hears Zamira without Zamira's even having to employ any words at all. (And, at any rate, Kiril does not understand Albanian nor Zamira

---

[5] Martin Heidegger, *Early Greek Thinking* (1975), 65.
[6] Hans-Georg Gadamer, *Truth and Method* (1979), 324, quoted in Gemma Corradi Fiumara, *The Other Side of Language: A Philosophy of Listening* (1990), 8.

Fig 4.1 Kiril (courtesy of Milcho Manchevski)

Macedonian.) Kiril thus listens to and hears not Zamira's words about herself and her situation, but rather Zamira herself, in her significance and her tragic predicament. Kiril's listening thus sidesteps, as it were, the realm of words and verbally engendered concepts—words that claim, for example, that Zamira murdered a Macedonian man—and goes back to the perhaps original relating outside or before language, the relating that should both precede and ground any relationship, the relating of proper listening and hearing. As Gemma Corradi Fiumara reminds us in *The Other Side of Language: A Philosophy of Listening*, "proper hearing" is explored in Heidegger's discussion of the Greek word *legein*: "Among the possible meanings of the verb *legein* (besides the prevalent ones related to saying) there are meanings of a different nature, such as to 'shelter,' 'gather,' 'keep,' 'receive,' which would surely be more conducive to a cognitive attitude based on 'proper hearing.'"[7] Such hearing is "listening, hearkening, attending to

---

[7]Corradi Fiumara (1990), 1. Corradi Fiumara here refers to Heidegger's discussion of proper hearing in his *Early Greek Thinking* (1975).

what is said (or unsaid)" and "is preeminently social," presupposing "the worldly condition of being-with-others."[8]

Silence and the Monastery

Let us step back for a moment to consider Kiril's environment, or the physical, social, spiritual, and artistic space that allows him to properly listen. The Orthodox monastery and church on Lake Ohrid (composed of several actual settings but presented as one location in the film), is itself a place quite "unreal, closer to a mythical land than to current-day Macedonia."[9] With its profound silences, this setting creates a unique environment in which one can hear properly. The classic Greeks distinguished *sigaô*, denoting a general absence of sound, from *siôpaô*, referring to the absence of human speech.[10] Adjusting these terms to modern times, it becomes apparent that the monastery creates both *sigaô*, the absence of the intrusive noise of modern life (traffic, industry, machines, media), and *siôpaô*, the absence of verbal noise. Situated in a breathtaking but rugged terrain accessible only by foot, the monastery offers the silencing of the modern world's noisy everyday life and its multiple voices and demands for attention, or, in other words, a reclaiming of that silence which has "today ... become an endangered species," as contemporary acoustic ecologist Gordon Hempton puts it.[11] In terms of the verbal noise or, as Corradi Fiumara calls it, the "environmental degradation ... with regard to the world of language," that is, "an unmonitored saturation of written or

---

[8] Gerald L. Bruns, *Heidegger's Estrangements: Language, Truth and Poetry in the Later Writings* (1989), 21.
[9] "In order to reinforce the fact that this is not a documentary about contemporary Macedonia, I treated the film—to a point—like a fable, stylistically. The country was made to look like a fairy-tale land in the way it was photographed. Blues and visuals suggestive of Byzantine art dominated the first third ... we wanted to create even more heightened reality composed solely of wonderful landscapes, a place obviously unreal, closer to a mythical land than to current-day Macedonia." Milcho Manchevski, "Rainmaking and Personal Truth" (2000), p. 131.
[10] J. H. H. Schmidt, *Handbuch der lateinischen und griechischen Synonymik* (1968), quoted in Silvia Montiglio, *Silence in the Land of Logos* (2000), 11–12.
[11] Gordon Hempton and John Grossman, *One Square Inch of Silence: One Man's Search for Natural Silence in a Noisy World* (2009), 1.

spoken words and ... a concomitant lack of silence," the complete absence of things such as electronic media allows the creation of *siôpaô*, or the silencing of this endlessly proliferating "saturation of words."[12]

Marked by the absence of non-diegetic sounds or the soundtrack music present in other segments, the parts featuring monks and their space contain long silences punctuated only by sparse diegetic sounds. At the film's beginning and after a sequence portraying the monks in prayer, the next sequence shows them walking together across an open area to their cells for the night, without any talking whatsoever. From the first shot of the church on a lake to the scene in which Kiril finds Zamira in his cell and gasps, and aside from the old monk's wishing Kiril goodnight, there is almost a full minute and a half in which the only sounds are crickets chirping, then Kiril's steps on the wooden floor, his undressing, and the pigeons' cooing on the roof above. Kiril's later outing with the old monk Marko is marked by another long stretch of silence, with only Marko's few words surrounded by almost two minutes of silence in which just a few diegetic sounds are heard. After Kiril's return to his cell, this silence is broken by Zamira's sparse "My name is Zamira. You are good." And the film's last sequence featuring monks, the one in which they take leave of Kiril and Zamira, contains another long stretch of silence punctuated by the music blasting from a boom box of one of Zamira's armed pursuers. Kiril ties his suitcase; as the monks look at him, he walks down the stairs; the old monk Marko embraces him; father Damjan fetches Zamira, slaps Kiril on the face and instantly afterward firmly embraces him, tells him "Good luck," to which Kiril responds with his first words, "Thank you, father. Forgive me." These remain the only words spoken by any of them as Zamira raises her eyes to look at the two other monks who return her look and then almost imperceptibly smile at each other, as the two young people leave. From Kiril's tying his suitcase to the onset of non-diegetic music accompanying the couple's final exit from the monastery, the silence lasts for what seems an interminably long period of three minutes and fifteen seconds.

The beginning of the second part of the film, "Faces," set in London, further emphasizes the monastery's silence by the loud

---

[12] Corradi Fiumara (1990), 98.

Fig 4.2 Zamira (courtesy of Milcho Manchevski)

contrast. The up-tempo soundtrack song, diegetic radio news, and telephone calls overlap with the rushed movements and nervous high-pitched voices of the people in Anne's office. After leaving her workplace, Anne appears in the background of a shot that foregrounds heavy machinery, traffic, and masses of people on the street, and is filled to the brim with all of their noise. Sharing a cab with windows closed, Anne and Aleks are depicted from the start as people who try to carve out not only their own space but also their own silence in the midst of this environment. And the fact that both a teen in a London graveyard and a member of the Macedonian search party are listening to the same abrasive tune underscores the "connection by noise" of these seemingly different spaces.

In opposition to such an environment and its ubiquitous "saturation of words," the only words spoken in the monastery are those uttered by the monks themselves, and their own speech is characterized by extreme pithiness and precision, allowing, as pointed out above, long periods of absolute silence. When they do speak, the monks' words are either familiar ones, yet to be considered over and over again (the words of prayers), or extremely limited and to the point. When the leader of the Macedonian search party, Mitre, announces that they are looking for an Albanian girl who killed one of the village men, Father Damjan responds: "In the monastery there have only been refugees from Bosnia. The Muslims. In front of God we are all the same," and when Mitre presses on, the abbot replies: "Turn the other cheek." The words the abbot directs to the other monks are also economical: "Did anyone see her? I just ask to know if she is here," with this particular line intimating that the monk is seeking to find out the facts, not to give the girl up to the irate men looking for her. Speaking in a calm and slow manner, the way all the monks do, he does not significantly increase either the volume or the pitch of his voice, and this delivery marks him as someone who is able to listen, contrasting him with the excited, loud, and non-listening villagers. The inflammatory nationalist phrases uttered by the men from the nearby village (for example, "they [the Albanians] will overwhelm us") are completely absent in the monastery. Aiding ourselves with another classic Greek insight about the ability of corrupt words to literally infect the listener—criminals in ancient Greece were not allowed to speak to the public lest their words contaminate others—we can see that the absence of such speech helps the monks remain impervious to the nationalist virus taking hold of the space outside the monastery. Though they ask Kiril to leave with Zamira, the monks themselves help the young pair escape.[13]

The monastery's silencing of external and physically audible noises allows the more important internal absence or silencing of the distracting noises of modern life on the one hand and of the voices of this or that dominant contemporary ideology, such as nationalism in this case, on the other. While the red-haired Macedonian youngster Stojan obviously just repeats the words he has heard a number of times and now uses as his own ("what about the five centuries of Turks [meaning Muslim Ottomans but now transferred onto Muslim Albanians]?"), the monks and Kiril

---

[13] Irena Makarushka's "Religion, Ethnicity and Violence in *Before the Rain*" sees this issue differently and reads the film's take on the monastery's seclusion and separation as mainly negative. Available online at http://www.manchevski.com/@page=press_essey&sub=therain&sub2=essays&body.htm (accessed 28 October 2011). My own sense is that the film as a whole perceives the monks and their space in a positive light: Kiril proves heroic in his hiding of Zamira, the monastery itself provides shelter to Bosnian Muslim refugees, and all the monks help Zamira and Kiril escape from the Macedonian men pursuing her.

are not possessed by, nor do they become the mouthpieces of, such internalized noise that would destroy the needed silence and prevent them from listening properly. The monastery thus creates an environment of deep external and internal silence conducive to better listening and hearing that enables the "transposition of hearing proper into the realm of spiritual" that Heidegger talks about.

And if such genuine hearing may also be diminished or tempered by the noise of one's own speaking, of one's own words, then a profound rebirth of listening as one's fundamental openness may sometimes require a complete cessation of speaking as well, something akin to a vow of silence. And it is precisely this vow of silence that characterizes and has deeply shaped Kiril who, when we first meet him in the film, has not spoken a word in two years.

Outside Language

A more detailed recounting of the chronology of events (in real time) may be in order: Zamira stands accused of the murder of a Macedonian villager Bojan by the man's relatives, who have assembled a band of armed men to search for her. (The film never reveals whether she has indeed committed this murder, nor does she speak about it.) She is captured by these men and guarded in a sheepfold, from where Aleksandar frees her; his cousin Zdrave shoots at the two and kills Aleksandar but the girl manages to flee, later arriving at the monastery where she hides in Kiril's cell. Startled when he discovers her at night, Kiril calms himself in a moment by crossing himself, and then looks at her as she tells him something in Albanian while protecting herself with her arms as if expecting a blow, before she turns off the light. Kiril leaves and goes to the elderly father's cell, presumably to alert him to Zamira's presence; just as he is about to knock on the monk's door he stays his hand and looks back toward his cell, where he sees Zamira looking at him through the bars of his window. When the other priest suddenly opens the door and asks Kiril, "What are you doing here?" Kiril neither speaks nor reveals anything but simply heads for the outdoor toilet with this monk who assumed that this was the reason of Kiril's coming to his door. Kiril stays in the latrine for a time, presumably pondering what to do next; still he does not betray Zamira and eventually returns to his cell, placing next to the girl, now lying on the floor, some tomatoes which she devours as soon as she hears him lying down. Nor does he reveal her presence the next day, when the Macedonian search party comes to the monastery looking for her, and he remains silent when the abbot asks if anyone saw her. Kiril pushes the armed man who he thinks is about to shoot Zamira (and who was actually about to shoot and kill a cat, which he does after hitting Kiril) and vomits upon seeing the horrible killing of the cat. The day after, Zamira is discovered by the monks, and the couple leave the monastery together at night. Fleeing the area and pausing for a moment in a mountainous landscape, the two are overtaken by Zamira's family the following day, and she is soon machine-gunned by her brother Ali while running after Kiril, who had been chased away by the men in her family.

As envisioned and embodied by the film, the strong connection between the monk and the girl is outside a shared ethnicity (he is Macedonian, she is Albanian), outside a context that could provide some more conventional character motivation (he does not know anything about her and only realizes that she is hiding and does not want to be found), and outside history: though existentially affected by current events, both Kiril and Zamira seem to exist apart from them, in a kind of a transhistorical realm where they are in a "world of their own." Their connection is also outside sexuality, partly because they both appear very young, almost like children, she with her boyish physique and very short hair, dressed in loose pants and blue Adidas T-shirt, and he appearing like a child among the other much older monks.[14] Their one touch is that of his hand briefly holding hers, their one kiss that of his brushing her cheek with his lips, and their one embrace, hers of him, is asexual and much too strong and direct to be sensual, like that of a child expressing love.

---

[14] As Victor A. Friedman clarifies, Zamira's wearing pants should not be interpreted as her being clad in men's clothing, because "çitjane or çintijane, a kind of loose pantaloon ... are characteristic everyday household wear of [rural] Muslim women in Macedonia and elsewhere in the Balkans." Friedman (2000), 136.

Their connection is, aside from all else, fully outside language: they share no common language and there is no verbal communication between them whatsoever.[15] If they can be seen as a symbolic Romeo and Juliet on account of their belonging to two feuding groups and forging the strongest connection despite their respective groups' total enmity, then they are Romeo and Juliet without words. He adheres to his vow of silence even in moments of profound shock, such as when he finds her asleep in his bed, and she quickly realizes both that they cannot understand each other, and that, for whatever reason, Kiril does not speak at all: "Are you dumb? ... You do not speak Albanian, I do not speak Macedonian." In addition to their not understanding each other's language, she assertively demands complete silence—the absence of any talking—at the beginning of their being together and at the end of their togetherness. Her first gesture to him in his astonishment at finding her in his bed is to quickly put her finger to her lips, whispering "shhhh!", and that very same gesture, now in slower movement, will also be the last one she will make for him as she lies dying with him touching her face and saying "forgive me." They hardly talk to each other in the period between her words at the very beginning of their initial encounter ("you do not understand me"), and his words at the end of their ill-fated escape ("afterwards, we will go to my uncle, in London ... no one will find you, no one ... you do not understand me?" and his final "forgive me"). Yet even these very few words function much more as a theatrical monologue for the audience, explaining things to the viewers, than as a communication between two young people who understand nothing of what the other is saying and who pointedly say as much at the beginning and end of their being together—Zamira's "You don't understand Albanian, I don't understand Macedonian," and Kiril's "You don't understand me."

The absence of speech and the presence of a deep silence mark their relationship and are crucial for their connection, which seems to appear, not despite of, but rather because of this silence. First,

---

[15] Friedman's article provides the historical background for this situation in which younger people of different ethnicities do not know each other's language, as opposed to their older family members who do: Zamira's mother and grandfather, Hana and Zekir, know Macedonian, and Aleksandar knows some Albanian. Ibid., 136-7.

Kiril's silence to the others with regard to Zamira's presence in the monastery, his repeated heeding of her first admonition to remain mute (about her, to the others), is his own act of heroism, showing Zamira that Kiril is "good" and selfless in his protection of her, that he loves her.[16] Second, silence profoundly imbues the very relationship between the two and allows proper listening. The silence of the world (their encounters happen at night), the silencing of the language around them (Kiril's non-acceptance of Mitre's assertion that "she [Zamira] killed our brother," and Zamira's own dismissal of her brother's violent words regarding all Macedonians), and the absence of language between them, actually helps the two young people to "hear" each other clearly. Kiril hears or heeds Zamira's need for protection, her basic innocence, and her claim on his love; Zamira "hears" Kiril's goodness. This genuine listening reveals itself to be stronger than the potentially divisive agencies of ethnicity and contemporary politics and in no need of a potentially connective pull of sexuality or language itself. Thus, the dying Zamira's admonition to Kiril not to talk and to be silent not only reminds him and us of the beginning of their connection; Zamira's final gesture primarily invokes the silence between the two of them that has so profoundly abetted their proper hearing of each other and their togetherness, a connection between the two that not only has been subjective and internal but was also acted upon decisively and with enormous personal courage.[17]

---

[16] Being silent in this way, Kiril becomes part of a vast and ancient community of those whose silence is "the expression of knowledge, willpower, or even heroism," as André Neher puts it. André Neher, *The Exile of the Word: From the Silence of the Bible to the Silence of Auschwitz* (1981), 13.

[17] The film complements its endorsement of silence by repeatedly showing the violent or even lethal potential of words when handled improperly in their making or their reception. The several instances of different, life-affirming uses of words, most notably in a conversation between Aleksandar and Hana (the woman Aleksandar loves and Zamira's mother), a conversation that leads to Aleksandar's rescuing of Zamira, are characterized by the presence of deep listening by the interlocutors, listening that hears not only the actually spoken words, but also the whole realms of another person's existence and one's own related ethical decisions. But the film repeatedly features "non-listening words" and failed communications; Venko Andonovski talks about the empty words and "damaged communication." Venko Andonovski, "Semiološkata fobija od tugoto: Semiotikata na sličnostite i semiotikata na razlikite vo filmot *Pred doždot* na Milčo Mančevski" (1995), pp. 21–7. Words are also associatively connected with or lead directly to death: Anne has

The Ways of Listening and a Reclining Body

Although Kiril shares all the silent times of the monastery and of the other monks as discussed above, he also creates—with his vow of silence—his own even more intensified practice of silence and listening. Introduced in a series of oppositions to at least minimally talking characters, Kiril keeps silent while walking with the older monk Marko who talks and also tells of Kiril's vow of silence, then during the monks' chanting, and later in his encounter with the (at first) briefly talking Zamira. His appearance alone creates silence: when he arrives late to the morning prayer, the prayer comes to an end and a silence more than twenty seconds long ensues, in which close-ups of frescoes are juxtaposed with close-ups of Kiril's face, as silent as the figures on these frescoes. Kiril is clearly likened to them, not only through this visual juxtaposition of his face with their figures and faces, but also through their shared silence. The sequences centering on Kiril are marked by long silences and the presence of only diegetic sounds characteristic of the monastery and its monks. In the second night of Zamira's hiding, the sequence showing Kiril in his cell is marked by almost complete silence, in contrast to the search party's talking and shooting on the outside. In the two scenes in which Kiril encounters Zamira that echo each other—the first one a dream, the second almost completely identical but real—they do not say a word, and the soundtrack during their silent, almost two-minute-long encounter(s) is a very few sustained notes on a violin, bracketing away and silencing the outside diegetic sounds, and marking the "heightened reality," as

---

an utterly nonfunctional verbal communication with her husband, punctuated by verbal outbursts and marked by what seems to be his total inability to hear her, which precedes the violence that erupts in the London restaurant and claims his life. The restaurant shooting itself appears to be caused by a conversation gone bad: the two men, speaking a variant of Bosnian/Croatian/Serbian, seem to be having a not unfriendly conversation that quickly veers into a quarrel, physical fight, and shooting. And it is not so much a concrete event, the murder of the Macedonian man Bojan, that, however horrible it may be, results in further acts of violence, but instead a specific set of words attached to it, alongside a very specific interpretation of these words, as will be discussed later in this chapter.

Manchevski calls it, of the two young people's connecting with each other.[18]

Not enclosed by noise and noise-making words, Kiril is fully "open" to and thus truly experiences, or hears on a highly sensitized level, the miracle of the giving and silent earth, the tomatoes he has nurtured and is now harvesting, the sun, and the gift of life these create together. As Corradi Fiumara puts it, "the speech act selects an aspect of reality simply by speaking about it"; that is, the words usher one out of a myriad of simultaneously coexisting aspects of reality, and thus prioritize that one aspect, thereby putting into the background of invisibility (or inaudibility) the unspoken realms.[19] With no words, Kiril's experience of the world is more bodily and direct, more in tune, as it were, with the matter itself, and less dependent—or perhaps not at all dependent—on the many possible conceptual or discursive constructions and self-confident words that may not be getting there at all, that may enwrap the matter and the living body in the cloak of invisibility, displace it, and replace it.[20]

Kiril is the one who retrieves and restores the "life-enhancing role of listening," because, to paraphrase Corradi Fiumara, he approaches in an accepting manner, or lets himself be accosted by, whatever faces him, and thus allows its existence and further articulation.[21] His listening and openness to the world around him—to plants, the sky, a landscape, the frescoes in the monastery, the other monks, the pigeons' cooing on his roof, Zamira—are marked by his responsiveness to, his receiving and sheltering of, this world, and these combine to allow him to properly hear this world.[22] A

---

[18] Manchevski (2000), 131.
[19] Corradi Fiumara (1990), 24.
[20] A prime example of such an erasure of the living body by strident words happens with the group of armed Macedonian men, who, by labeling Zamira an "Albanian whore," become unable to grasp that in a way she is still just a child.
[21] "We can retrieve and restore the life-enhancing role of listening. To the extent that we approach in an accepting manner, or let ourselves be accosted, we allow the existence and further articulation of whatever faces us." Corradi Fiumara (1990), 16.
[22] To repeat: "Among the possible meanings of the verb *legein* (besides the prevalent ones related to saying) there are meanings of a different nature, such as to 'shelter,' 'gather,' 'keep,' 'receive,' which would surely be more conducive to a cognitive attitude based on 'proper hearing.'" Corradi Fiumara (1990), 1.

precondition of saying, a precondition of doing, or even of seeing, listening is gathering, sheltering, heeding, and the path to proper hearing.[23] This silent listening and proper hearing come first, as the origin of anything that follows; the next step (saying, doing) may or may not arrive, but the initial hearing as sheltering has to be the source, the root of whatever comes next. Literature or philosophy cannot themselves be the silence and the wordless listening to whatever faces us. They can talk about or even tell this way of being (as in poetry), but they cannot themselves be this silent, wordless mode: by speaking or writing, through the use of words, they can talk about silence but cannot be silent themselves. Though sometimes brought about by words, as the "unspeakable" brought about "by clearly displaying the speakable" (Ludwig Wittgenstein), this silent being is, as silence, the absence of language; its silence excludes language. The medium of film, on the other hand, can create something that language-based forms cannot. Film has the capacity to put before us and shape the silent listening that is called for and talked about by the philosophers. Their ideal concepts get their embodied, concrete reality in *Before the Rain*.

Consider the following two fragments from Heidegger's *Early Greek Thinking*, and a third from Corradi Fiumara's *The Other Side of Language: Philosophy of Listening*:

> Who would want to deny that in the language of the Greeks from early on *legein* means to talk, say or tell. However, just as early and even more originally ... it means what our [German] similarly sounding *legen* means: to lay down and lay before. In *legen* a "bringing together" prevails, the Latin *legere* understood as *lesen*, in the sense of collecting and bringing together. *Legein* properly means the laying-down and laying-before which gathers itself and others.[24]

---

[23] Saying that proper hearing is a precondition of seeing may sound counterintuitive: after all, we see what we see and that's that. But things are not that simple: one sees what one thinks one is seeing, and the presence or absence of hearing what one is looking at is a crucial component in the creation of what one thinks one sees. For more on this topic, see a discussion of *Chinatown* in Gordana P. Crnković, "From the Eye to the Hand: The Victim's Double Vision in the Cinema of Roman Polanski" (2004).

[24] Heidegger (1975), 60.

Legein ...means just this, that whatever lies before us involves us and therefore concerns us.[25]

This ... perspective is characterized by the requirement that we dwell with, abide by ... that we aim at coexistence with, rather than knowledge-of.[26]

In *Before the Rain*, the notions of "laying-down and laying-before which gathers itself and others" or of "just this, that whatever lies before us involves us and therefore concerns us" come back from their abstracted philosophical meaning, where the literal laying down of the physical bodies before us becomes the figurative "laying down" of something in front of our minds. *Before the Rain* returns these abstracted notions to earth, where laying down and laying before—and receiving, sheltering, and co-existing with—become the basic descriptive words expressing the relation between two living, human, and increasingly connected bodies. The two night scenes involving Kiril and Zamira in his cell can best be described as scenes of Zamira lying in front of Kiril or laying down before him. On the first night, she lies sidewise on the bare wooden floor, her body curled, with her hand under her head, parallel to Kiril's bed and his body; the two are turned away from each other. On the second night, she again lies on her side on the floor parallel to him, but the two are turned toward each other. This time Zamira props her head on her hand and just looks at him lying on his bed, his face and body turned to hers, looking at her. She looks at him for a long time and then smiles. From a point behind the triangle made by her arm propping her head, a long shot emphasizes her perspective: Kiril is seen through that triangle made by Zamira's body and is framed by her supine position.

Not standing, moving, or even sitting, a reclining body is the furthest removed from movement and action, the most unprotected and vulnerable, the most open to whatever it lies in front of. Zamira's body lying in front of Kiril is not a sexual body, nor a body in simple repose; it is the body that is "laying in front" of Kiril in the most profound way that "involves" him and "therefore concerns" him. Kiril "receives," "shelters," and "keeps" Zamira,

---

[25] Heidegger (1975), 62.
[26] Corradi Fiumara (1990), 15.

and he dwells with and abides by her, shaping his being with her as a coexistence rather than an indifferent distance and noninvolvement. Such coexistence implies a shared destiny of flight and exile, marked by their now shared physical appearance: having relinquished his monk's robe, Kiril becomes like Zamira, dressed in a pair of pants and a striped Adidas T-shirt, the same as hers except that his is red and hers is blue. Slapped or threatened by both the Macedonian and Albanian pursuers of Zamira, Kiril indeed shares her fate, and, in the end, it seems like chance that she is killed rather than him or both of them.

Silent Children and Nature, Talking Children and Their Games

Although young adults, Kiril and Zamira can also be seen as symbolic children on account of their youth, lack of explicit sexuality, and childlike appearance. Zamira's extremely sparse talk, even with her own family's male members, also likens her to a child who does not explain or argue but only repeatedly asserts the most basic and important things. After eating the tomatoes Kiril brought her, Zamira lies down on the floor and says: "My name is Zamira. You are good." When eventually apprehended by the men in her family and repeatedly hit by her grandfather Zekir who accuses her of killing Bojan and being a "whore" for having been accompanied by Kiril, she simply states: "He saved my life, grandpa, he hid me," and keeps repeating, despite Zekir's slaps, "He loves me. He loves me. He loves me." Zamira never tries to explain that Kiril is a monk, that he never touched her until he gave her that light kiss on the cheek seen by her family's men, that he did not reveal her hiding in his cell despite the grave danger to himself, that he got beaten by a Macedonian man and left his monastery because of her. Her talk is not discursive, explanatory, argumentative, or apologetic; she utters only the most basic truths: "You are good." "He helped me." "He loves me."

Furthermore, Kiril and Zamira's predominantly silent, wordless existence helps strengthen both young people's metaphorical closeness to the quiet of nature, plants, and animals, a closeness intimated by both the film's narrative elements and its visual articulation of scenes featuring the two young people. From the very start Kiril is associated with the cultivation of plants, and with the silence that connects them to him, a being equally mute. A poignantly long close-up shot of Kiril's well-tanned hands picking ripe tomatoes opens the film, and his very first contact with Zamira, the first thing he does for her, is place tomatoes on the floor next to her—as many tomatoes as he could carry. In the same way in which he has worked in the monastery's garden, Kiril is now caring for and protecting Zamira. She is in turn repeatedly associated with a cat or a hunted animal. The party of Macedonian men searching for her is introduced with a close-up shot of a man's boot stepping right next to a cat and scaring it away; one man's looking for the cat echoes his search for the hidden girl, and the final brutal killing of this cat with a machine gun reflects the desire to kill Zamira, echoes the chronologically earlier (though later in filmic time) shooting at Zamira that missed her but killed Aleksandar, and prefigures her eventual murder. Like a cat, Zamira is nocturnal, able to hide and move well at night, meeting Kiril and being sheltered by him the first night, making contact with him the second night, leaving the monastery in search of rescue and safety the third night, and being overtaken and killed in the full light of the day after, deprived of her nocturnal protection. Zamira's body language is catlike as well: she is flexible, quiet, capable of being still for a long time, and she crouches like a cat, on all fours, while looking through the barred window at Kiril walking to the senior monk's cell, presumably to inform on her.[27] Tamed like an animal would be, with food (she eats the tomatoes Kiril brought to her using both hands simultaneously, hungrily biting into one tomato and then into another), Zamira is pursued by one (Macedonian) group of armed men and then found, captured, and killed by another (Albanian) group of armed men. Both of these groups resemble hunting parties, whose long-distance

---

[27] The association between Zamira and a cat is also clearly present in Manchevski's vision of her character, as evidenced in, among others, the published fifth revision of the screenplay for *Before the Rain*. In a description of one scene that did not end up in the final version of the film, Zamira, while running, gets hit by a branch and licks blood off her hand, "like a cat." Milcho Manchevski, *Before the Rain/Pred doždot* (2002), 189. Manchevski also mentions the "feline quality" of the actress Labina Mitevska in his director's commentary on the Criterion DVD edition of *Before the Rain*.

weapons are trained on a single defenseless creature. Her death has the overtones of a ritual sacrifice as well, as she has been likened to a newly born lamb: right after observing the birth of the two lambs, we see the two girls on the hill above the sheepfold, one of whom is presumably Zamira.

The film's "fairy-tale" mode ("the film is shot, seen, colored ... like a fairy tale"), strengthens this associative connection between, or the metaphorical sameness of, two silent children and silent plants and animals.[28] After all, fairy tales often include the archetypal relationship between children or good (innocent) people on the one hand, and animals and plants on the other. (A familiar fairy-tale motive is that of a young girl who has to remain silent and not speak a word for a certain number of years in order to break an evil spell; while under her own vow of silence, the child is approached and befriended by meek forest animals—such as squirrels, birds, and a doe, who help her and feed her, accepting her as one of their own.) In the film's screenplay, the opening scene showing Kiril's hands picking ripe tomatoes includes a simple event in which the hands identify and then prop up a broken twig with a stick, thus in effect healing the plant, and also ascribing the character of cultivator and nurturer to the young man. The poignant metaphoric association of the two silent children with plants and animals endorses Kiril and Zamira by making them fluent with nature and also opens up the scope of the film toward broader insights into ways in which the humans' specific relating to other humans corresponds to their relating to nature. The non-listening aggressive violence toward Kiril and Zamira is related to the non-listening aggressive violence toward nature, the violence that is as unwilling to hear and heed this nature (killing the cat and turtles) as it is unwilling to hear Kiril and Zamira.[29]

---

[28] Milcho Manchevski, in a director's commentary on the Criterion DVD edition of *Before the Rain*.
[29] The rendering of nature in *Before the Rain*, and this link between the two main characters and plants and animals in particular, could be a topic of another whole work focusing on the issues of eco-criticism, whose insights deeply concern listening and silence. Identifying Maurice Merleau-Ponty as one of eco-criticism's main predecessors, for instance, Louise Westling writes that "Merleau-Ponty called for a reawakening to the world around us, that requires listening to the other voices that

Before the Rain's contrast between life-affirming ways of silence and listening on one hand, and the violence of non-listening and speaking on the other, is also embodied in a profound division between "silent" and "talking" children. The two silent children, Kiril and Zamira, are contrasted to the talking children, who do not merely aid the Macedonian men's pursuit of Zamira but actually initiate that pursuit with their words. After all, no one (including us, the viewers), ever sees what actually happens to Bojan or who kills him; as the writer and director Manchevski comments, "the film never shows us anything; we see two girls on the hill near the sheepfold and yes, one of them is Zamira, but the film never gets a close-up of her, so we can at best only surmise that it is she, not know it."[30] With its vagueness and lack of clear information, the film accurately articulates the situation on the ground: there was no factual knowledge or any positive eyewitness' account that identified Zamira as a murderer. Instead, there were only very specific words, allegedly spoken by children—"the children saw her [Zamira] with him"—and then received and interpreted in a very specific way by a group of Macedonian villagers—"Zamira is Bojan's murderer"—that lead to the pursuit and capture of Zamira, and the killing of Aleksandar who frees her. And it was another set of words disclosing Zamira's hiding place (Mitre's "the children told me she hid in the monastery") that led to the search of the monastery, the escape of the two young people, and the eventual death of the girl.

The children use words to first focus the men's shock and disorientation upon finding the murdered Bojan by singling out Zamira as the suspect, and later to direct the men's hunt with a new piece of information regarding her hiding place. Even though we never see these transactions of words between children and grown-ups and can thus assume that, for example, the children only truthfully answered questions posed to them by the elders, the way these children were previously introduced in the film (in their brutal game of taunting and then killing two captured

---

we have forgotten to hear, voices that arise in what we may have formerly assumed to be silences." Louise Westling, "Literature, the Environment, and the Question of the Posthuman" (2006), 39.

[30] Milcho Manchevski, in a director's commentary on the Criterion DVD edition of *Before the Rain*.

turtles), the fact that we have observed two girls—not one—near the sheepfold (although the children allegedly mention only one girl, Zamira), and the way in which the scenes involving these children's words are filmed (as if an absent master gives an order, "the children tell me ... [and thus I am here]"), combine to convey the uncomfortable impression that these children are more than the omnipresent eyes of the grown-ups appearing in a number of scenes.[31] Instead of being solely the adults' surveillance tool, the "talking children" themselves initiate the adult hunt and direct the search with their own words—the hunt so much like playing tag, the search so much like hide-and-seek—with the real puppet masters, the children, appearing barely but ominously as distant handlers of the grown-up executors of their games.

These talking children not only symbolically command and cause adult aggression: their own violent games repeatedly mirror grown-up games, creating a rich internal echo in which the children's games acquire an unmistakably grown-up aspect, and adult pursuits have a childish side, in a way that corrupts and perverts them both. The children reveal the potential to be cruel in an "adult way," with real bullets and real killings: they surround two turtles with a circle of brushwood, play with them pretending that the two turtles are two tanks fighting each other, and then set the twigs around them on fire and throw bullets into it. The scene ends with a close-up of two turtles on their backs, dead and burning, and with the sound of children's laughter. This killing of animals prefigures the killing of people associated with defenseless animals, such as Zamira, and is shown as a part of the chain of murders that includes the cat, Bojan, Aleksandar, and Zamira. While the children behave like violent adults, the adults themselves appear like unaware children in their seeming inability to control their weapons or be conscious of the predictable consequences of their use. Echoing the symbolic dynamic of the film, a man is separated from both his silence and his animal, a small donkey whom he

---

[31] We see a boy taking a photograph of the double funeral of Bojan and Aleksandar and then turning around and seeing Kiril running down the hill, which would seem suspicious and could lead to the discovery of Zamira's being in the monastery; the two boys observe Aleksandar's visit to Zekir and Hana, and a few boys emerge from behind the rocks when Zekir hits his granddaughter Zamira, which indicates that it was perhaps again the children who watched her and informed on her movements.

holds in an embrace, by being given a gun that literally seems to take hold of him, making him shoot into the air (the sound of the machine gun mixed with that of the laughter of nearby children) or at the cat on the roof. Aleksandar's cousin Zdrave is also unable to hold a gun without using it and eventually shoots at Zamira, only to end up killing Aleksandar; and Zamira's brother Ali, unable to hold his sister back with his voice and also unable to control his gun, shoots at and kills Zamira. In both of these killings, the men end up doing something they never intended to do—killing their own cousin or sister—and looking like dumbfounded children when faced with the real effects of their use of these weapons. After shooting at Zamira with his machine gun (after she starts running after Kiril), and seeing her felled, her brother is in a speechless, wide-eyed state of shock, as if it indeed never occurred to him that shooting someone could actually kill them even if this was unintended. And after shooting and gravely wounding Aleksandar, Zdrave exhibits an even more childish reaction, leaning in disbelief over Aleksandar and repeating "Don't you worry, Aleks, you'll be fine," as the bleeding man lies dying on the ground.

Mirroring each other with the same absence of listening, the violence of words and action, and fascination with weapons, both adults and children end up corrupted by a disturbing hybridization with the other realm, with children appearing like masked grown-ups and adults like perverted children. The fatal outcome of this mutation, where children are not children anymore and neither are adults adults, is most clearly revealed in its final results, which are classically known as the grossest violations of nature—the murders of close relatives, of a cousin or a sister. Adults stop being adults when they allow themselves to be led by children, real or symbolic, and thus become unnatural children themselves, obsessed with new toys/guns and exciting games and unable to foresee the consequences of their violent actions—unable to answer Aleksandar's simple question, "And what after?" Children stop being children when they start playing their games—hide-and-seek and tag—in the adult arena, playing with infantile adults and playing the adults as their own tools of finding and catching. Using words to fuel and direct violent games, these "talking children" are contrasted to the silent children (Kiril, Zamira) and the children who bring silence—as the boys' choir in a London church does, echoing the Macedonian monks' prayer and space and bringing a moment of peace and composure to the pregnant Anne. But it is the adults, of course, who preserve and protect the spheres of both adulthood and childhood by preserving and protecting the separation between the two or, rather, by protecting the environment in which children are allowed to grow and ripen in silence and thus learn and nourish their own ability to listen and hear, which they can carry into adulthood as their own best foundation. The adults either affirm the sanctity of childhood and its silence, disarming the children and asserting their distinctiveness (Aleksandar's taking the guns away from young Stojan and a little boy and his repeating that Zamira is a "child") or, on the contrary, draw the children into the sphere of corrupted borders by arming them, as Mitre does when he gives a gun to his nephew Stojan and to a somewhat feeble-minded childlike man who later shoots the cat.

The division between the silent and the talking children is another embodiment of the film's symbolic division between life-affirming listening and aggressive non-listening. The choice between silent hearing and loud shouting-down of what is in front of us lies much deeper than the sphere of adult politics and begins much earlier, during the period in which a person establishes her or his grounding in the world. Only by recognizing and protecting the sphere of childhood as the sphere where silent listening to the world is learned can one hope to foster a lifelong listening attitude that may resist distracting or aggressive noises and be capable of opposing violence.

Inner Listening and the *Daimon*

Before the Rain is an inspiring and profound cinematic meditation on silence and proper listening and their opposition to the advent of the world of noise, violence, assertive words, and the lack of hearing. Not listening to and not hearing nature and people creates the first, original erasure of them, and the "real" physical destruction often comes about as a consequence of that primary erasure. The "non-listening" words produced by objectifying discourses, and those that initiate and shape the violent games, make a large part of the noise that destroys the silence necessary for proper listening. *Before the Rain* can thus be experienced as implying the overall need for the reclaiming of silence and the possibility of proper listening allowed by that silence.

The Macedonian villager with cropped hair who shoots in the air and kills the cat is characterized by his noticeable inability to endure silence once he gets pulled into the vortex of violence—he is always making noise himself or else wrapping himself fully in it, as when he puts a boom box turned up very loud right next to his ear. He is a metonymic representative of an environment in which noise works against any possibility of sensing and recognizing the need for proper hearing against and outside this noise. The silence in *Before the Rain* thus involves, first, a removal of the listening garbage that distracts and explodes the person.[32] Kiril's silent monastery allows such an absence of noise; Kiril can thus "hear" outside and beyond his time with its distracting or violent noises. In a sea of silence, the daily prayers are basic and make one, perhaps, ponder their meaning and scope over and over again; Kiril's silent ways thus help him hear Zamira properly and immediately.

Second, silence can also bring the removal of one's own talking, or the need to verbally justify or explain oneself when no words are available. Kiril's vow of silence thus allows both his openness to whatever or whoever accosts him and the removal of the imperative to immediately explain, justify, put into words, or verbalize himself. This imperative is crushingly hard in novel situations that do not yet have proper words or with the dominant discourses pushing their own words. As Simone Weil puts it, "the effort of expression has a bearing not only on the form but on the thought and on the whole inner being."[33] Being able to not speak, Kiril does not have

---

[32] As Corradi Fiumara puts it, our noise-laden environment may cause a person's numbness or the complete "inhibition of our listening potential," which happens simply in order for one to survive or "protect one's inner self." Corradi Fiumara (1990), 82. Or, this environment brings about the subconscious metabolization of the large volume of messages, which can again mightily distract one from his or her own proper hearing and being in the world; or one can deal with this dense and overwhelming noise critically, but then dealing with it may make one spend so much of oneself and one's time in this sphere that there is much less chance for the development of the proper listening to the voices that become audible only when noise is silenced.

[33] Simone Weil, "The Power of Words," a non-referenced quote from Weil in Siân Miles's preface to this essay, in Siân Miles ed., *Simone Weil: An Anthology* (1986), 239.

to translate his hiding of Zamira into words intended for the senior monks, an act that may have in itself been so painful and difficult for Kiril that it could have stopped him from doing the right thing and helping Zamira.

Third, silence allows not only hearing the world around oneself and other people but also the more original, primary, or basic listening to oneself or to one's own "messages from within." Silence can thus facilitate the rebirth of listening to one's own "inner self," or what one may call the Socratic *daimon*.

In her chapter "On Inner Listening," Corradi Fiumara writes:

> And at least *one* of the salient features of Socrates the philosopher can be identified in his relationship with the inner *daimon* to whom he constantly listens. And if this type of relationship tends to disappear during subsequent flights in our philosophical history, perhaps we do not ask with sufficient curiosity why it is that, after Socrates, messages *from within* which inspire, advise and direct us are no longer "audible" ... we become compulsively dependent on external messages and incapable of letting any inner message spring to life. ... Possibly the apex in the trajectory of Western thought, our culture does in fact tend to ignore this voice, whose only concern is for the "health of the soul." And thus the most credible voice is ultimately represented as the most negligible. ...
>
> Rather than proceeding toward it, therefore, one should simply let oneself be approached by it.[34]

Being "approached by it," sleeping Kiril hears the voice speaking the 23rd Psalm: "Yea, though I walk through the valley of the shadow of death, I will fear no evil: For thou art with me." "Thou" is God as love and the deepest me, in the identity between the God and the *daimon*, the divine and the demonic. "Plato, in the speech of defense, even makes Socrates connect the two and call the phenomenon 'a divine and demonic element' ... and even 'the sign of the God.'"[35] Kiril then dreams that he is waking up in his

---

[34] Corradi Fiumara (1990), 127–31 (emphasis in the original).
[35] Paul Friedlaender, *Plato. I. An Introduction*, trans. H. Meyerhoff (London: Routledge and Kegan Paul, 1958), 33, quoted in Corradi Fiumara (1990), 130.

bed and that he sees Zamira in front of the window filled with rain: the "you" of Zamira is now connected with the "you" of God, of Kiril's own innermost voice or *daimon*, with his love flowing to "you." The silence of the monastic life, of the exclusion of the external noises of society and of Kiril's own words, has allowed the real listening and heeding of "you" (God, love, Zamira), being at the same time the profound listening and heeding of his own innermost voice, his *daimon*.

Before the Rain participates in and reinvigorates a long and rich tradition of the philosophical, spiritual, and artistic emphasis on the need for nourishing silence and the proper listening enabled by it. Evading the noises of the world, of assertive speeches, and of one's own words, young Kiril is able to properly listen to and hear himself and his own clear inner voice, to hear Zamira, to love and help her, and to show us that a way out of the circle of violence has to include the reclaiming of the environment and the state of mind of deep listening, which many of us have forgotten ever existed.

5

Foundations II
Eternal Realms and Individual Victims in Ivo Andrić's *Ex Ponto* and *Unrest*

> But I have never forgotten a human face, a beautiful human face lit up with the shine of reason and with only human sadness because of what is seen.
>
> IVO ANDRIĆ, *EX PONTO*[1]

Founded in 1990, Zagreb's publishing house Durieux was named after German theater actress and writer, Tilla Durieux (1880–1971), who left Germany in 1933 and lived in Zagreb through World War Two and until the early 1950s. The title of one series of this publishing house—"Ex Ponto"—dedicated to publishing contemporary Bosnian literature in exile, invokes Ovid's classic work but also an early twentieth-century work of the same name, written by Yugoslav writer Ivo Andrić (1892–1975). A Nobel laureate whose main works revolve around his native Bosnia, Andrić was arrested on charges of activities against the Austro-Hungarian state when he was 21 years old, "on 4 August 1914, the week after Austria-Hungary declared

---

[1] Ivo Andrić, *Ex Ponto. Nemiri [Unrest]* (1975), 164. This translation by Gordana P. Crnković.

war on Serbia."[2] He was imprisoned in Maribor until March 1915; the experience is invoked in the first part of his *Ex Ponto*.

Andrić's early works, *Ex Ponto* (1918) and *Unrest* (*Nemiri*, 1920) have often been considered artistically less accomplished than his later acclaimed historical novels, *The Bridge on the Drina* (*Na Drini ćuprija*, 1945) and *Bosnian Chronicle* (*Travnička hronika*, 1945).[3] *Ex Ponto* and *Unrest* might indeed at times cause aversion in the contemporary reader with their exalted neo-romantic tone, hypertrophied subjectivity, and archaic pathos. However, despite these perhaps initially alienating aspects, these two early works "surpass" Andrić's celebrated later novels when viewed with regard to the articulation of a dynamic between individual victimization and the minimizing of this victimization through the soothing realms of "eternal art."

Ex Ponto and *Unrest* are short, fragmentary, and poetic pieces commonly described as poems in prose. They were written during or immediately after World War One. *The Bridge on the Drina* and *Bosnian Chronicle* were written during World War Two.[4] These two groups of works, early and late, differ in their artistic responses to myriad individual victimizations of the world wars and to the question of how literature relates to these victimizations.

---

[2] Wayne S. Vucinich, "Introduction: Ivo Andrić and His Times," in Wayne S. Vucinich ed., *Ivo Andrić Revisited: The Bridge Still Stands* (1996), 29.

[3] *Ex Ponto* was originally published by Književni jug (Zagreb) and *Nemiri* by Naklada St. Kugli (Zagreb). In both cases I shall cite the 1975 edition published by *Svjetlost* (Sarajevo). Translators and scholars have used both "Anxieties" and "Unrest" for Andrić's title *Nemiri*. I prefer "Unrest" because it seems to me that it better captures Andrić's meaning(s) even though it loses the plural of the original that is preserved in "Anxieties."

[4] *The Bridge on the Drina* was "written quickly, between July 1942 and December 1943" (Celia Hawkesworth, *Ivo Andrić: Bridge between East and West* (1984), 124). While most of *Bosnian Chronicle* was also written during the war, "Andrić began work on this, his first novel, in 1924, seeing it as a study of contacts between East and West" (ibid., 142).

"Above The Victories" in *The Bridge on the Drina* and *Bosnian Chronicle*

In a part of *Unrest* entitled "Above the Victories," Andrić writes:

> God holds his hand on the crown of the head of those who are conquered, and the victor is alone and his mirth burns and goes out. All the hope, comfort, and beauty in the world is revealed to the eyes of those who are won over; the victors are blind; they tremble and burn and have nothing other than their wild flaming mirth, which leaves ashes behind. ...
>
> The winds travel and the rains go, good and fertile, always the same, and the flags slowly disintegrate and tear; and colors get pale and everything is forgotten, but a man remains always the same, bent under the pain and persevering in work; wreaths wither and the flags rot and what remains is a man who sows and works and the rain which helps him. Who will win over a man?[5]

Indeed, who will win over a man? By constructing a sphere of lasting humanity ("what remains is a man who sows and works"), Andrić's text articulates a space "above the victories." In this space, specific historical "victories"—such as the ones in the war, which cause the victimization of numerous individuals—lose their weight, finality, and reality ("the flags rot"). When these victories cease being the only reality that exists, the victimization of those who are won over by these victories is also diminished. With an emphasis on the space in which a man—as humanity—is invincible, the destruction and victimization of many individual human beings becomes less important. They might cease to exist, yet humanity itself remains. The history of particular events, of "victories" in which some ascend to power while others die or are profoundly damaged, becomes less urgent when viewed from the standpoint of the eternity of humanity.

---

[5] Ivo Andrić (1975), 123. As noted, citations from both *Ex Ponto* and *Unrest* will be taken from this edition. Unless noted otherwise, translations here from these two works are by Gordana P. Crnković.

While the above fragment from *Unrest* explicitly displaces particular individual victimizations through the sphere of persisting humanity, *Unrest* as a whole is characterized precisely by the opposite thrust of asserting the urgency of individual victimizations and refusing the consolation of the immortality of humanity or art. The poetics of displacing and minimizing the victimizations of particular individuals by the creation of a space of everlasting humanity or community, however, shapes *The Bridge on the Drina* and *Bosnian Chronicle*. In the former, specific destinies and tragedies, narrated in detail, lose their weight under the sheer scope of the historical novel. The span of four centuries turns any individual existence into solely one of the many elements of the persisting life of the *kasaba* (small city), thus depriving this existence of the urgency and importance of unrepeatable and unique life:

> Life [is] an incomprehensible marvel, since it was incessantly wasted and spent, yet none the less it lasted and endured "like the bridge on the Drina."[6]

The continuing life of community, this "incomprehensible marvel [which] last[s] and endure[s]," a life intertwined with and also symbolized by the persistence of a functional and beautiful object, the bridge, receives primacy over the specific lives that constitute this one life "in general" and which themselves "waste" and "[are] spent." These particular individual lives become the building blocks of the enduring life of community or humanity, and thus the horror of individuals' passing away is diluted by a repeated assertion of the persistence of life in general and of the immortal work of art, the bridge:

> Thus the generations renewed themselves beside the bridge and the bridge shook from itself, like dust, all the traces which transient human events had left on it and remained, when all was over, unchanged and unchangable.[7]

---

[6] Ivo Andrić, *The Bridge on the Drina*, trans. Lovett F. Edwards (1977), 81.
[7] Andrić (1977), 93.

But misfortunes do not last forever (this they have in common with joys) but pass away or are at least diminished and become lost in oblivion. Life on the *kapia* [part of the bridge] always renews itself despite everything and the bridge does not change with the years or with the centuries or with the most painful turns in human affairs. All these pass over it, even as the unquiet waters pass beneath its smooth and perfect arches.[8]

Andrić's own calm and unperturbed realist narrative, moving onward systematically and forcefully regardless of the tragedies and individual victimizations that are being recounted, is the main device of articulation of this life "in general," which goes on ineluctably and victoriously. The very title of this novel is coined from part of a folk proverb, "*Ostade kao na Drini ćuprija*" ("It has stayed like the bridge on the Drina"), which refers to something persistent and invincible.

Andrić ends *The Bridge on the Drina* with the thoughts of the dying Alihodža, who, after seeing the bridge wrecked by an explosive, thinks:

> So be it. ... If they destroy here, then somewhere else someone else is building. Surely there are still peaceful countries and men of good sense who know of God's love? If God had abandoned this unlucky town on the Drina, he had surely not abandoned the whole world that was beneath the skies? They would not do this for ever. But who knows? ... Anything might happen. But one thing could not happen; it could not be that great and wise men of exalted soul who would raise lasting buildings for the love of God, so that the world should be more beautiful and man live in it better and more easily, should everywhere and for all time vanish from this earth. Should they too vanish, it would mean that the love of God was extinguished and had disappeared from the world. That could not be.[9]

The bridge is destroyed, and Alihodža dies. But this departure of one man, ending *The Bridge on the Drina*, is carried onto the plane

---

[8] Andrić (1977), 101.
[9] Andrić (1977), 313.

of humanity and creation in general, in which the final victory of destruction or death simply does not exist: "That could not be."

Although narrated in detail and providing the theme and body of *Bosnian Chronicle*, the specific events in the Bosnian city of Travnik (events connected with the rise and fall of Napoleon), as well as individuals acting in, experiencing, and verbalizing these events, are all finally displaced and minimized by the "persisting life of community" in this novel as well. Sorting out his old papers, for example, Daville, the French consul in Travnik and a main character of the novel, finds:

> ... a sheaf of those encomiums and verse letters penned on various gala occasions and celebrating various men and regimes. Poor orphaned verses, dedicated to lost causes and personalities who today meant less than the dead.[10]

Given a large enough scope of the narrative, all the personalities who shaped and ruled the world yesterday would of course "today [mean] less than the dead." Specific history, although chronicled and recorded in detail, eventually loses out in front of the ahistorical persisting community, in which, as Andrić put it in *Unrest*, "flags rot and what remains is a man who sows and works." Thus in the epilogue of *Bosnian Chronicle*, Travnik's oldest and most respected *bey*, Hamdi Beg, reflects on the life which will be the same as it has always been before Napoleon's intrusion into these parts of Europe:

> "Seven years, eh?" Hamdi Beg said thoughtfully, drawling a little. "Seven years! And do you remember what a hue and cry there was over these consuls and over that ... that Bonaparte! Bonaparte here, Bonaparte there. He was going to do this, he was going to do that. The world was too small for him. His strength was boundless, no one could match him. So this infidel rabble of ours lifted up their heads like some cobless corn. Some hung onto the coat tails of the French Consul, others to the Austrian, and the third lot waited for a Russian. The rayah went plain off their heads and ran amuck. Well, that was that

---

[10] Ivo Andrić, *Bosnian Chronicle*, trans. Joseph Hitrec (1993), 424.

and it's over. The emperors got together and smashed Bonaparte. Travnik is sweeping out the consuls. The people will talk about them another year or two. The children will play at consuls and kavasses down by the river, riding on wooden sticks, and afterwards they too will forget them as if they'd never existed. And everything will be the same again, just as, by the will of Allah, it has always been."

Hamdi Beg stopped, as his breath gave out, and the others remained silent in case he had anything more to say. And as they drew on their pipes, they enjoyed their relaxed, victory-scented silence.[11]

The Bridge on the Drina ends with the destruction of the bridge and the turmoil of war, and *Bosnian Chronicle* with the establishment of the "old ways" in which "everything will be the same again, just as ... it has always been." But despite such different endings of two historical narratives, in both of them the plane of permanence—of the established ways of society (in *Bosnian Chronicle*) or of humanity and art (in *The Bridge on the Drina*)—asserts its primacy over the specific contingent instances of history. Specific historical realities and concrete individual destinies are displaced and minimized by the poetic articulation and explicit assertion of the consoling eternity of humanity, community, and art.

Ex Ponto

Returning to *Ex Ponto* and *Unrest*, we see that in them art (as storytelling) and eternal humanity are not yet asserted as harmonizing forms that narrate or contain, but at the same time transcend and thus minimize specific individual existence. In these two works, there is an uneasy tension between the outcry of individual destiny and victimization, on one hand, and the consoling eternity of humanity, community, or art on the other.

Ex Ponto is divided into three parts, consisting of poetic prose fragments, each fragment being only a few paragraphs long.

---

[11] Andrić (1993), 429.

As previously mentioned, the first part of *Ex Ponto* is related to Andrić's imprisonment in Maribor (Slovenia, then Austro-Hungary) at the beginning of World War One for suspected political activity against the state. As opposed to *The Bridge on the Drina* and *Bosnian Chronicle*, *Ex Ponto* is not written from the point of view of an omniscient narrator but rather in the first person, conveying the reflections and various subjective states of the poetic "I" of the text:

> Last night it was particularly cold. I could not fall asleep, a kind of rage at myself overtook me and I—thought about suicide.
>
> I was ashamed and I repented at the same moment, but I thought vividly and for a long time. With some black ecstasy I thought about death, which is something wonderful, easy, and beautiful, but something that should not be. ...
>
> When I woke up, it seemed to me like I was reborn. That was the hardest night in solitary confinement.[12]

The various fragments of *Ex Ponto* are connected by the same subject of speech and by the dominant thematic concerns, tone, and (especially in the first part) the context of writing (imprisonment in Maribor). However, these fragments do not constitute a unified text. The empty space between consecutive fragments emphasizes their relative independence, confirmed by the fragments' varied motives that do not create a more integrated unit. For instance, the first fragment takes as its theme the writer's reminiscences of home—a kitchen with freshly baked bread and a mother who was growing old; the next fragment focuses on the writer's (inmate's) recurrent dreams of traveling; a third fragment depicts the clash between resignation and rebellion in the writer's mind, and then the following fragment dwells on a woman from the writer's past: "Whom is that young woman loving now?" (28–9)

By such a lack of unity and fragmentation, *Ex Ponto* recreates the disjointed speech of the victim himself, rather than the narration that tells of victimization but also cancels it at the same time, by existing above and independently from the victim's "I," as a realm

---

[12] Andrić (1975), 26. Further citations from these titles will be marked by the page number in the body of the text, referring to this publication.

in itself which cannot be affected, ruptured, or stopped by any of its tragic contents. The speech of *Ex Ponto*'s "I" does not create the unperturbed progress of the calm narration of the grand historical novel. It is not founded on—and itself does not create—the certainty and comfort of the persistence of narration or community. Rather, this is an "unfounded" speech, made by one "under whose feet the ground is slipping away."[13]

The fragmentary and open form of *Ex Ponto* articulates the "I's" individual life very differently from the epic narration that shapes—and transcends—the individual lives in *The Bridge on the Drina* and *Bosnian Chronicle*. The text of *Ex Ponto* does not create the organic unity and wholeness of the work of art that transcend the specific parts of the work or its particular thematic motifs, such as a concrete individual victimization. Here motifs are not "smoothed out" by the harmonizing wholeness of the work of art. For example, a fragment about the funeral of a peasant, Nikola Balta (49), is placed between a fragment that contains reflections on the nature of a melancholic person (48) and one about the soul's unrest at night (49). The funeral fragment thus stands out, not connected to anything, and therefore not a part of something larger than itself that could minimize the gravity and importance of this individual life and victimization ("He was only 54 years old") by making it only a part of a larger continuum.

> The flags were not put at half mast, nor were the drums beating covered with black fabric ... nor did the bell ring, because we have not had a bell since the fall; everything was ordinary and calm when the peasant Nikola Balta died.
>
> His wife, taciturn and old before her time, cried the whole night and the next day until afternoon, listening to how they hewed boards in front of the house, and when they lifted the dead man and took him along to the graveyard, she swooned and two women stayed with her to rub her with apple vinegar and consecrated salt.
>
> The funeral was going up the hill and slowly, because the old people who carried the coffin were weak, and there were few

---

[13] Ivo Andrić, *Ex Ponto* (1918), 9. As quoted in Hawkesworth (1984), 54. Translated by Celia Hawkesworth.

of them so they could not alternate. The priest, a solicitous and sickly man, dragged his boots with difficulty, but he sang the psalms beautifully and loudly. The women prayed the rosary.

They carried him on the village road, on the side of which the fruit trees blossomed and bent their branches equally mercifully above each passerby.

They buried him quickly and dispersed, and right after that a fine and plentiful spring rain fell; on the grave earth spilled off and settled, the earth with which he had battled and dealt his whole lifetime.

Thus they buried the peasant Nikola Balta.

He was only 54 years old. (49)

The ruptured text of *Ex Ponto* creates a tension between individual fragments that assert their relative independence from the larger unity of the text and the text as a whole, being the realm that transcends the individual fragments. This dynamic can be seen as articulating a tension between un-transcended, often victimized, and desiring individual life ("this always thirsty 'I'") and the larger realms of narration, immortal art, divinity, or humanity:

> All the painful exertions to elevate oneself above oneself and outside of oneself are not but one torment. They—woe to me—mix with the unsatisfied demands of life and create one unbearable chaos. (58)

The attempt to participate in the non-individual realms above and outside of oneself is mixed with the opposite thrust of the individual life and its "unsatisfied demands." There is no resolution offered to this conflict, which leads to "unbearable chaos." The text goes back and forth between the two opposites.

The comforting presence of divinity is invoked in reflections such as "in God there is the end of a thought which to us disappears—desperate infinity." (24)

Ex Ponto's "I" also goes through moments of exalted demands to be "delivered from oneself":

> Let this pain sent from God burn up everything mine in me, let it consume by fire the blazing I as a wound, and let it heal me from stumbling on the road of wishes and imaginings.

Everything, everything that fetters me and that is called: mine, let it disappear so that I be pure, strong and free. (83)

Individual victimization is displaced in reflections such as: "I know that God bestows horrors on us when He becomes grievous over our soul and when He decides to rescue it." (81)
Or:

And this fall, with the ring I shall never lose, with the pain of a victim, fate tied me to humanity, which through suffering goes to meet truth and goodness. (34)

Truth and goodness are asserted as the goal, or *telos*, of victimization, which is thereby minimized and also in a way justified as a necessary step in the process of attaining this final goodness. Victimization and suffering themselves can thus be seen as good because they lead to the achievement of this good result:

All who suffer and die for their truths are one with God and humanity and are the inheritors of the eternity which exists only for those who believe and suffer; they are the cornerstone of the future building of a new humanity which will, after all the toil and delusions, nevertheless realize itself as God's thought on earth.

Why do we need this life of fifty years (and one harder from another!) if one sacred truth does not give it the strength and beauty and does not prolong it into one shining eternity? (79)

An individual life is meaningless without its "sacred truth": the purpose of life is not in life itself, but in that which transcends this life and "prolong[s] it into one shining eternity." The horror of some having to "suffer and die for their truths" is mitigated by the assertion that this suffering is not just a suffering, a victimization that cannot be undone, a final end followed only by the emptiness and nonexistence of the one who died. The individuals do not die in vain: they create a "future building of a new humanity" and are "one with God and humanity."

When life is victimization, reality is characterized by "weight and bitterness." But instead of attempting to change this reality, one can completely renounce it:

All that is lost is in my consciousness, only without the weight and bitterness of earthly things; I have again everything that I lost, transformed and beautified—in memory. And more: I have the great freedom of one who has nothing and the peace of one who grieved and finally took leave. (46)

Ex Ponto's fragments that explicitly emphasize the comforting notion of the eternity of humanity, community, or art are countered by fragments whose theme is the importance of individual lives and victims:

Do people ever think what the night is like of a mother who knows that her only son is captured by iron and by the stranger's merciless hand? ...
In the room in which I was—in the wrong moment!—born, You wake and pray and in the humility of your heart ask: "Jesus, is it for tears that our children are given to us?" (25)

In a scene in which the inmate's mother prays for her jailed son, her presence and pain outweigh the certainty of the presence of God. The mother is addressed as "You," written with a capital letter, and thus equated with "God," written the same way. The simple statement, "I am sorry for my mother and for her futile pains, torments and hopes," (25) declines the consolation of a possible higher purpose of this suffering. The mother's pain is futile.

A few passages of *Ex Ponto* rather sharply emphasize individual victimization. These include, for example, passages on the funeral of the peasant Nikola Balta (mentioned above), on a disastrous drought in a village (64), on the waking of a hungry child at night (91), or on a conversation between two tired soldiers (96). These sparse narratives bring out hardship, poverty, and exploitation. God—as a symbol of a possible transcendence of these victimized existences—is depicted as absent: after she has managed to put her hungry child to sleep, a mother grabs her rosary and starts to pray, quickly moving her lips. The pain of the hungry child negates the presence of God, and this absence of God or of any transcendental, redemptive sphere in the victimized world resounds even more in a room filled with desperate and hurried prayer that is not being answered.

"It is certain that many people during their entire lives do not even surmise the existence of such vastly unhappy people in the world," states the narrator, (39) concluding his brief account of a chance encounter with a passenger in a train. The statement ends the anecdote and does not lead anywhere, emphasizing a bare fact that is not mitigated by the claims that (for example) its sheer saying helps or that the unhappiness of these people leads to some higher future goal.

Specific individual life is not realized by its presence within the realm of eternal humanity or by its being narrated or transformed into art. The fragment depicting the jailed writer's reminiscences of home, for instance, creates "home" as a brief narration: "As I sit leaning on the window, I have a vision. ... Mother has, like every Saturday. ..." (28) But this fragment also creates a sharp contrast between writing, in which home exists, and reality, in which home is taken away. There is no reconciliation by which thinking and telling about home makes its absence any less painful or real. Andrić also writes:

> And when life is over, silence, a good mother, will put her pale hands on my eyes and this whole wretched story will be drawn into darkness, as the short and incomprehensible sound dies in silence. (44)

The image of the end of the poetic "I" (the writer's "I") is not that of a continued existence through eternal writing that remains after the "I" departs, but rather that of a temporal sound—the "I's" unique real-life existence—that disappears completely in the silence of "I's" non-being. Thus, the most important thing is to simply live: "The sheer fact that I live bestows on me calm happiness." (103)

In the constant tension between eternity (transcendent divinity or immortal humanity or art), on one hand, and the unique individual life on the other, each side displaces and unbalances the other. Consecutive fragments of *Ex Ponto* verbalize the primacy of one or the other. The tension is present on all levels of the text; not only among the fragments, but also within them, and even within many single sentences (e.g., "Oh, God, for what is all this torment of the eternally thirsty and eternally conscious I?" (62)).

The tension between individual victimization and general salvation in the eternity of humanity or art is also present in the contrast of two brief statements about history. In one, all human history seems "as a slaughter of the innocent, as the black chest whose key is thrown into the sea" (39)—that is, like the ongoing repetition of senseless victimization of individual human beings. In the other, humanity "goes through suffering to meet truth and goodness," (34) so individual suffering is transcended and neutralized, as mentioned before, by its *telos*, its leading to final salvation.

Working through the tension between the two opposites, *Ex Ponto* at the end affirms the primacy of individual lives and victimizations over the soothing eternal realms. The epilogue poses the opposition between "strong earth" and "eternal sky," on one side, and "weak and short-lived" man on the other. Choosing between these two, the "I" of the text resolutely affirms his allegiance to a unique individual life, thus explicitly confirming its primary importance, an importance articulated by the fragmentary and ruptured textual form itself:

"What did you see, my son, in the summer day?"
I saw that this life is a painful affair that consists of an unequal exchange of sin and unhappiness, that to live means to pile illusion upon illusion.
"Do you wish to sleep, my son?"
No, father, I am going out to *live*. (105)

Unrest

Unrest can be read as relating, among other things, specifically to the unrest resulting from the tension between individual mortality and the eternity of divinity, of humanity as a whole, or of art: "Flickers the unrest of all the worlds in which a man once thought about God for the first time." (161) In this work one finds a more direct articulation of this tension than in *Ex Ponto*, as well as a stronger endorsement of unrepeatable human existence.

The tripartite structure of *Unrest* takes as its direct theme the tension marking Andrić's two early works. In the first part, "Unrest of Eternity," Andrić specifically reflects on the existence of God and questions of eternity; the second part, "Unrest of the Day," gives very short narratives of specific individual victimizations; the third part, "The Hills," asserts the primacy of the cursory life, of a "beautiful human face with its desire for happiness," (164) over the eternities of words or gods.

In the first part, a divinity that is reflected upon "ripens" and radically changes:

> You are not the same in the morning and in the evening; with the minutes Your form ripens; in vain I knew You yesterday, because You grow, and they say different things about You every day. (117)

At the beginning, God takes one away from the world ("And that was You wanting to wean me away from the world as one-year-old children are weaned from the breast") and puts his "invisible hand" between "me and the world." The writer is God's and is thus separated from the world; God is an obstruction that "hurts and consecrates." (112)

As the reflections progress, the certainty and comfort of the existence of divinity gradually disappear: "He keeps silent so well that one already thinks he does not exist." (115) One searches but does not find the consolation of divinity; God is fast asleep: "I have to get up at night, to look for You and ask.... How weak are human hands and how fast God can sleep." (116) At the end of the first part, eternity and divinity have completely departed: "The sun and the thought about God have set and left me alone." (118)

In the second part of *Unrest*, Andrić posits the tension between the soothing realm of persisting humanity and the outcry of individual victimization and asserts the primacy of the latter. Fragments of this part are given titles (e.g., "A Night on a Train," "Children"), unlike anywhere else in *Unrest* (or in *Ex Ponto*), and this procedure highlights the attention given to specificity. For example, even though *Unrest*'s fragment "Above the Victories," cited at the very beginning of this chapter, neutralizes specific victimizations with its pronouncement that "what remains is a man who sows and works," and the rhetorical question, "Who will win over a man?", a photographically precise and relentless account of starving children in the fragment immediately following, titled "Children," erases any consolation that the notion of the eternity of humanity in "Above the Victories" might have produced.

> The small city teemed with children. They waded the brook passing in front of the military slaughterhouse and hunted for the little pieces of bowel and entrails that were thrown into the water; they gathered the pits of dry plums, beat them on the cobble pavement and ate their bitter core; on the garbage piles behind the officers' kitchens the children seized thrown away empty cans, washed them with hot water and drank that; to trick the hunger, the children chewed on the elder's marrow until the blood gushed forth from behind the teeth; they tasted the primrose's leaf and the fern's bread; at night they crept into newly tilled gardens and with their fingers dug out the potatoes sown yesterday from the soft garden beds; they asked alms, stole, took by force, but all of that was not enough to get full and stay alive. (126)

"Children" begins and ends with the mention of a specific time period, "April of the year 1917," and asserts that "[i]t is hard to forget these children for those who saw them even only once." (127) In this way, a reader is called upon to remember these very specific victims, and the remembrance should not be softened by considerations of eternal humanity, which, after all, continued to exist.

Another fragment from the second part, "Funeral Poem," briefly describes the killing of a burglar:

> He was killed by one who was stronger than he was—and the stronger ones have the right!—he was shot by one of those who serve the power, and they shoot well. (128)

The fragment is a "poem" about injustice ("And above him [the killed burglar] my poem burns in indignation and pity" (129)), but there are no reflections on the immortality of poetry in general, or this poem in particular, that would make this specific injustice, the killing of a man who resorted to burglary as perhaps the last means of survival, seem smaller. Nor does "Funeral Poem" offer any reflections on the potential consolation that could come from pondering upon the immortality of humanity. On the contrary, those who survive and perpetuate this "immortal humanity" are themselves victimizers: those "who [are] stronger," "who serve power," "[who] shoot well."

Thus, as we read in "The Hills" (the third part of *Unrest*), "There is no truth but one: pain, and no other reality but that of suffering, pain and suffering." (143) There is no transcendent realm, such as art, which could record but also at the same time minimize the pain as the only truth of individual existence.

In "Unrest of the Day," specific individual destinies and specific subjects' victimizations claim their primacy over and over again. In the fragment entitled "A Night on a Train," for example, Andrić depicts the transportation of prisoners, himself among them, in an overcrowded train traveling by the Adriatic seaside.[14] Glued to a window, the writer sees in the sea "all the new shine and new colors" and a "beauty which [he] never surmised." This infinite beauty allows him to "[forget] what is behind [him]." (121–2) However, in the end it is not beauty, art, or eternity that assert their presence beyond an individual's life or death. The fragment ends with the approach of night and with falling darkness that prevents a passenger from seeing the enchanting beauty of the sea. In the light of the lamp the writer now only sees his own face on the window:

> I saw, on the glass behind which lies the night, my face—and nothing else but my very own face! ... In vain I closed my eyes; I was condemned and had to always again look into my eyes. (122)

Beauty does not transcend individual life. Rather, it is the individual life that, not realized by that which transcends it, comes back to claim its own. Victimization and pain are "like a stone," hard, unchanging, and the sole reality: "I dream that a pain passed away ... And when I wake up, look, yesterday's pain is in its place, like a stone." (143)

The third part of *Unrest* reconfirms the nonexistence of comforting and persisting realms of humanity, art, or, in this case, divinity:

> I, who have no Gods. ... stopped for a moment and was small and alone with the unspeakable sadness of the bright short days known only to a man. God and the world kept quiet. (135, 137)

---

[14] For details of Andrić's arrest, incarceration, and internment, see Vucinich (1996), 29–30.

Big world. Big burden and big exhaustion. Deep night. And a lone man. (156)

The temple of God, of eternity and divinity or of eternal art or lasting humanity, is empty. Now the most specific and passing things—"the lines of the houses ... tram tracks ... calm trees, the arch of the eyebrow of some unknown woman, one male profile"—create a "temple of swaying and transitory shapes." (144)

The aspect of eternity is not fully erased from the last part of *Unrest*. One reads, for example, "that there is one tide of creation, and we grow, we grow!" (151) However, the tension between the soothing realms of eternity and the victimization of mortal and unique individuals ends with the assertion of the primacy of the latter:

> But I have never forgotten a human face, a beautiful human face lit up with the shine of reason and with only human sadness because of what is seen.
> Behind all my bitter words hides, in the end, always a human face with its desire for happiness. (164)

Behind the words is the beautiful human face with its desire for happiness. These words, as literature or storytelling, are one of the expressions of immortal humanity that keeps existing regardless of the disappearance of any particular individual. But these words are not a goal in themselves. Rather, they are one of the ways in which individuals seek happiness, fulfillment, and life. The image created here is that of an individual life that attempts to be realized with the help of words and literature, and not that of transcendent literature or eternal humanity that displace and neutralize the sense of individual victimizations or lack of individual realization.

Continued Relevance

While one can see *Ex Ponto* and *Unrest* relating, among other things, to the carnage of World War One by marking the victimization of numerous individuals, Andrić's *The Bridge on the Drina* and *Bosnian Chronicle* can be seen as relating to World War Two by creating a realm above and outside the wars ("above the victories"), a realm in which both victimizations and the victimized lose much of their weight and importance. Yet it is crucial to remember the early works' sense of the supreme value and urgency of present individual lives, and not just of the life of humanity in general or of eternal storytelling, including Andrić's own.

In time, the names of "higher causes" to which individual lives need to be subordinated, or in the name of which they have to be victimized, change. What was once, for example, an imperative of History, can now be called a necessity of national security or the free market or "development," a word that has in a seemingly unnoticed manner replaced the word "progress." But every time the individual life and its many needs and potentials are treated as anything less than the ultimate goal of these broader "indispensable" realms that tend to take off with interests of their own, we are back again in the turmoil that Andrić was wrestling with. Whenever that happens, the tenor and sentiment of Andrić's *Ex Ponto* and *Unrest* should be invoked.

In 1992, the centennial of the writer's birth was celebrated in a dark atmosphere. Following the war in Slovenia and, on a larger scale of destruction, in Croatia, the year 1992 saw the start of the war in Bosnia and Herzegovina, which was being destroyed in a campaign of terror and genocide. At the conference in honor of Ivo Andrić's centennial on 22 November 1992, organized at the USA's Stanford University by Professor Wayne S. Vucinich, I ended the speech on which the present chapter is based with the following:

> The tension of Andrić's early works between the individual's mortal reality and the eternity of humanity or art should not be lost. We should not only embrace the latter moment of this duality and say that "we have all we lost, transformed and beautified—in the memory," or that "we have the great freedom of the one who has nothing and peace of the one who grieved and finally took leave." While honoring the memory of a great writer and his work, let us not disregard the cries of those all-too-mortal victims of the terror that is at this very moment destroying the Bosnia that Andrić loved and wrote about. Let us

not allow our sense of gratitude for the preservation of lives and culture in Andrić's work to "smooth out" our sense of urgency of struggle against the current destruction of lives and victimization of real individuals, those unique and unrepeatable "I"s, that are now vanishing into silence.

6

"The Truthful Road to Me"
Short Takes on Six Bosnian Films

You have decided to wipe me out whatever the price
Yet nowhere will you find
The truthful
Road to me

MAK DIZDAR, FROM ROADS[1]

Ways of Seeing[2]

It is a summer night, and two men are talking across a wooden table set under a tree in the garden by a house, one older and one younger, their faces lit by the flickering shadows of a small fire. The two are father and son. The conversation goes on and the scene is quite ordinary, except for the fact that the young man,

---

[1] Mak Dizdar, "Roads," transl. Francis R. Jones, in Rabia Ali and Lawrence Lifschultz (eds), *Why Bosnia? Writings on the Balkan War* (1993), 69. I have replaced the word "real" used in the translation with the word "truthful," as this is the more literal translation of the original's *istinski*.

[2] This phrase is meant to invoke John Berger's seminal book *Ways of Seeing* and its influence on the perception of visual arts and visual culture in their often inconspicuous "ways of seeing" things. See John Berger, *Ways of Seeing* (1972).

Fig 6.1 Zaim and his son Adnan, *Fuse* (2003)

Adnan, is dead—has been for some time now—killed in the war, no one knows exactly where or how. Yet the son's death does not stop his father Zaim—and the audience of Pjer Žalica's film *Fuse* (*Gori vatra*, 2003)—from seeing him in the flesh as he appears now at the family's garden table, now on a tree branch, now on a balcony, having short conversations with his father who himself becomes increasingly drawn towards his dead son and away from his two living children, a beautiful girl bursting with life and a well-meaning young man with an open and bright countenance.

This poetic device, having dead and absent people appear casually before us, is one of those things that art can do. It is unrealistic in literal terms, yet as realistic as can be in the existential, social, and psychological sense. After all, the dead and violated of the recent war in Bosnia and Herzegovina (1992–5) are not absent but still present, not just in the past but also in the evolving Bosnian present—present memories and minds, fears, politics, in grief and cynical manipulations; in that present that sows the seeds of the future at every moment. And what better way to show that strong presence than through dead people mingling with the living and talking to them, affecting their thoughts and actions, right here and right now?

This manner of articulating something (in this case the presence of dead people) in a very specific, original way that makes the viewer really see it as if for the first time, or become aware of it in a different way than before, this manner of even making something previously invisible or unknown become apparent through an unusual, unaccustomed way in which the world is re-told or re-seen, a certain specific take on or view of things that may show previously unknown aspects of the present or even potential future of something, is an important aspect of aesthetic works, of literature or art or cinema. London's Hyde Park as Monet painted it is quite different from the Hyde Park of a tourist's photo; the siege of Sarajevo, as seen through the lens of the first post-war Bosnian feature film, *Perfect Circle* (*Savršeni krug*, 1997), is quite different from the CNN coverage. It is a way of seeing that decides not only how we see but also what we see, what becomes apparent in our mind's eye, and what remains invisible, or is pushed to the margins. And it is this way of seeing created by the new Bosnian cinema, or its many ways of seeing, quite remarkable in both their originality and cinematic execution, that profoundly re-evaluates both the world at large and contemporary Bosnian realities, changing the perspective on what is desirable and what despicable, acknowledging bleak realities but also discovering unacknowledged blessings and unseen potentials. While touching on a few other films, this chapter, then, will flesh out in more detail these "ways of seeing" created in the films *Armin*, *Snow*, *At Uncle Idriz's*, *All for Free*, *Summer in the Golden Valley*, and *Grbavica: the Land of My Dreams*.

Referring to "Bosnian" films, one should probably clarify that these films are shot and made in and out of Bosnia, with both financial support and entire film crews often being multi-national rather than solely Bosnian (multi-national production being a feature shared by much of recent European cinema). What makes these films "Bosnian" is the story, which is related to Bosnia in some way, then usually the Bosnian setting (real or pretended) of the film, and commonly the director and/or screen-writer, who may or may not live in Bosnia at the time of making the film, but usually has a Bosnian affiliation. Indeed, while *No Man's Land* (*Ničija zemlja*, 2001) won the Academy Award for best foreign film as the official Bosnian entry, it is a French–Belgian–British–Italian–Slovenian co-production shot in Slovenia; but its screen-writer and director, Zenica-born and Sarajevo-schooled Danis Tanović, obviously used his own "intimate knowledge of the Bosnian war … honed from direct experience, from making award-winning documentaries on the subject, and from being responsible for the Bosnian Army's film archives."[3] The film also concerns the Bosnian war and features Branko Đurić Đuro, one of the main creators of the 1980s Sarajevan cult series *Surrealists' Top Chart* (*Top lista nadrealista*). Furthermore, films such as *All for Free* (*Sve džaba*, 2006) and *Armin* (2007), seen by some as clearly a part of the new Bosnian cinema, are commonly seen by other critics, including myself, as—also—a part of the new Croatian cinema.[4] The latest project by Bosnian director Jasmila Žbanić, in process at the time of this writing, is an adaptation of the novel *Hotel Zagorje* by Croatian writer Ivana Simić Bodrožić. In this new film, the story revolves around the experiences of a Vukovar child who fled her home city with her family and spent years in exile in other parts of Croatia. Despite the fact that established institutions or notions often require that films be identified with one country of origin, especially when it comes to the newly independent Yugoslav Successor States, it thus seems that both artistic and economic tendencies push film-makers here and elsewhere towards artistic collaboration across borders, so that the two mentioned films could more appropriately be seen as new cinema of *both* Croatia and Bosnia.

---

[3] Daniel Goulding, *Liberated Cinema: the Yugoslav Experience, 1945–2001* (2002), 220.

[4] *All for Free* is written and directed by Antonio Nuić, who was born in Sarajevo (in 1977) and relocated to Zagreb in 1992, a few months after the beginning of the siege of Sarajevo. He studied film directing in Zagreb, where he now lives. The film is a Croatian, Bosnian, and Serbian co-production, the story is squarely about Bosnia and Bosnians, the film takes place in central Bosnia, and the actors come from Bosnia, Croatia, and Serbia. *Armin* (Croatia, Germany, Bosnia and Herzegovina) was nominated for the Academy Award by Croatia; it is written and directed by Croatian director Ognjen Sviličić, and largely set in Zagreb. Yet here also the story revolves around Bosnia and Bosnians, it is on a literal level about who tells the story of Bosnia and how, one of the producers is Ademir Kenović, and the central actor of the film is the excellent—and so omnipresent in the new Bosnian cinema as to literally become its symbol—Emir Hadžihafizbegović.

The Pull of the Past, the World of Success: On Nostalgia and *Mimesis*

Two pre-war lovers who are about to be reunited after the peace has been re-established and the girl returns from exile in Germany will not do so in *Fuse*, as she steps on a landmine outside her home. Another pre-war couple who seem likely to reunite (in *At Uncle Idriz's*), following the woman's return to Sarajevo from New York, may not do so either, as we are made privy to the information unknown to the joyful man that the girl is already looking into buying tickets to return to the US. A present solely based on the past, as in the beginning of *All for Free*, where the main character Goran spends all his time with his three childhood friends, will not be allowed to last either: a desire for change and novelty will lead one of the friends to betray the other and cause a tragedy for them all.

When it comes to the past, both personal and that of Bosnia and Herzegovina and of the former Yugoslavia in which one lived, it seems that the new Bosnian cinema acknowledges both the presence of that past in the present (dead people mingling with the living, the focus on the children orphaned or conceived in the war, omnipresent memories and comparisons with the mythical "before"), and the fact that, after all, much of the world of Bosnia existing before the 1991–5 violence is in many aspects destroyed and cannot be resurrected. The unique mosaic celebrated and lived by so many has been broken up, with many pieces shattered and others displaced or changed into something quite different from what they were before. Although some films linger for a moment on the desire to go back in time and recreate the past, they inevitably show that the present cannot be attempted as an imitation, repetition, or continuation of the past. It is impossible to go back through the walls of time separating us from our past, impossible to make it as it was, the new Bosnian films seem to say.

The films acknowledge, however, that it is even harder to stop dwelling in the past and fully commit to the present if this move also feels like the desertion of loved ones who lived in that past but are no more. Departing from the past, then, appears like a betrayal of the dead who, with their bodies lost and with the material objects bearing witness to their past existence often destroyed, seem to claim their presence in the memory of those who loved them as their last shelter. Still, the imperative of leaving this past or, rather, dealing with it in a different way is again affirmed. In *Snow* (*Snijeg*, 2008), an emaciated woman's mental holding onto the past through her metonymic fixation on a few remaining relics—a photograph, a shaver—from her murdered sons and husband, her elevation of these objects and the past into a sacred realm ([Let these things go!] "This is sacred!"), where all the spirituality, love, and meaning is contained, and thus her emptying of the present into a realm of mostly apathetic survival, saps her strength and distracts her from the potentials of the current moment: she almost causes the death of the orphan girl whom she has adopted. Another woman's frequent dwelling in the past ("how beautifully we lived!") makes her vulnerable to those willing to exploit her sense of the present as only barren and in need of replacement at any cost.

While the father in *Fuse* decides to join his dead son and the past by eventually committing suicide, his younger son chooses to go on living, and asks his visiting dead father and brother to "stay away for a while." This commitment to life and the present affirmed in a number of Bosnian films, however, also includes a question of how, actually, is one to live that life, now that the previously established patterns of living have been shattered. One of the possibilities seems to be a "mimetic" one, that is, the option of emulating "Westerners," getting close to them and perhaps being accepted by them.[5] *Armin* (Croatia, Germany, Bosnia and Herzegovina, 2007,

---

[5] The symbolic "West" appears in a number of Bosnian films, but it is in most cases both clearly separated from the Bosnians themselves and physically placed within Bosnia. The West is often seen as indifferent to or largely complicit in the past Bosnian tragedy, as self-serving or clearly mercenary, or else with individuals (such as French UN soldiers and British journalists in Academy Award-winning Danis Tanović's *No Man's Land* (*Ničija zemlja*, 2001)) genuinely wanting to help, but being disabled by their own inert and malfunctioning institutions. The visual objectification by the Western media during the war is also thematized (e.g., in Jasmila Žbanić's documentary *Images from the Corner* (*Slike s ugla*, 2003) or in *Armin*), and the recurrent films' motif concerns the sense of the developed West, so close and yet so far, as calmly moving away from Bosnia, unconcerned and uninterested. A beautiful jet plane increases its speed as it flies over the Sarajevo valley, to flee as fast as possible "the sickness of misery" (*bolest bijede*) in *Summer in the Golden Valley*, shiny UN vehicles and Western embassies' parties appear untouched by the suffering

written and directed by Ognjen Sviličić, Croatia's official entry for the Academy Award for the best foreign film), delves into this possibility and all that it entails.

Fourteen-year-old Armin (Armin Omerović) and his father Ibro (Emir Hadžihafizbegović) leave their small Bosnian town of Orašje to spend a few days in Zagreb, the capital of Croatia, where Armin is to audition for a role in a new German film about Bosnia during the war. While *Armin* has a few other obvious thematic concerns (e.g., the cinematic construction of the Bosnian war), the film's most interesting aspect is its turning back of the camera lens, so to speak, not only on those who are allegedly focusing on the boy Armin, but, more importantly, on the whole world that is metonymically and to some extent symbolically represented by this little slice of it. This includes interiors of the modern hotel in Zagreb, its spaces, lights, colors and sounds, the people who work there; Zagreb streets at night; the ways in which the film crew works and the ways in which this work affects the way they are, the way they have become. Not so much through its story as through its visual language that creates a distinct, specific atmosphere of this world, the film looks at and sees the world of modern professionalism, efficiency, productivity, a world which is supposed to be the "best of all possible worlds," as Voltaire, ironically, and our current global ideologies (without irony), would proclaim it to be. *Armin* looks at the world which is the object of the outsiders' desire to become a part of it, or at least of the outsiders' conviction that they can survive only by becoming a part of it.

As Armin and his father interact with people in Zagreb, the two discover that these people are quite different from the ones they have known before. The officious receptionist snaps at Armin's father for trying to circumvent minor rules; a vacuuming maid does not acknowledge their presence, rushing to finish her work; the good-looking Croatian woman, working as an intermediary for the German crew, has no time to stop for a moment and tells them

---

around them in *The Perfect Circle* (*Savršeni krug*, 1997, the first post-war Bosnian film directed by Ademir Kenović), and President Clinton's limousine, bringing the president to visit the Bosnian town of Tešanj in *Fuse*, ends up just passing by without ever stopping or even lowering its metallic windows.

Fig 6.2 Armin and his father, *Armin* (2007) (courtesy of Maxima Film, Zagreb)

all she needs to say in passing; the photographer looks at Armin only as much as necessary in order to make a good photo of him, focusing more on his equipment than on the visibly uncomfortable child in front of him. Everyone is tense, doing his or her job all the time and becoming identical with that job in the process of the film: Armin's dejected father gets his last drinks from the hands of the waiter who has become solely his (working) hands and legs—we do not see the waiter's face, and even though the father asks him a question, we hear no answer in return.

There is no human, non-functional excess in the world of *Armin*, which is that of, as it were, hyperrealistic seeing, where all the aspects of modern professional environments, rules, and people, are simply put together, without any soothing interlude that would dilute their combined effect. Placed under a magnifying glass and a grotesque dystopian light, these aspects appear larger, more potent and more ominous, in visual terms, than they literally would be. Yet, precisely by using this cinematic device which turns average hotel spaces into claustrophobic traps, and people doing their jobs into disturbing automata, *Armin* creates a penetrating view of this world, which corresponds with the mute experience of this world acquired by the hastily appraised and belittled father and son. Not a friendly city this, not friendly streets, not friendly people: the lights of the film are bluish-cold and metallic, the real lights of large hotels the world over, with a sun that never shows itself in the enclosed inner spaces; the rooms impersonal and indistinct, profoundly uncomfortable; the elevators full of men of the same stature in the same business suits and set expressions. And it is these cold objective lights, these quietly moving elevators, these huge buildings and walls and machines, that make these people, rather than the other way around. The people obey and "succeed" by their obedience, gradually becoming parts of the system with a bit of the system's power—a receptionist, a film director, a producer—doing their job while losing all the other aspects of life and of possible joy, which become vague and distant.

The filming of the interiors of the hotel, with the people in them seen in long shots much more than in close-ups or medium shots, indicates this containment and the creation of the people by that environment, this inability of people to take themselves out of their overwhelming background or context and become known heroes of the motion pictures. No one is larger than life here, and everyone is always a part of her or his place—a part of the bar, of the crew, of the elevator, or of the restaurant. People are the elements of a system which shapes both their external and internal features, such as in the scene where a long shot sees all of the many auditioning young boys reciting the exact same lines, and thus all symbolically becoming the same thing.

After refusing the German director's offer to make a documentary film about Armin's epilepsy, father and son reclaim the bond with each other and with their home in Bosnia, now seen not only as a place of absence of all the things present somewhere else, but also as a place of many invisible but supremely important things that have now been seen as missing and forgotten in that other world. In contrast to his previously having said "this [the film] cannot be dumb if it's a foreign film," the father now simply asserts that "they don't know a thing." And the regaining of some inner peace and joy accompanies the acquisition of this new set of eyes, so to speak, on both the presumably superior alternative mode of life somewhere else, and on the life here and now in Bosnia.

"Find Peace inside Ourselves and then Breath it Out"

In his essay "Vermeer in Bosnia," Lawrence Weschler writes how he "happened to be in The Hague a while back, sitting in on the preliminary hearings of the Yugoslav War Crimes Tribunal."[6] One day, he had lunch with Antonio Cassese, an Italian jurist who had at that point been the court's president, and Cassese was "rehearsing for [Weschler] some of the most gruesome stories that have crossed his desk," and that dealt with the specifics of what was done to the individual men, women, and children during the ethnic cleansing in Bosnia.[7] After reading about only one of such cases, one understands why Weschler asked the jurist how he could bear his dealing with such things.

"'Ah,' [Cassese] said with a smile. 'You see, as often as possible I make my way over to the Mauritshuis museum, in the center of town, so as to spend a little time with the Vermeers.'"[8] As Weschler will come to realize, Vermeer's paintings not only "radiate 'a centeredness, a peacefulness, a serenity' (as Cassese put it)," but they do so in the midst of a radically opposite environment.[9] "When Vermeer was painting these images," Weschler recognizes, "*all Europe was Bosnia ... awash in wars ... violence and cruelty.*"[10] It is on account of this context that "[i]t's almost as if Vermeer can be seen, amid the horrors of his age, to have been asserting or *inventing* the very idea of peace."[11] And the same practice of the invention and creation of the peace "within" which one then puts "without" is then discovered in the past moment of Weschler's own life, when, amidst a group of heated students, a visiting religious historian told the story of Jesus on the Waters,[12]

---

[6] Lawrence Weschler, *Vermeer in Bosnia: Selected Writings* (2005), 13.
[7] Weschler (2005), 13.
[8] Weschler (2005), 14.
[9] Weschler (2005), 14.
[10] Weschler (2005), 14.
[11] Weschler (2005), 16.
[12] This story (from Matthew 8:23–7) concerns the crossing of the Sea of Galilee by Jesus and his disciples. They embarked on a small boat, Jesus fell asleep, the storm rose, and his disciples, increasingly horrified, kept waking him up. He went on calmly telling them not to worry, and kept going back to sleep. The last time they woke him up, now "beside themselves with terror, [Jesus said] 'Oh ye of little faith'—that's where that phrase comes from—and then proceeded to pronounce

and calmly concluded: "It seems to me ... that what that story is trying to tell us is simply that in times of storm, we mustn't allow the storm to enter ourselves; rather we have to find peace inside ourselves and then breathe it out."[13]

Written and directed by Aida Begić, the film *Snow* (*Snijeg*, 2008) is set in eastern Bosnia's village of Slavno, in the vicinity of Srebrenica, in 1997. This region experienced some of the worst ethnic cleansing of Bosniaks during the 1992–5 war; it is now part of *Republika Srpska* and predominantly ethnically Serbian. The story takes place rather soon after the cessation of the violence in 1995. A handful of survivors has stayed in their village, still largely in ruins; a few women are accompanied by the only two men who survived the cleansing, a village imam and his grandson, and by the surviving daughters of their own or adopted girls orphaned in the war. Led by Alma (Zana Marjanović), a young widow, the women are trying to reclaim their existence by the collective production of all kinds of pickles and preserves. At one point an international real-estate corporation, represented by a Serbian man from a neighboring village, offers to buy the entire village—the women's homes and their surrounding agricultural land—thus dangling a great temptation before the women: a possibility to take the money, leave, and start a new life elsewhere.

While the women are often seen working together or spending what little free time they have with each other, the camera is focused on Alma as she lives her days from waking up for morning prayer to going to bed at night. Marked from the start as the hardest worker, Alma also seems to be the one who wants to make a break with the past: she stays distanced from the charade in which other women impersonate their missing men, and does not engage in her colleague's day-dreaming about how "it would be so nice to be at the seaside now," recalling past summers at the Adriatic Sea. Instead of allowing herself to imagine this now impossible reality, Alma firmly explains how the women will use their first money to buy a car that will help them transport their products, build their

---

'Peace!' Whereupon the storm instantaneously subsided and calm returned to the water." Weschler (2005), 17.
[13] Weschler (2005), 17–18.

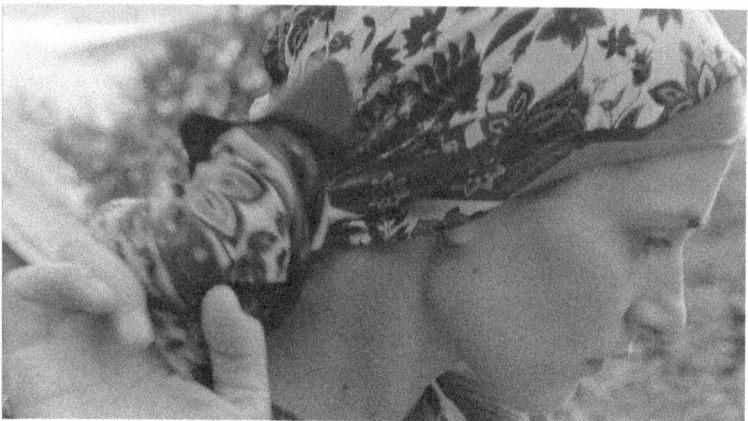

Fig 6.3 Alma, *Snow* (2008) (courtesy of Elma Tataragić and Mamafilm, Sarajevo)

food enterprise, and finally "feed half of Bosnia." Alma also seems to be one of the few women, and the only one among the younger ones, who has recently embraced Islam: an old photo of Alma with her husband shows her in Western-style clothes with her long dark hair uncovered; she now dresses modestly and covers her hair. Repeated a few times and providing a rhythmic pulse to the film is a scene of her walking briskly to prayer, shot in close-up from the side, with her blue headscarf waving in the wind creating a poetic visual image.

As the film progresses, it becomes clear that the vision of Alma, and the vision shared by *Snow*, is that of the need for one's utmost focusing on the potentials of the present time and place. The young woman's prayers do not distract from the here and now, but, on the contrary, provide her with much-needed rest—praying and going to bed at night are the only moments when she stops working—and the regular re-focusing on this here and now. The prayers seem to help Alma re-commit to do the most that can be done with the things that are present here and now, rather than flee into religion seen as only transcendence and consequently devaluation of this world's realities, or into the dreams of the past or the tempting "elsewhere" of the offered emigration. *Snow* thus articulates a possible social and individual dynamics where the available people and resources have to be seen differently, not just as parts of the whole that was destroyed in the past and that is now and forever lacking, but as a potential in its own right for the present and the future. These people and their resources can transform themselves into a functioning and resilient community providing both material and spiritual nourishment to all, *if* they see that they can do it and if a proper impetus is provided—an impetus which Alma gives with her unwavering commitment. Quick to recognize possible openings for the village's enterprise, Alma counters the corporate men who sneer at the women's labor and plans. In response to a woman who emphasizes the seemingly obvious negatives of their situation— "just see where we live, in the twentieth century!" (alluding to the villagers' hardship and the lack of modern amenities previously taken for granted), Alma says: "It is pitiful what life is [means] to you." Challenged to state what life means to her, she underscores tersely yet profoundly the vision built by the film and embodied in her character: "This what I have. The village. We."

It seems that *Snow* shows a few devout Muslims as the strongest characters who are more "in the right" than the non-devout ones, and this may be problematic for some viewers. Alma has a vision for the village and the strength to carry it out; her mother-in-law (the other devout woman of the film), will do the right thing at the decisive moment, and the village's imam will be the one asking a crucial question about the village's missing men. All of this happens in opposition to the more secular and more easily distracted or persuaded other women, who are manipulated into selling their land. Yet, although seemingly endorsed, *Snow*'s Islam is far from imperial, power-attracted, or opportunistic. There are no Saudi-financed mosques here, but only a small open-air platform with a few people praying; and there are no political or economic favors or preferences coming to Alma on account of her faith, which stays individual, intimate, and a purpose unto itself. Islam ends up being seen as primarily a helping tool for one's utmost focusing on the worldly life and the absolute commitment to the here and now. With regard to the past, *Snow* implies that, instead of not being able to leave the past or yearning for the transcendent otherworld in which the past is cancelled and the innocent victims revived, one's constructive attitude towards the past includes the closure of that which should be closed, with the village women's final reclaiming and burying of the so-far missing remains of their murdered men and the creation of a graveyard for them. Both organizing and appropriating the landscape, the new graveyard embodies a new attitude towards the dead and the past: it is a collective and spiritual space housing the dead, in the midst of the living yet separated from them, so that the living can be both connected to and separated from their dead ones and their own past. The proper attitude towards the past also includes the nurturing of the fertile seeds that got passed down—it was Alma's dead husband's wish, it turns out, that their village become the breadbasket of Bosnia. Alma's refusals to reconnect with the past through the futile wishes of getting that past back or through its painful re-enactment are in the end seen as her commitment to reconnect with the past through honoring its unfulfilled dreams.

While *Snow* literally addresses the plight and the possible resistance of eastern Bosnia's Bosniaks, decimated in the past and pressured to leave their homeland in the present by both the largely non-Bosniak powers-that-be of *Republika Srpska* and by global "free market" forces, implied as working in conjunction with the Bosnian Federation's government,[14] the film's main strength is of a broader scope. *Snow* articulates a desire to stay in the past because this past is perceived as so much better than the present, and because one does not want to leave those who were forced to stay in that past and not live on into the present times. The film explores a temptation to finally succumb to the relentless adversarial forces and to give up, and a yearning to be someplace else and live some other life in some other time. *Snow* identifies these very real problems, yet also shows how much can be made out of the present if one sees its potentials, puts the proper spin and energy into it, and affirms the commitment to "this what I have," and to the place and community I have: "[Life for me is] this what I have. The village. We."

Another film articulating the potential of reviving individuals and their community by a proper vision and impetus is *At Uncle Idriz's* (official English name *Days and Hours*; *Kod amidže Idriza*,

---

[14] The film's corporate characters claim that the Federation's government supports the sale of this land in its supposed desertion of eastern Bosnia and its Bosniaks; but these characters have been shown as non-truthful in other cases, so the statement, as far as the film goes, is ambiguous.

2004, directed by Pjer Žalica), a film awash in the warm light of a Sarajevo home. Oranges, dark reds, yellows, wool, carpets, and subdued lighting produce a lively play of light and shadows on the faces and in the rooms, a lit-up area that is often gradually darkened at the edges so as to soften the sharp square frame and make a rounded space, in some shots distantly reminiscent to that of Rembrandt's paintings, an area of the unique warmth of this world. Fuke (Fuad; Senad Bašić) arrives at his aunt's (Semka Sokolović-Bertok) and uncle (*amidža*) Idriz's (Mustafa Nadarević) house to repair their broken water heater. The three spend some Saturday afternoon hours together, talking, drinking coffee and eating, trying unsuccessfully to fix it, with Fuke also visiting the elderly couple's neighbors whom he knows well. Fuke's car breaks down so he stays the night in the room that belonged to the son of his uncle and aunt, an only child, who was killed in the war, the room that has remained unchanged ever since. There are intimations of a relational break-down between the two old people and their widowed daughter-in-law, who relocated to the city of Tuzla with her daughter, their only grandchild. In the morning,

Fig 6.4 Fuke, *At Uncle Idriz's* (2004)

Fuke leaves with his apparently repaired car, only to return with the couple's granddaughter and daughter-in-law, whom he had obviously talked to and urged to come the day before. The family is reunited in the house's garden, the previous misunderstandings dissolved, and the neighbors from surrounding houses join in, adding various instruments to Idriz's mandolin and playing and singing together.

At Uncle Idriz's is a lesson in how a static scene (much of the time people just sit and talk), simple long takes of medium or close-up shots of these rather motionless people, and a story that is so minimal that it is all but non-existent, can produce a gripping film that captures the viewer with intensity and authenticity of the world it creates. All of the talking in the film—and there is a lot of it, with conversations becoming a distinct character or agency by itself—all this talking and all the many apparently small gestures which people do for each other, gradually weave an almost tangible "net" of criss-crossed ties and connections amongst family members, their friends and neighbors, a web of great mutual concern, care and warmth, an energy field that both builds on the previously long-lasting, mutually nourishing web of such connections on the one hand, and reinforces and re-adjusts this living web for the future on the other. Aside from talking with each other (often not about themselves but rather about the people dearest and closest to them, thus bringing these people into this community largely built on conversations), people also help or treat each other in a myriad delicate ways, with needed help, special foods, with the mending of broken water heaters, shattered personal ties, and forgotten musical instruments. Fuke repairs his uncle's mandolin so that Idriz can play again when the reunited family and friends close the film with a song. The many conversations and small caring gestures create not a world of self-centered monads concerned primarily with themselves, but instead a fluid and energized world of people whose most genuine concerns project out of themselves and revolve around the well-being of the people they care for. And given that people at uncle Idriz's actually still know how to feel that deep concern for others— which feeling, as we saw in *Armin*, can be a lost talent in some other environments—and they also act on it, one can experience the palpable "densening" of the web of care and concern going from one person to another, back and forth, and the "warming up" of the threads connecting and deeply nourishing these people. And an unofficial but strong community based on that web grows, a community that includes the dead who live on in the others who love them, but also enables the living to reclaim and, with help of others, mend their lives.

Innocence Unbound: Unpredictability and Disempowerment

Ushering in a liberating unpredictability, the apparently irrational behavior of the main character of the *Summer in the Golden Valley* (*Ljeto u zlatnoj dolini*, 2003, written and directed by Srđan Vuletić) breaks down the seemingly fixed chains of causality and of the characters' motivation. The assumed causality in which the bleak, drug- and prostitution-infested post-apocalyptic landscape of Sarajevo's devastated spaces, mostly filmed at night, would of course produce teenage boys who can easily be drawn into crime and violence, crumbles, as the two main characters, long-haired Fikret (Haris Sijarić) and his best friend Ramiz (Svetozar Cvetković) start out as predicted, but then change course and act in seemingly inexplicable ways. The boys agree to help kidnap a young girl, Sara (Zana Marjanović), for ransom, an action arranged by a crooked cop, in order to pay off Fikret's family's supposed debt of honor, but they do not follow the plan once they have the girl. Finding themselves unable to harm her or assert any dominance over her, the two release her and form a close if transient relationship with her. Following a series of what seem highly improbable—but not impossible—events, all ends well, with the girl saved and the two boys alive and ethically uncompromised.

The character motivation in *Summer in the Golden Valley* goes from an assumed desire for power and power-based relationships to a desire to disempower oneself; from forcing someone to do or give something to allowing that someone to be free to leave if so wished, or else to give or do something of their own free will; and from rational and predictable motivation to a seemingly irrational one. Both rationality and at least recognizable motivation (you do something to achieve something, or at least to survive) are gone, as Fikret repeatedly does things that—in the light of any

Fig 6.5 Fikret and Sara, *Summer in the Golden Valley* (2003)

rational calculation—seem sure to destroy him. Yet these irrational actions end up doing the opposite and actually save him. Had he followed through with the seemingly rational and previously planned actions, he would have ended up dead. No amount of calculation could predict or map the causality in which a crooked policeman ends up killing himself, in which a kidnapped girl gives the money to Fikret of her own will, and in which Fikret eventually fares well. His behavior is not based on any future projections or "objective" calculation; instead, the boy behaves in a way that seems "right" to him at any given moment, even though he does not understand or have reasons for this feeling. The only consistent traits of his actions seem to be his inability to hurt anyone, and his doing exactly what feels right. And then his "irrational" actions impact upon and change the seemingly fixed chain of causality itself, and in the end it is as if he were literally "walking on water," getting the happy ending against all odds, and with the film intimating that even though one does not know how one's proper action will lead to a good result—and even when it looks like the right action (ethically proper or simply feeling right) will bring a bad outcome—one should still stick to it and do the right thing, leaving all else to providence.

Based on the relinquishing of power, an inability to hurt anyone, and doing what feels right no matter how counterproductive for one's own previously assumed goals this may be, the main character's "other-worldly" attitude does something to and within others as well. It is as if this attitude embodies and calls upon the other people's forgotten but deeply authentic element of the often "absurd" goodness, activates this element and makes it build a very different story with a very different ending for everyone involved. Unabashedly participating, to a degree, in the realm of fairy-tale, *Summer in the Golden Valley* suggests that the fairy-tale's counterfactual aspects are not only a means of escapism, but can also be the imagining of the paths we may want to pursue.

Another film foregrounding unpredictability, or the open possibility for people to go in a different direction from the one expected and socially established, is *All for Free* (*Sve džaba*, 2006, Croatia, Bosnia and Herzegovina, Serbia, written and directed by Antonio Nuić). After losing his three best friends—who were his only family—in a crime of passion, Goran (Rakan Rushaidat) sells his house in Vareš and buys a dilapidated luncheonette on wheels. He travels from town to town (Prozor, Breza, and so on), setting up shop in the town squares, and not selling but rather giving away assorted drinks for free. "Many places are better," says Goran, "but not a single one is cheaper." And also: "I have never earned anything, so it is right that I do not have anything." Staying one day in each town and drawing to his "All for Free" bar an assortment of characters (including those played by Pero Kvrgić, Vanja Drach, and Josip Pejaković) embodying different Bosnian destinies with different attitudes towards their lives and the situation in Bosnia that largely affects those lives, Goran with his "dumb," as many call it, or apparently irrational but certainly unique attitude works as a catalyst for these people as well. Some open up to him because of it, some affirm their own non-realistic (in the sense of not expected or uncommon) choices, and some, thanks to Goran, change themselves in unpredictable ways.

All for Free sees unpredictability—or basic historical openness, individual and social—as playing a crucial role in a search for a new and liveable present. This unpredictability fosters a dynamic in which the usual beginnings do not lead to the usual endings, but to something else that cannot fail to be surprising and liberating in its display of the real possibilities that have not before been visible. Such a dynamic is often played through a two-part

Fig 6.6 Goran and Fara, *All For Free* (2006) (courtesy of Propeler Film, Zagreb)

structure, in which the situation is set to go in one (established or dominant) direction, but then goes in another. For example, Goran's handsome old house is the only asset he has, but instead of preserving it or even using it as an investment, he sells it and then sets on the road to literally have strangers "drink the house" down. Contrary to the profit motive, and contrary even to basic self-survival impetus, Goran chooses a seemingly completely absurd gift-economy. Instead of the principle of earning and accumulating, he embodies the opposite of dissipation and giving away—knowing full well how short-term and irreversible this is. His unpredictability then at times emphasizes or catalyses the unpredictability of the people he interacts with, who either reassert their own exit from the realms of expected, or else are inspired to imagine and attempt a future that is different from their past and present. The two-part structure—setting expectations and then going in a surprising direction—is evident in these cases as well. In one scene, two men in a warehouse, one Bosniak and the other one Serb, introduce themselves by saying that each of their brothers killed the other man's father, setting up what seems like a recognizable pattern of violence and revenge. But the conclusion of the warehouse pair, like Goran's, does not seem to be calculated predictably from the given premises: "And what should we do now? Kill each other?" The answer being a clear "no," the so-called Balkan (and Bosnian) cycle of violence is interrupted, and a board game and everyday companionship between the two are taken up instead.

All for Free's central character's own unpredictability is, like the unpredictability of Fikret and Ramiz in the *Summer in a Golden Valley*, mostly characterized by a contrary-to-expectations thrust to relinquish power rather than empower oneself—the giving away of one's assets, refusing to arm oneself, weakening and exposing oneself instead of strengthening and shielding oneself. For instance, threatened with violence by a local bar owner, Goran does not protect himself but instead gets drunk and passes out in his wide-open truck, becoming even more defenseless than he had been before, and he repeats the same surprising refusal to strengthen himself after he does get beaten up: he declines a gun offered to him for future protection.

The unpredictability whereby the first part of a situation is not followed by the expected second part, but instead goes in a different direction, sets up an alternative reality in which behavior is not based on the established "rules of the game," of how something is done or how something seemingly develops or goes a certain way on its own. Once one element of the environment shows that things can go otherwise, not according to the given parameters (e.g., self-interest, profit, exploitation or alienation of the others or of oneself), but differently, other elements—whether they be individual lives or political patterns—can be "inspired" to try to find different directions as well. "Well, let's do something... live," as Goran, not very eloquently but nevertheless correctly, puts it to his would-be girl-friend Maja (Nataša Janjić), who asks in disbelief, "how did you imagine that?" In other words: Is it possible, just like that, to leave behind history, not just the individual history of that which happened to us, and the history of us as formed and established in that past that stretches up to this moment, but also the broader history of the set ways of doing things that always present themselves as the only ones, inevitable and necessary? It is possible, shows Goran, asserting that the first step of doing the new thing is simply stepping into it and trusting that it could be found and done, even though we may not know in the moment of getting off the beaten path exactly where the next step will lead us, or how this "new thing" will look.

The Question of the Future

At first glance, the story and themes of *Grbavica: the Land of My Dreams* (*Grbavica*, 2006, written and directed by Jasmila Žbanić), though dire, are simple enough. Set in Sarajevo, the film centers on Esma (Mirjana Karanović), a single mother, and her teenage daughter Sara (Luna Mijović), whose father had been killed while defending Sarajevo and is thus considered a *šehid* (martyr). The cost of Sara's school trip could be significantly lower if she furnished a document confirming the circumstances of her father's death. Esma, who just took a job as a night waitress in a seedy club, maintains she cannot find this certificate, and in the final showdown with Sara discloses the secret—that she was interned in a prison camp and repeatedly raped, and that Sara is not the child of a brave defender of the city but of one of her mother's captors. The fate of rape victims such as Esma, and of their children, is the foregrounded concern of *Grbavica* and of Jasmila Žbanić herself in her public endeavors. However, focusing on this issue alone means looking into the one-time event which, though horrific, is as a specific past event relegated to that past, and safely, at least for the time being, enclosed there. Although it greatly affects the present of those women who were directly victimized, as well as of many people connected with them, the reality itself of the rape camps has stayed in the past.

And yet, despite the obvious intentions and themes, perhaps the most poignant aspect of *Grbavica* lies in its creation of the multiple indirect echoes of Esma's past victimization in the present—and not simply in the obvious dramatic role, as the events which will remind Esma of her previous experiences as well as alert us as viewers to the side of her life undisclosed until the film's end. In a scene of heated and highly sexualized group-dancing to "turbo-folk" music in the club where Esma works, a Ukrainian woman "animator" lets the UN patron of the club pour beer all over her breasts and then lick it off while she shrieks and dances with him, looking as if she were having sex with him in the midst of the cheering club patrons. Upon seeing this and similar events, Esma runs away, gets sick, or cries. But while functioning as reminders of Esma's slowly unraveling past, these visual echoes also bring that past into the present, or show what of that past is still very much alive in the present. The context and some crucial elements are of course radically different, with the Ukrainian woman not fearing for her life and forced not by violence but by economic necessity to become a sexual object, and not being repeatedly raped but instead professionally engaged to render "animation" services. Yet these scenes reverberate with Esma because they seem so much like the ones from her past that they become equated or made parallel to them in profoundly disturbing ways.

The rhythmic progression of the film alternates scenes of mutual support and care with those of objectification of or direct violence over the others, constructing a clear contrast and, as it were, a permanent conflict between the two options. The scenes are initially recognizably gender coded, with feminine standing for support and masculine for violence. Thus, the opening scene with a slow panning of the camera over the faces and bodies of women leaning on each other and sitting on a colorful carpet, with their eyes closed listening to one of them singing, and ending with a close-up of Esma suddenly opening her eyes and looking into the camera, is juxtaposed with a scene of a smoky club with aggressively loud music, women dancing provocatively, and with Esma trying to get

Fig 6.7 Esma, *Grbavica* (2006)

a job with the owner, Šaran, who immediately assumes the position of intimidating dominance and approves of her having no husband or children (as she tells him). The following sequence, beginning with a close-up of a young girl's hand stroking a woman's hand and the girl's voice calling "mom, mom, wake up", and with Esma and who we now see is her daughter Sara having their playful pillow fight, is followed by scene in which Sara gets repeatedly pushed by a boy during a soccer game, and responds by getting into a fight with him. Different spaces are both gender and value coded as well, with the women's support center and the all-female shoe factory[15] where Esma's best friend works being spaces, despite their own issues and problems, of mutual support and care, and with the night club being a space of often predatory masculinism. But soon this straightforward dichotomy becomes much more complex, as the two spaces and ways of being and acting in the world start to battle it out within both scenes and their characters. The joyful playfulness of Esma and Sara on a walk is destroyed by Esma's aunt's subtly sadistic behavior. Sara is fascinated with the gun of the boy who fought with her before but then becomes her friend, and she is also throwing snowballs at a cat, in a scene reminiscent of one in Roman Polanski's *Two Men and a Wardrobe* (1959), where the stoning of a cat leads to violence towards people. On the other hand, a scene in which the bodyguard Pelda (before the war an economy student, a past defender of the city, and now working for the war profiteer Šaran whom he despises), shows the capacity of gentleness and care by patiently nudging his mentally declining mother to have a bite of food, and by covering her in kisses, is juxtaposed with the following close-up shot of a punching bag and the boxing gloves-clad hands of this same man punching with passion.

The tension and the battle of *Grbavica* are not only about coming to terms with the past so that one can move on with the present, but also about the past as repeating or echoing itself in the present and in the unfolding future; in other words, it is not so much about the rape victim Esma, though she is the central character, but rather about Sara and her future. Asleep and hugging her stuffed bunny,

---

[15] The setting of a shoe factory may invoke the communality of a similarly all-women shoe factory in Miloš Forman's classic *Loves of a Blond*.

still a child in many ways, Sara is repeatedly shown "montaged" with and within the often disturbing scenes of different women's present lives, her inquiring look into her face in the oval mirror echoing the same inquiring look of her mother into her face in the same mirror, so that one increasingly senses the implied question which the film poses. Is Sara going to end up like Esma, an ambitious student of medicine who was derailed into an often humiliating existence? Or like the Ukrainian woman animator, who may have had to choose between going hungry, or worse, and living from her sexuality, re-enacting some of the images that still haunt Esma? Or, perhaps, as a woman who attempts to protect herself by taking on the masculine skills of fighting and using a gun? The space of possibilities for Sara's future is a space that contains much of Esma's past: too much violence, dire need, injustice, legitimized and illegitimate but present aggression and exploitation is still around and not going away either, and too many times these forces translate into the victimization of innocents.

"If I am your friend [i.e., if you see me as your friend], you will leave this gun with me. It will stay with me until you cool down," says young Sara to her beaten up and enraged friend, asking him to disarm himself lest he does something irrevocable and out of proportion in response to the offense done to him. He agrees and surrenders the gun, and later on, learning of her mother's past and having previously been told that her hair is the one thing she has in common with her father, Sara shaves her head, thus visually and symbolically, if unwittingly, asserting her being on the opposite pole to the Ukrainian woman night club animator who dons a wig for her job. He is disarmed and she is in a way de-feminized or at least visually de-sexualized and made even more like a "tomboy" than she usually is, and it is on this middle ground that they meet and kiss for the first time, re-enacting their first act of peace when they both made a few steps towards each other at the same time. Disempowerment on one side—an individual's inner and outer disarmament—has to be matched with the expulsion of the destructive aspects of the past (rapist father's hair, a will for revenge) on the other, and with the rejection of the destructive aspects of that past still existing in the present (shaving head in opposition to the woman animator's "putting on" of her hair), but also with the reclaiming of the kindness and love of the past: Esma tells Pelda that he needs to stay in Bosnia in order to recognize and reclaim his dead father's body.

After being asked to take on a hit job, Pelda's partner muses: "Damn it if the people did not love each other more in the war!" The love that is referred to here is not just a particular individual love of one person for another, but more a principle of a society, infusing—or not—that society and its many various relationships and people. *Grbavica* does not find any love in the political bodies or activities, which are never even present in the film in any way; and it does not find any love in religion either, as murderous deals are made in front of a large white mosque, unhindered by it in the least, with the call for prayer serving only to cover-up violent plots.[16] But real and potent love does exist in the minute sphere of private relationships—mother and daughter, son and mother, potential and real lovers, friends—and within the wider groups of women who share the past and the present and who help each other: it is the shoe factory's women workers who will in the end collect the money that Esma needs. The question, of course, is whether this love can expand and win over, in individuals and in the society, the broader well-entrenched ways of profit and objectification, of the powerful and the powerless, and save those who are now still children?

"The Truthful Road to Me"

Bosnian films introduce new ways of seeing reality and new possibilities of being an individual. The focus on and respect for the here and now, with a critical look at the presumably superior modes of life elsewhere and with a healing and productive attitude towards the past, the exhilarating possibility to be unpredictable

---

[16] One could argue that the use of a so-called *ilahija*, a song that repeatedly calls out Allah's name and is thus a blessing and help in itself, in a crucial scene in the women's center in which one woman sings the *ilahija* "Procvali su behari," and then this singing segues into Esma's first public recollection of her past, intimates that the religion is a vehicle for getting in touch with oneself and facing up to one's past, thus hopefully coming to some grips with it. While Russell A. Berman, in his speech "After Europe: Islamism in Bosnia," argues along these lines, my reading of this scene is different.

and pursue new directions, and a thrust to disempower oneself (opposing the adoration of power present in mainstream cinema), are all aspects of Bosnian cinema's vision of a new and necessary individual and society. Compassion and poetry, not discussed at length in this chapter, are also seen as necessary for one's being and becoming—again—both a Bosnian and a full human being in the vastly different circumstances of the past two decades. As Mak Dizdar put it:

> The hardest wrestling
> The real wars
> Are in your very core.[17]

With their fresh and giving vision and their often inexplicable joy despite it all, Bosnian films help viewers become aware that there *is* such a "wrestling in one's core" in the first place, and that it may be possible to at least imagine, for start, the "truthful road to me."

---

[17] As quoted in Amila Buturović, *Stone Speaker: Medieval Tombs, Landscape, and Bosnian Identity in the Poetry of Mak Dizdar* (2002), 99. I have somewhat modified Francis R. Jones's translation.

7

Under the Star of Orwell
Jurica Pavičić's *Plaster Sheep* and Ante Tomić's *Nothing Should Surprise Us*

> *Now, it seems to me that you do less harm by dropping bombs on people than by calling them "Huns."*[1]
>
> GEORGE ORWELL

If one employs the sometimes helpful distinction between a more socially engaged literature (say, Charles Dickens), and a more *l'art pour l'art* literature (e.g., Vladimir Nabokov), re-thought in recent times by Richard Rorty as a distinction between "Orwellian" public and human liberty, and a "Nabokovian" private and aesthetic bliss literary project,[2] it may not be surprising to find that much Croatian literature from the 1990s and the early twenty-first century, roughly speaking, has been made under the star of Orwell. His saying, "you cannot take a purely aesthetic interest in a disease you are dying from,"[3] relates to much of the literature written in this period, and it is only in recent years that the more clearly "Nabokovian" texts are making a clear comeback in Croatian letters.

---

[1] George Orwell, *The Collected Essays, Journalism and Letters*, volume 3. *As I Please, 1943–1945*, edited by Sonia Orwell and Ian Angus (2000), 199.
[2] See Richard Rorty, *Contingency, Irony, and Solidarity* (1989), 145.
[3] Rorty (1989), 145.

Some Croatian literature has particularly engaged the proliferation of lies within the new (post-1990) Croatia, which have proven both literally lethal for some people as well as destructive of the overall health of social life. Orwell wrote:

> I cannot feel that mere killing is all-important ... War damages the fabric of civilization not by the destruction it causes ... nor even by the slaughter of human beings, but by stimulating hatred and dishonesty. By shooting at your enemy you are not in the deepest sense wronging him. But by hating him, by inventing lies about him and bringing children up to believe them ... you are striking not at one perishable generation, but at humanity itself.[4]

Words can be more deeply destructive than "mere killing," lies worse than outright physical destruction, because lies cast their shadow far and wide in space and time, recasting the past and present and often directly causing a string of future killings and devastation. In Chapter 2 I discuss the destructive potential of the words of *Fama*, or Rumor, as seen in Alenka Mirković's 1997 memoir *91.6 MHz: With the Voice Against the Guns*. The violence that erupted in the Yugoslav Successor States in the 1990s can itself largely be seen as a direct result of numerous lies, including the ones of "Serbia's politicians' [manipulation of] ... historical memory."[5]

---

[4] Orwell (2000), 199.
[5] Sabrina P. Ramet, *Serbia, Croatia and Slovenia at Peace and at War: Selected Writings, 1983–2007* (2008), 31. Here is a larger excerpt (originally published as part of an article in *Foreign Affairs*, 71(4) (1992), 79–98), from Ramet's book:
> Western officials and publications circulate myths that perpetuate misunderstanding about the nature of the war and render any effective countermeasures more elusive. Of those myths, the most popular are these: the conflict between Serbs and Croats is "centuries old"; the war is primarily a "religious" war (between Orthodox Serbs and Catholic Croats or Bosnian Muslims) ...
> Regarding the first myth: Serbs and Croats have, in fact, lived together peacefully for centuries prior to the twentieth century. There was no rancor until after World War I, when the two nations united in a single state. ...
> Second, the war is not a religious war. The war is about land, not religion ... Religious differences did not impede interethnic social contact in either republic until Serbia's politicians began to manipulate religious sensitivity and historical memory to kindle collective hatred for non-Serbs.
>
> (Ramet (2008), 30–1)

It was these lies, and not "ancient ethnic hatreds," that started the war.⁶

However, the regime and society of the newly independent Croatia were also burdened with a proliferation of various kinds

---

⁶In *The Myth of Ethnic War* (2004), V. P. Gagnon demonstrates that the convenient trope of "ancient ethnic hatreds" is a lie or a "myth" itself, not in sync with the situation on the ground in the Former Yugoslavia. This myth was convenient, and thus more maintained than debunked, in justification of some of the Western policies that worsened rather than relieved the crisis and the war. Gagnon's book is one of the must-read volumes for understanding of the causes of the Wars of Yugoslav Succession. Here is Gagnon summarizing his findings:

I show that the violence of the Yugoslav wars of the 1990s was part of a broad strategy in which images of threatening enemies and violence were used by conservative elites in Serbia and Croatia: not in order to mobilize people, but rather as a way to *demobilize* those who were pushing for changes in the structures of economic and political power that would negatively affect the values and interests of those elites. The goal of this strategy was to silence, marginalize, and demobilize challengers and their supporters in order to create political homogeneity at home. This in turn enabled conservatives to maintain control of existing structures of power, as well as reposition themselves by converting state-owned property into privately held wealth, the basis of power in a new system of a liberal economy.

The wars and violence seen in the 1990s were thus not the expression of grassroots sentiment in the sites of conflict. They were also far from being the democratic expression of the political and cultural preferences of the wider population. Rather, the violence was imposed on plural communities from outside of those communities by political and military forces from Serbia and Croatia as part of a broader strategy of demobilization.

... I am not arguing that ethnicity was meaningless. ... The approach in this book recognizes ethnic identification as a social fact. That is, many people in the former Yugoslavia did identify as Serbs, Croats, or Muslims. But the meaning of that identity was contextual: it was not homogeneous nor was it unchanging. Along these lines, sociologist Martijn van Beek describes the tendency of observers of conflicts that are framed and described as ethnic to focus on that ethnicity in their explanations. [Martijn van Beek, "Beyond Identity Fetishism: 'Communal' Conflict in Ladakh and the Limits of Autonomy," *Cultural Anthropology* 15, no. 4 (2002): 528–529.] He labels this tendency "identity fetishism," or a fixation on "the imputed stability and irreducibility of identity and the groupness it supposedly reflects." Such a focus, van Beek argues, "leads to a 'misrecognition' of social identification, obscures the processes and conditions that give rise to conflict, and reproduces the logic of discrimination that it seeks to resolve." These fallacies are exactly what this study is attempting to avoid.

(Gagnon (2004), xv–xvi)

of lies, many of them creating an atmosphere that threatened and alienated many, and that made war more rather than less likely. Charged with something similar to Orwell's insight, Croatian literature has consistently exposed and engaged those lies. Some writers did it directly, such as Dubravka Ugrešić in her collection of essays *The Culture of Lies* (1996). Others crafted fictional stories and novels that, as Christa Wolf would put it, "invented something ... that was needed to tell the truth", that is, created bits of truthful reality that in turn exposed some of the lies promoted in public discourse.[7]

In his collection of stories *I Forgot Where I Parked and Other Stories* (*Zaboravio sam gdje sam parkirao i druge priče*, 2001), Ante Tomić engages the falseness of the descriptions of Croatia in the 1990s, promoted by the official regime, in which the achievement of national independence and statehood was supposed to be the be-all and end-all of the country's life. This focus made all other problems lose importance and also made any pointing at these problems look like criticism of the new state—which in itself was proclaimed to be anti-patriotic. Tomić's stories simply and effectively bring into the

---

[7]Interviewed by Tomislav Čadež (2005) about the new generation of Croatian writers who came to the prominence in the late 1990s and after, Croatian critic Velimir Visković said:
They are really characterized by a deep feeling of reluctance, and even deep disgust, toward the easy use of big words like patriotism, Croatianness [*hrvatstvo*], state. These are most often writers, poets ... who saw the war from up close, and some of them were themselves on the war front. And yet, they were watching other people who never went to the war or saw the war, but have operated with big phrases and became owners of the factories that laid people off en masse. They were watching the fervent social stratification which brought wealth and all the power in the society to the one narrow circle of people, which all happened with the blessings of the very top of the government. In short, that generation rebelled against the nationalist rhetoric and oligarchic governance of the country. The commonality of that generation is not of a political character, it is more apolitical: despising of any empty rhetoric, above all the right one but the left one too ... They all talk about the war and post-war reality strongly and without lies. They tear down the facade of the national pathos behind which outright material greed and theft are hidden. At the end of the nineties and today the disgust of our new writers with politics and political elites—of all parties—reaches the pinnacle ... [T]heir literary heroes are small, ordinary people from the outskirts of the city who felt the walk of the new times on their own skin in the hardest and most direct way.
(Tomislav Čadež (2005), 63)

field of vision many bleak facets of the new Croatian society, from emerging poverty to government corruption and crime and drug problems in a place where, suddenly, heroin became cheap and "looked to the kids as innocent as cold cuts."[8] The story "With the Help of Tricks, or How the Serbs of Croatia Disappeared" *("Pomoću trikova, ili kako su nestali Srbi u Hrvatskoj")*, engages two other still rather present (though considerably less so than in the 1990s) social lies. The first one is the one of the generalizing nationalist discourse in Croatia, proclaiming all the Serbian people to be the enemies of Croatia. The second lie concerns the official presentation of the action "Storm" (*Oluja*, August 1995, Croatia'a military operation that regained a large part of Croatia's territory occupied since 1991), which had until some years ago largely avoided or minimized any mention of the Serbian civilian victims of that operation. Tomić returns the lost subjectivity, presence and humanity to Serbian characters by depicting the "Storm" from the point of view of a young Serbian man, a magician, taking care of his terminally ill father in one of the towns of the *Krajina* region, and refusing to leave him in the path of the advancing Croatian troops. The story focuses on an encounter between Croatian soldiers and a young Serbian man, Radojica, which reveals that the soldiers are not Serb-hating killing machines, and Radojica is not a brutal *chetnik*, as portrayed by the respective propaganda machines. Instead, they are just young men terrified for their lives in a situation that they can hardly control.

The emphasis of Slavonian writer Julijana Matanović's pseudo-autobiographical collection of integrated stories, *Why Did I Lie to You* (*Zašto sam vam lagala*, 1997), although including some references to past and present politics as well as to the 1990s war, is squarely on one's own intimate past. It is this past and its secrets that explain one's unusual present, and that are of supreme importance for the first-person narrator of this text. *Why Did I Lie to You* recalls the whole past era from the 1960s to the present, and depicts this era's average life that, from the perspective of the turn of the millennium, seems static, limited in options and frustrating in some aspects, but also vibrant, fulfilled, and in many ways joyful.

---

[8] Ante Tomić, *Zaboravio sam gdje sam parkirao i druge priče* (2001), 184. Trans. by Gordana P. Crnković.

In a world not dominated by career or politics, work is important (the author mentions all the effort she put into her studies and her chosen profession), yet the book's emphasis is on the development of intimate relationships of all kinds, and on the pleasures of a slow-paced life, food, family, reading, thinking, socializing, all considerably enabled by some of the guaranteed benefits of the socialist era. Matanović's text recreates sounds, smells, rhythms, tastes, and words of that time, which bring back its tangible fullness and warmth, and makes a lie of the official descriptions of the Yugoslav past that present it primarily and most importantly as an absence of something. Readers are obviously finding something that resonates with them in this text too: at the time of this writing it has gone through 13 editions.

The following passage gives a taste of the texture and tone of *Why Did I Lie to You*:

> In the village where my father's mother lived the pub was called 'the reading room'. I do not know to this day, and I am sincerely sorry for it, who named it this way. Perhaps this was done by my grandmother Kata who, although she never read a single book herself and who up to her dying day signed the most important contracts with a cross, heard so many paragraphs from the more important literary works that she was ready to beat even the most educated villager in some competition in this field. And she was taught by her son, my father Ilija, who, even after becoming independent, visited her every week-end and always prepared for her a short literary seminar during his visit. For years his favorite book was Faulkner's *As I Lay Dying*, and grandmother was most surely the only old woman who did not know how to read and who, although she never left her house, built in the woods far away from the main traffic roads, could say how Faulkner reacted when he was told that he was the winner of the Nobel Prize for literature.[9]

The two novels that I now turn to are *Plaster Sheep* (*Ovce od gipsa*, 1997) by Jurica Pavičić, and *Nothing Should Surprise Us* (*Ništa*

---

[9]Julijana Matanović, *Zašto sam vam lagala* (2002), 150. Trans. by Gordana P. Crnković.

nas ne smije iznenaditi, 2003) by Ante Tomić. The first takes as its theme one tragic and still under-discussed aspect of the Homeland War (*Domovinski rat*) of the 1990s, and the other revisits the era of the late 1980s, right before the break-up of the Socialist Federative Republic of Yugoslavia. Both novels are written in an accessible, popular style, and are a pleasure to read. *Plaster Sheep* is a fast-paced thriller, and *Nothing Should Surprise Us* is marked by a humorous tone characteristic of Tomić, though with increasingly dark tenor and high stakes towards the end. Both novels were well-received and made into films by prominent Croatian directors, Pavičić's novel into Vinko Brešan's *Witnesses* (*Svjedoci*, 2003; this film is discussed in Chapter 8), and *Nothing Should Surprise Us* into *The Border Post* (*Karaula*, 2006), directed by Rajko Grlić.

Garbage and the Girl: Jurica Pavičić's *Plaster Sheep*

> The city kept stinking like a dead fish in a warm southern wind, overfilled with people like worms moving about ... He felt all of it, but did not think about it. He was getting used—more and more each year—not to think about the things he could not change.[10]

The story of *Plaster Sheep* begins with a prologue that takes place in June 1991, somewhere in eastern Herzegovina, where five Croatian soldiers on an unidentified mission enter a minefield due to a mistake by their leader Krešo. Two of the soldiers die, and Krešo loses a leg. The main part of the story takes place in 1992 in the coastal city of Split, the home town of these soldiers where, one evening, fueled by alcohol and hate speech, a few of them decide to bomb the presumably empty house of a local Serbian merchant. Their action miscarries and they end up killing the man and kidnapping his young daughter, the only witness to the murder. The novel revolves around the ensuing panicked and distracted efforts of the group to decide what to do with the child, in the process of which different individuals gradually move in

---

[10] Jurica Pavičić, *Ovce od gipsa* [*Plaster Sheep*] (1998), 121. All translations here from Pavičić's novel are by Gordana P. Crnković.

different directions, with one of them (Vojo) eventually trying to save the girl, and another (Slave, whose brother died due to Krešo's mistake) apparently making up his mind to kill her. Their erstwhile commander Krešo, who was not involved in any of this, gradually discovers what is going on and attempts to save the girl with the help of his sister, the journalist Lidija. In a parallel plot, Lidija's boss Galjer, the editor of the crime section of the local newspaper, is pressed by a local bigwig, Dr. Matić, the city's mayor and a close relative of one of the involved soldiers, not to deal too much with the case, in exchange for which Dr. Matić promises to ensure that Galjer's wife Vera, gravely ill with cancer, receives treatment in the Split hospital that may perhaps save her life.[11]

Pavičić's novel creates a world that is in many aspects the direct opposite of the ideal one of Platonic connectedness of truthfulness, goodness, and beauty. *Plaster Sheep* descends straight away into the sphere of lies, evil, and ugliness, where lying words are materialized into their final ugly, murderous reality. The unintended murder of a Serbian merchant and the kidnapping of his daughter are both

---

[11] Aside from symbolically referring to all of the Serbian civilian victims of such assaults, *Plaster Sheep* may particularly bring to mind two specific cases. One is the well-known case of the Zec family, in which father Mihajlo, mother Mirjana, and their 12-year-old daughter Aleksandra were killed by members of the Croatian reserve police forces in the vicinity of Zagreb. Pavičić's characterizing his novel's child Mila as having "some twelve years" and his mentioning the case "when the family of that butcher at Sljeme was killed" testify to his keeping in mind this case as he was writing his novel. Pavičić (1998; 43 and 63). Sljeme is a mountain near Zagreb onto which the northernmost part of the city has spread.

The second case this novel can be more specifically related to took place in Split. As Slavica Lukić writes: "[I]n the night between 7 and 8 February 1992, in Zrnovica by Split, a young married couple Đorđe and Vesna Gasparević were taken from their house and afterwards liquidated on the Zrnovica garbage site. They agreed to quietly leave the house with their liquidators, probably in order not to wake the children who were sleeping in the house, thus saving these children from death. The inspector of Split's police, who was assigned the case and who traced the killers, was kidnapped by masked men and beaten up for a few days at an unknown location next to Split. The inspector had to escape out of the country, and today he still lives abroad." Slavica Lukić, "Crna knjiga Domovinskog rata" ["The Black Book of the Homeland War"], in *Globus* (10 August 2005), p. 29. In the same article Lukić talks about the "destinies of the citizens of the Serbian nationality who in 1991, after the start of the rebellion in the region called *Krajina*, remained living peacefully in the areas under the control of the Croatian government, and were afterwards taken from their homes and have disappeared or been killed." (p. 26).

caused by a string of interlaced lies, including those of radical nationalism on one hand, but also particular "daily" lies claiming, among others, that the man in question was out partying every night and his daughter was out of the country altogether. And lies are connected not only with ethical and political evil, but also with the physical environment of varied ugliness: the opening events take place in the unpleasant eastern part of Split, and the novel closes with a scene on the city's huge garbage dump, in which another murder—of the child witness—is predicated on an acquiescence to another lie, as will later be elaborated.

> Around them a wild settlement was spreading, a typical landscape of eastern Split, which people from the western parts see once or twice a year ... The illegally built and mostly unfinished family houses were scattered for kilometers around, with no order whatsoever. They were so alike: unpainted, gray ... all the access paths were in mud and silt, bordered with channels taking cloaca into the sea. If it were day, Joško would be able to see, from the spot on which he waveringly stood, the inextricable labyrinth of the telephone and electric lines through which the houses that had legal telephone and electricity passed on some of that blessing to wild habitations for the appropriate fee.[12]

Plaster Sheep creates a strange dynamic between the clear plot with the things related to it, and the environment where the story takes place. The environment of the city engulfs the plot and the characters, and pushes itself into the foreground of the text, surrounding and in a sense threatening to "drown" and stop the story. The realm of the city is affected by the war that does not directly claim it, but whose shadow and reverberations profoundly transform this social, urban, and psychological space. The 1991–5 occupation of a part of Croatia largely cut the city off from the northwestern parts of the country, and Split in 1992 is depicted as literally imprisoned "in the thick and blind intestines, a faraway channel submerged in war and lack of honor."[13] "Submerged

---

[12] Pavičić (1998), 36–7.
[13] Pavičić (1998), 121.

in war", the city is overwhelmed by both the war's voracious needs—for young men, various resources, people's work, fortunes, and nerves—as well as its refuse: corpses, invalids, thoroughly changed personalities, poverty, general addiction to the news from the front. The wretchedness of the city penetrates all of its parts: people's own homes are surrounded by "piles of garbage, paper cups, pieces of glass,"[14] the cars they drive have a "peeled exterior and not much better interior,"[15] and people themselves feel like they have been "thrown into the corner where [they] now squat, humiliated and powerless."[16] Unpleasant and unruly, the familiar yet new environment of the city appears as a dominant presence in the story, as the material embodiment of that "shadowy" presence of the war beyond its literal confines in space and time.

The physical environment of *Plaster Sheep* is characterized also by its own immanent falsity. The material reality is of course truthful in the sense that it exists, but it is a lie when compared with the original idea of what it was supposed to be. The hospital to which Galjer brings his wife, for instance, is described as an idea which, "like many other good ideas in Split, also turned into a monstrosity [*ruglo*]." While the man-made material reality can often be seen as in some ways an imperfect mimesis of the original guiding idea, in this case this imperfection is pushed to the extreme, and the reality thus created becomes a grotesque parody or even the direct opposite of the beginning idea, a "lie" of this idea. As commander of a small military unit on a mission, Krešo was guided by the concept of keeping his men safe; instead, a chance occurrence and his own mistake made him cause the death of two of them. The five embittered Croatian soldiers planned to damage the house or car of a Serbian merchant, and instead ended up killing the man and kidnapping his young daughter. In the same way in which the idea of a new hospital turned into a "monstrosity", the ideas of Krešo and his former fellow soldiers were perverted. In Pavičić's novel, the people are not in control of the matter, of what happens with and around them; rather, the matter—originally made by people but now out of control—lords over the people:

---

[14] Pavičić (1998), 49.
[15] Pavičić (1998), 50.
[16] Pavičić (1998), 125.

badly built hospitals, cars of poor quality, growing garbage heaps, intentions of harassment that end in dead bodies and kidnapped children, the war itself. The foul environment is also a metaphoric embodiment of the invisible network of social contacts criss-crossing the city and country on one hand, and the network of lies and gossip with potentially deadly effects on the other. Regarding the social network: the "bad guys" such as Dr. Matić are plugged into the give-and-take of a mutual support network, whereas the lack of such networking marks those who are at distance from such an environment—former commander Krešo, his sister Lidija, and editor Galjer are all "loners," connecting only in extreme situations like this one. The surplus of substantial subjectivity, of that which could anachronistically be called the "inner beauty" of these characters—however compromised it may be by the environment in which they live—creates an automatic tendency to distance oneself as much as possible from the repugnant environment, and thus most often prevents self-interested networking. Galjer "knew that he was not one of those in the circle, that they can manage without him and that they had already managed without him."[17] The second network, that of lies, is also metaphorically embodied in the unruly and organically growing unpleasant physical environment, and has in itself falsehoods of different kinds and levels. There are omissions and silencing (such as the media omission of the sheer fact that there was most probably a young daughter in the house of the murdered Serbian salesman), active and manipulative lies (e.g., by Dr. Matić), lies forced on someone (e.g., on Galjer), and even lies used by the "good guys" because the truth would not be believed. Aside from these individual and interrelated lies, however, there are also greater and more fundamental lies of radical nationalist discourse coloring the whole space, homogenizing and vilifying all of the Serbian people into enemies or *chetniks*. Without an identified original source, speech reflecting such an attitude is being reproduced by many willing mouths and heard throughout the city. It is encountered for the first time in a group of Krešo's fellow handicapped soldiers, where one man explains how "he will kill the Serbs who go to class with his kid"; it reappears on a city bus where a

---

[17] Pavičić (1998), 24.

drunken man carries on a monologue which includes the invective that "one should kill all the Serbs in Split", and similar talk ends up being the main thing that prompts the group of Croatian soldiers to attack the house of the Serbian merchant: "after being mad and threatening and downing vodka for three hours, Jakus thought it up that they should go and kill all the Serbs."[18]

> Tišma deserved to be a target of revenge. Joško never doubted whether Jakus spoke the truth. And Jakus told to Joško and the boys such things about Tišma that Joško had no reason to pity him. The whole neighborhood, he said, knew Tišma was a thief who had gotten rich by cheating his customers. It is also known that he is a pure *chetnik*, who traded with Krajina until the last moment. Jakus claimed that Tišma was also seen on the barricades at Baljak. A part of all this, they knew, did not make much sense. But the rest was enough to not feel sorry for him.[19]

The moment in which the Serbian salesman Tišma becomes a victim is not the moment when he is shot, but the much earlier one in which his self (his life, his humanity, his commonalities with the others), is completely displaced by such talk about him, and he himself is no longer seen. When Tišma appears at the door of his own home with the gun in his hand, the five attackers can see a big man with a gun in his hand—which fits the speech about him—but, significantly, what they "could not see was his appearance full of fear."[20] The kidnapped daughter of the slain salesman, Mila (meaning "the dear one") is precariously positioned to move in the opposite direction, from being the sign of negativity and danger in the nationalist discourse toward the real existence, emerging out of the discourse and into the experience, traveling from being a word solely, *četnikuša*, to being "just a girl." Her silence throughout her ordeal, the silence that unnerves even the most resolute character who says he is ready to liquidate her, puts the whole burden of decision and responsibility squarely on the side of the soldiers, without the girl pleading for her life or saying anything else

---

[18] Pavičić (1998), 28, 106, 80.
[19] Pavičić (1998), 39.
[20] Pavičić (1998), 41.

whatsoever. This silence is astounding: it does not battle one kind of speech (nationalism) with another (pleas, persuasions), but rather lets the sheer presence of a young girl speak for her and against the now prominent lying language about her.

> *She passed this trailer hundreds of times. White, scratched, and filthy, it looked by day like a meeting place of loafers [and a site of] misery and social cases. Now, at night, it would greet its Cinderella's ball. The only brightly lit abode in the dark street, a "mobile shop for simple food service" (that was written on it), it would become the princess of the industrial zone.*[21]

The pervasive presence of the environment of physical ugliness, of perverted ideas, contacts and lethal lies in *Plaster Sheep* takes over the focus of the text and creates a dynamic in which the progress of the plot and the characters' action (or for the large part the lack of such action, omnipresent indecisiveness, paralysis, and confusion), have more to do with the people interacting with this environment of ugliness of all kinds in which they find themselves, than with them interacting with each other or trying to pursue their own goals. In other words, the actions of Krešo, Vojo, and editor Galjer appear primarily as a heavy interaction with this *milieu*. A person is reduced from being a presumed subject of his/her actions to being a "worm"—"city ... filled with people like worms"—much less in charge of anything, which "move[s] about and budge[s]" through this environment.[22] Only in cases of extreme focus and exertion do people manage to actively engage with and even struggle against this environment, thus elevating themselves to the level of ethically driven subjects. To do so, people must first get out of the state of being overwhelmed by this environment, the state which paralyses them and turns them into passive observers who become "more and more used to not thinking about the things [they] could not change." They must fight the uphill battle against the environment's momentum to pervert good ideas, attempt to take control of this contaminated and amorphous space, and break away from the

---

[21] Pavičić (1998), 195.
[22] Pavičić (1998), 121.

networks of both mutual support and deadly lies. Krešo thus has to fight his own passivity and despondency, start believing that something good and important can in fact be done and that he is the one who can do it, and then attempt to actually accomplish it. He must also part ways with his comrades and turn his back to the whole network of solidarity of the "brothers in arms," as well as refuse his support for yet another lie that would cause another loss of life.

In the final part of Krešo's struggle, taking place at the city's large and unruly garbage dump, Slave, who is apparently about to kill Mila (standing, still silent, right between him and Krešo), asserts: "I will, right now, kill the little one, because I have to do that. I'll let you go, this moment, if you only promise that you'll keep silent."[23] Krešo is offered life in exchange for his agreement to perpetuate the web of lies—metaphorically equated with the garbage site waiting to claim another life and engulfing the entire city—by only one omission of speech, one silence. His survival entails his acquiescence to lies and to the ugliness that embodies them; in turn, his acquiescence to lies would facilitate another murder. Krešo eventually refuses to do this with a simple "'No' ... Whatever happened, he knew he could not take it."[24] Krešo's inability to participate in the lie that would cover up in the future—and thus allow in the present—the murder of a girl, severs his presumed connection with Slave. Krešo has now firmly allied himself with Mila, a child in need of protection, come what may. Faced with the sudden necessity of a double murder, Slave collapses and leaves, and Krešo helps Mila get out of the garbage heap and out of the country.

The ending of the novel, however, coming in an epilogue after the positive resolution of the girl's destiny, is bifurcated and more ambiguous. Putting his life on the line, Krešo again had the good luck to avoid death and also, this time, to save one other life. However, editor Galjer, who was also trying (unbeknownst to Krešo) to save the girl in his own way by directly confronting the corrupt Dr. Matić, ends up being physically overpowered by Matić and tied to his car, embodying a lie incarnate, looking not

---

[23] Pavičić (1998), 212.
[24] Pavičić (1998), 213.

like a person who tried to save a child's life, but rather like a thief who tried to steal Matić's car. When Galjer finally manages to detach himself from the car, he hurts himself badly and starts to bleed, and the car's alarm goes off loudly and endlessly. The end, thus, contains both victory and loss. The double ending of *Plaster Sheep* is significant in its avoidance of a simple ending. Such an ambiguous ending points to the fact that things, in short, are more complex that that. Even a victory, like Krešo's, can be accompanied by Galjer's loss in the very same battle, and the "at least temporary" victory of truth can be accompanied by the newly-minted embodiment of a grotesque lie (Galjer tied to Matić's car). This bifurcated ending indicates that victories cannot be perfect and all-inclusive, but one should nevertheless keep struggling. The novel suggests that, even if the ugliness of the environment of lies stays right there at the very moment of a great victory, one should go on fighting for what may be the most we can get in certain situations, a temporary whiff of better times or, as the novel puts it, a temporary spell of a healing and refreshing northern wind, *bura*, after the days of oppressive and headache producing southern *jugo*.

While Pavičić's novel indirectly fleshes out many lies proliferating in the contemporary Croatian social sphere, its main thrust lies in its unsentimental depiction of the war *milieu* in a city not directly involved in military operations, yet still profoundly affected by the war. The environment created in the novel is that of bleakness, paralysis, self-interested networking, various lies, things that get out of control, and sheer physical ugliness; it has elements often covered up by the officially promoted grand epic of the achievement of national independence. The characters' actions or inactions are primarily carried out in relation to this whole complex environment, which often overwhelms and paralyses them. However, *Plaster Sheep* also shows that an individual, in pursuit of a goal based on sheer humanity, is at times able to go against this environment and perhaps even reach the level of heroism. In so doing, such a person, like Krešo, reshapes the environment itself and literally creates a "better world"—temporary and partial as it may be, but real nevertheless.

Rebellion and Conformism:
Ante Tomić's *Nothing Should Surprise Us*

Published in 2003, Tomić's *Nothing Should Surprise Us* [*Ništa nas ne smije iznenaditi*], was a very popular novel in Croatia. The story takes place in the 1980s, in a small military station of the JNA (Yugoslav People's Army) in the mountains of Macedonia, close to the small Macedonian town of Struga and the border with Albania. Given that the Army was arguably the only place of intensive ethnic, professional, and social mixing of young men from all of the six republics and two autonomous provinces of the Socialist Federative Republic of Yugoslavia, this setting allows Tomić to explore both interpersonal and international dynamics as it develops in this small and constrained place. Amidst the young soldiers are two main characters—a 26-year old newly-minted physician from Split, Siniša Siriščević, and a charismatic 19-year-old Belgrade cab driver, Ljuba Vrapče, which means "Ljuba the Sparrow." Other characters include a Montenegrin, Danilo, nick-named "Vladika", a Macedonian called Milčo, a Bosnian folk music star, Hasan Šišmiš, a Slovene known as Lanišnik, a Roma man, Miša Bajramović, and so on. Siniša and Ljuba develop a close relationship based on shared essentials such as a "passion for cartoons and contempt for soccer, but above all ... the Ramones, the Cramps ... Iggy Pop ... a bunch of irreverent music in which the army's reality somehow revealed itself as absurd and monstrous,"[25] but also based, even more, on mutually attractive differences: "[y]et, what probably made Siniša and Vrapče closer than anything else, was that they were actually completely different people."[26] Ljuba constantly invents various mischiefs that steadily increase in intensity and effrontery, and which result in increasingly harsh consequences for the young man. His pranks are always more or less directed against his immediately superior officer, the unit's young commander Imre Nađ, a Hungarian from Subotica. The novel follows two parallel narratives: Vrapče's increasing provocation and challenging of Nađ, and Siniša's secret medical treatment of Nađ, suffering from

---

[25] Ante Tomić, *Ništa nas ne smije iznenaditi* [*Nothing Should Surprise Us*] (2003), 12. Trans. by Gordana P. Crnković.
[26] Tomić (2003), 14.

syphillis, as well as his clandestine affair with Nađ's wife, the charming Mirjana from the town of Ruma (in the Serbian province of Vojvodina). By setting its story in the late Yugoslav period, the novel takes a fresh look at that time and also reveals some of the falsifications or simplifications of the contemporary rewriting of that period. Most obviously, and opposed to the reframing, dominant in the 1990s and still rather present, of the social space both past and present in mostly national terms, with those of one nation being regarded as having always had more in common with each other than with people from other nations, the connections which the characters in this novel establish among themselves are emphatically non-national based. The Croatian Siniša from Split is the best friend of Belgrade's Ljuba Vrapče and the lover of a Serbian woman; he also instantaneously connects with the urbane and cultured Bosnian physician from Sarajevo, Esad Rešidbegović, helps Montenegrin "Vladika" despite a chasm of cultural differences, and so on. The very language of this novel challenges the officially much promoted notion (in Croatia) that proper Croatian language has to be as different and distinct as possible from Serbian or Bosnian. Unusual for the time in which it was written, *Nothing Should Surprise Us* vigorously incorporates many of the numerous variants of the language that was called in Croatia, in its latest incarnation, "Croatian or Serbian" (*hrvatski ili srpski*), and which is used in its different variants in Croatia, Bosnia and Herzegovina, Serbia, and Montenegro. One feels the writer's almost physical delight in having found a narrative theme that allows the inclusion—or re-inclusion—of the non-specifically Croatian variants of this language (which is now considered by many linguists "one [at least for the time being] but not unified", and known as "BCS", "Bosnian/Croatian/Serbian").[27] Tomić includes spoken replicas of

---

[27] Bosnian, Croatian, and Serbian are now the three recognized languages in the region, but there is a push for the acknowledgment of the Montenegrin language as a separate language as well, and some places already use it as such (e.g., a Montenegrin periodical *Crnogorski književni list* [*Montenegrin Literary Magazine*], which notes on the front page that it comes out in "Montenegrin, Serbian, Croatian, and Bosnian language" [*Crnogorski književni list* (Podgorica), 15 June 2002, p. 1], and the other institutions in Montenegro. The same move is evident outside of Montenegro as well, for instance in the literary award "Meša Selimović" from Tuzla,

various characters which display all the richness of the numerous variants: Ljuba Vrapče talks in an idiosyncratically enriched Belgrade slang, Mirjana in a Serbian dialect, Siniša in Split's dialect, Slovenian Lanišnik uses his own variant of the Serbian language (non-native to him), and Esad speaks in the Bosnian of Sarajevo. By presenting so many variants of the individualized language of oral speech, Tomić shows the immense internal diversity and richness of this language, the existence of numerous regional and local variants, and in addition, the existence of a rich variety of the specific cultural sub-groups' slangs or languages which transcend national boundaries but are often incomprehensible to members of the same nation but of a different cultural subgroup. Siniša and Ljuba even communicate in "their own" language that is largely incomprehensible to others from either of their nations who do not share their specific cultural *milieu* and code.

Similar to Vrapče and Siniša, who got to like each other mostly because they were "actually entirely different people", the distinct variants of language in Tomić's novel relate to each other in ways that are marked, again, by an aesthetic enjoyment of differences, which can be erotically colored as well. When the two soon-to-be lovers, Siniša and Mirjana, meet for the first time, it is their play with the language and with the differences of their two variants of that language which opens up a space for intimacy, with Mirjana asking what the line of a popular Dalmatian folk song actually means, and with Siniša expertly translating "*kad Nadalina noge toća srid dvora u maštilu*" into something like "*kad Nadalina noge pere u sredini dvorišta u koritu,*" meaning "when Nadalina washes her legs in the middle of the courtyard in a bucket." This is a more generic "Croatian or Serbian" language version understandable to

---

Bosnia and Herzegovina, which is given for the best novel written in either Bosnian, Croatian, Montenegrin, or Serbian language). For a clear summary of this complex problem I would recommend a book by Ronelle Alexander: *Bosnian, Croatian, Serbian, a Grammar: with Sociolinguistic Commentary* (2006). The sharing of the same grammar as well as easy understanding between the speakers of various variants allow these variants to be called one language when language is seen as a communication system. Seen as a "symbolic icon ... representing ethnic/national identity", as Alexander puts it, they can be seen as different languages, but with the caveat that this is far from a simple situation in which, for example, all the Bosnian people speak the Bosnian language, etc.

Mirjana. The literary genealogy of this novel, which Tomić notes in the postscript, also goes beyond the realm of only Croatian literature. The author explicitly states his gratitude to Serbian author Dragoslav Mihailović, from whose *Kad su cvetale tikve* [*When the Pumpkins Blossomed*, 1968], a "superb novel" as Tomić calls it, he borrowed the character of Ljuba Vrapče.

The story, relations among the characters, and the language of this novel all question or reveal as a lie the still widely-held stereotype (at least until a very few years ago) that Yugoslavs were by and large affected by omnipresent ethnic animosities or at least deep incompatibilities, rooted far in the past and spiraling out of control in the last years of Yugoslavia. What comes to the forefront, instead, are two other aspects of the late Yugoslav era. One of them concerns the inadequacies of the political system. The one negative aspect of the 1980s late Yugoslav system pointed at by Tomić's novel seems to be the preservation of social, political, and cultural forms which had once been functional and had a meaning, but would now have to be filled with different content or done in entirely different ways to do or mean the same thing. Such outdated forms are exposed as lies because they simply do not keep up with the life and changes of the society and people. For instance, though Belgrade's Ljuba Vrapče reshuffles the letters of Tito's famous slogan, "*Čuvajmo bratstvo i jedinstvo kao zjenicu oka svoga*" ("Let us keep brotherhood and unity like the pupil of our eye"), placed on the barrack wall, to make the name of a popular Belgrade band at the time, *Električni orgazam* (Electric Orgasm), he is actually promoting the mentioned "brotherhood and unity" on an important intimate level by developing his friendship with Split's Siniša Siriščević. The system, embodied in commander Nađ, however, does not care much about the substantial relationships called for by this slogan, or about what this slogan may really mean, but is instead capable of understanding and upholding this maxim mostly as a literal keeping of an empty form, the words on the wall.

"Healthy conformism," as Tomić ironically terms it at one point, seems to be implied as another enabler of the political decline of the country, and refers to those many educated young people who clearly observed the system and its problems, but had no motivation to try and change things. Siniša and Vrapče carry two lines of plot and also two ways of behaving. While Vrapče initiates things, opposes a system, pays for it, but also affects some real changes (Nađ is eventually replaced by a better commander), Siniša accepts things as they come to him, but his makeup does not seem to include any impulse to change or get involved in anything beyond his immediate life concerns. Genuinely likeable Siniša is characterized by irony and "healthy conformism" towards the alienated political sphere (both local and more general), and his subjective distancing from it goes along with the objective acceptance of the current state of affairs.

The comparison with Dragoslav Mihailović's novel *When the Pumpkins Blossomed*, from which Tomić borrowed the character of Ljuba Vrapče, set in Belgrade in the 1940s and 1950s, underscores this emphasis on conformism as an important aspect of the late Yugoslav environment present in Tomić's novel. Tomić's Ljuba Vrapče shares many similarities with Mihailović's Ljuba: he is a young, brave, and charismatic guy from Belgrade's Dušanovac district; he boxes and shares with his predecessor the knowledge of a fatal blow in the heart; he also engages his antagonist in ever more serious duels and, following the last encounter with this antagonist, he also emigrates from the country. But the attitude of the narrative itself towards its most engaging character is different in the two novels. Ljuba of *When the Pumpkins Blossomed* is the main character who both does things and talks about them; the novel is the first-person narrative in which the middle-aged Ljuba, now a long-time emigrant in Sweden, talks about events in his youth and the things he himself did that made him emigrate. Mihailović's novel is an account by someone who does things, a doer, and the emphasis is on someone doing and having done all kinds of things. In Tomić's novel, on the contrary, the third-person narrative creates the position of a narrator who is an observer of the character who does things (Ljuba), and the attitude of another main character, Siniša, replicates the narrator's attitude in the sense that he also mostly observes that one person who initiates something while he himself "falls into" things. The switch from Mihailović's doer of the 1940s and 1950s, who later remembers and tells what he did, to Tomić's sideline observer of the mid-1980s, who observes from the side what the lone doer does the way Tomić's narrator and Siniša observe Ljuba, may also imply a profound shift in society away from an era of "doers" to an era of more conformist observers.

8

The Museum Spills Out on the Square, the Past's Challenge to the Present
The Films of Vinko Brešan

The point is that you push the limits, then there's a fuss over it, but it has happened and there is no going back. That's a good thing all around.[1]

Vinko Brešan has emerged in the last two decades as one of the most interesting new Croatian film directors, and the most popular contemporary filmmaker among domestic audiences.[2] His four

---

[1] Aida Vidan and Gordana P. Crnković, "A Conversation with Vinko Brešan: No Aesthetics Without Ethics" (2011). Available online at http://www.kinokultura.com/specials/11/int-bresan.shtml (accessed 3 November 2011).

[2] An excellent source for a critical and systematic overview of the recent Croatian film production is Tomislav Kurelec's *Filmska kronika: zapisi o hrvatskom filmu* [*The Film Chronicle: Writings on Croatian Film*] (2004). A number of Kurelec's articles giving overviews of the specific year's film production was published in English in the *Variety International Film Guide* (years 1993 to 2004). English-language readers could also consult some high-quality web articles, such as a succinct overview of 1990s Croatian film production given by Jurica Pavičić in his article "Moving into the Frame: Croatian Film in the 1990s" (2000), available online at http://www.ce-review.org/00/19/kinoeye19_pavicic.html (accessed 3 November 2011), and a

feature films to date have all been daring forays into new artistic, ethical, and political realms, opening up new vistas and possibilities to their audiences, and taking considerable risks in the process. Brešan's first film, *How the War Began on My Island* (*Kako je počeo rat na mom otoku*, 1996), is a comedy made at a time when laughter was all but prohibited in relation to the subject of the Croatian Homeland War (*Domovinski rat*, 1991–5; also referred to abroad as the "Croatian War of Independence"). He proceeded with another comedy at the end of the decade, *Marshal Tito's Spirit* (*Maršal*, 1999), staging a hilarious conflict between the socialist past and post-socialist present, in which both come to be seen in ways very different from the dominant ones of the time. Brešan took the unexpected turn of leaving his successful comedy path to make an internationally acclaimed and cinematically masterful war drama, *Witnesses* (*Svjedoci*, 2003), and a post-war love story with elements of a thriller, *Will Not End Here* (*Nije kraj*, 2008). At the time of this writing, he is marking his return to comedy with making of his newest feature, *The Priest's Children* (*Svećenikova djeca*).

The Renaissance Touch of *How the War Began on My Island*

"*... banish plump Jack, and banish all the world.*"
Falstaff to Prince Henry, *King Henry IV*

The popular success of *How the War Began on My Island* can perhaps be preliminarily attributed to one thing: the film returns to laughter and comedy, which were sorely absent in the cultural landscape of the first half of the 1990s, affected as it was with the high drama of profound changes: the proclamation of Croatia's independence, war and the attendant material destruction, human losses and displacements, immense social changes connected to transition from socialism to capitalism. The solid assertion of laughter and playfulness in Brešan's first film was embraced *en*

---

volume *In Contrast: Croatian Film Today*, ed. Aida Vidan and Gordana P. Crnković, *KinoKultura* Special Issue #11, available online at http://www.kinokultura.com/specials/11/croatian.shtml (accessed 6 December 2011).

masse by the Croatian audience that made this the most watched Croatian film in Croatia since its independence, responding enthusiastically to a comedy that departed from realism into the realm of parody and caricature.

The plot of the film revolves around a small island community which, at the very beginning of the war in Croatia, is trying to persuade the commander of the Yugoslav People's Army base to release from military service all of the young men stationed there, as well as to give up all of the ammunition. The commander, Aleksa, an ethnic Serb, is hesitating to decide the matter and is also rather inept, preferring to wait for orders while watching the island folk address him day after day in (usually unintentionally) funny ways, from a stage they have erected in front of the base. Eventually, a daring action by the people on the outside works out: the father of one of the soldiers impersonates an officer of the Yugoslav People's Army, and orders Aleksa to fill the trucks with ammunition and put his own son in one of them. The loaded trucks successfully manage to get outside of the post, but once Aleksa realizes that he was tricked, he orders the indiscriminate shooting of people, which causes the death of one of the citizens.

Some of the reviews of the film criticised or else praised the humanization of the enemy figure, which went against the simplification and demonization of all real and proclaimed enemies, present at the time in the officially-promoted nationalist discourse. In other words, commander Aleksa is shown as imperfect, ordinary, often funny, and far from either inhuman or even unlikeable. He is torn between the people and the army once the institution he belongs to, "The Yugoslav People's Army," breaks down, with the *people* of the small unnamed Croatian island (his own wife, friends, neighbors, and his home of many years), falling on one side, and the *army* and its premise of obeying orders on the other. More than because it shows an ordinary man in extraordinary times and put in a predicament of torn loyalties which he cannot solve, and thus re-humanizing the "enemy figure," however, the film is interesting because of a subtle subversion of the more general paradigm of seeing history as a result of a chain of necessities.[3] The

---

[3] This intellectual habit sees private stories as affected by contingencies (e.g., romantic affairs started by a chance encounter), but more broadly national

nationalist discourse in Croatia in the 1990s used to its advantage this "necessity paradigm," repeatedly asserting, for example, that the former Yugoslavia *had* to break apart (rather than, say, re-constitute itself as a democratic confederation), and Croatia *had* to become independent because of some deep underlying reasons, political, historical, economical, and so forth, not because it just happened to happen that way on account of various contingencies.[4] But, as Wittgenstein succinctly put it: "The insidious thing about the causal point of view is that it leads us to say: 'Of course, it had to happen like that.' Whereas we ought to think: It may have happened *like that*—and also in many other ways."[5] In accord with Wittgenstein's insight, in *How the War Began* ... it is not a predestined chain of events, but precisely a combination of various contingencies that make things happen the way they do and that lead to the ultimately fatal resolution—the war.

Brešan's film repeatedly emphasizes the role of contingencies through its own unpredictable twists of plot and the characters' own unforeseeable "changes of heart." The commander's wife, talking to him from the improvised stage, reminisces about their first meeting, their happy marriage, and his love of her *pašticada* (a local specialty). She starts to soften Aleksa, who is wiping away tears and may end up surrendering, but then all of a sudden she remembers his past infidelities, which makes her suddenly fly into a rage—all of that on the stage and in front of the microphone—and

---

or collective history as caused by greater necessities which both explain and justify this particular history as necessary and thus unavoidable. In other words, what happened is seen as what had to happen given some underlying causalities.
[4]These contingencies include, of course, human agency as its very important element.
[5]Ludwig Wittgenstein, *Culture and Value* (1984), 37e. Other theorists have also wrestled with the problem of the tenacity of the causal point of view. Ernesto Laclau and Chantal Mouffe talk about the "morphological necessity" versus "narrative contingency" in their *Hegemony and Socialist Strategy* (1985), and literary critic and theorist Gary Soul Morson writes about "structural givens" versus "narrative freedom," presenting each point in time as a space of many possibilities. The fact that only one possibility is utilized in any given moment does not mean that others could not have been realized; in other words, the fact that something happened the way it did does not mean that it had to happen that way and that it could not have happened otherwise. See G. S. Morson, *Narrative and Freedom: The Shadows of Time* (1994).

Fig 8.1 *How the War Began on my Island* (1996) (courtesy of Vinko Brešan)

causes her husband to make the sensible decision to remain safely inside the post rather than face her wrath. The plot did not have to end with Aleksa becoming so mad that he orders the shooting at the civilians outside. This whole story leading to war did not have to happen the way it did, its twists and turns were caused by a number of contingencies (including decisions made by individuals), rather than by any underlying causality, and the film's emphasis on these contingencies in its answer to that title question ("how did the war start?") throws a wholly different light on the master-narrative of the country's history that was being created in that period by those in power and by the kind of nationalist discourse they promoted. If history is largely created by contingencies (including human activity that could have proceeded differently), rather than by major underlying causalities, then existing conflicts and problems could have been dealt with in different ways, and the whole recent history did not have to happen the way it did.

The main aspect of this film, however, may not be the subversion of the perception of history as necessary rather than largely happening on account of a number of contingencies, but instead a "Rabelaisian" moment of a carnivalesque affirmation of and return to humanity as such, non-reducible to any nationalist identity. In *Rabelais and His World*, Mikhail Bakhtin writes that, during the carnival, "[p]eople [are], so to speak, reborn for new, purely human relations,"[6] and "discover the gay relativity of [political] events as well as of the entire political problem they presented."[7] Laughter, unpredictability, and playfulness characterize this unruly humanity. People on the island are attractive not because they are heroes or embodiments of this or that idealized nationalist trait, but because they are themselves—and that to an exaggerated extent which turns these people into the over-sized caricatures of their own idiosyncratic individualities, and creates a comic effect as well as gives a welcome respite from the relentless realism of both real life and art at the time.

The imminent danger to the whole island makes people put everything aside and try to deal with this danger through performance rather than through confrontational action. Much of the film's action takes place on the stage. People sing, play, plead, make *ad hoc* speeches, and so on. The moment is carnivalesque, creating a time outside of ordinary life, a unique realm with its own rules. "Carnival is not a spectacle seen by the people; they live in it ... While carnival lasts, there is no other life outside it."[8] People performing often forget their intended audience (commander Aleksa), and come fully into their own being in these performances: a poet (Ivica Vidović) is that, a poet who recites and walks in a dream-like state; and similarly the wife of the commander is primarily a wife, who forgets her patriotic mission of softening her husband the moment she remembers his affairs.

The liberating laughter of *How the War Began ...* undermines the ideology of nationalism and the dominance of the nation over the individual. The inimitable individualities of the island's folk assert themselves to the fullest against all nationalist identity constraints in a series of comic mishaps and in moving performances. At the end, this "poetry" of individualism retreats, faced with violence. As the shooting starts, the island people flee the stage; the only person who gets killed is the old poet who does not exit the stage,

---

[6]Mikhail Bakhtin, *Rabelais and His World* (1984), 10.
[7]Bakhtin (1984), 448.
[8]Bakhtin (1984), 7.

continuing to recite his poetry. This ending is obviously symbolic: when the bullets fly, poetry dies, and not only that personified by the old romantic poet, but more importantly human poetry of every individual's unruly uniqueness.

Vinko Brešan's first film acts as a powerful reminder to people of who they are, aside and above nationalist frames, a reminder that they will destroy their own humanity and spirit if they stop laughing and asserting their absurd, playful and wonderful personalities.[9] In addition, the film makes a clear distinction between home and nation, and gives primacy to home. "Our island" from the title is emphatically not our nation but rather our home, because the island as a home can include other nations (islanders keep telling the Serbian commander Aleksa that this Croatian island is his home), whereas nation, though larger, constructs itself as a much more exclusive concept. Also, "home" is a tangible place of one's everyday life and daily interactions, and not an

---

[9]The light laughter of *How the War Began on My Island* was therapeutic in the bleak 1990s, and although its particular side-effects—liberating display of multifaceted humanity as opposed to one-dimensional identity defined primarily by national denomination—were probably not consciously apprehended by many who saw it, they were arguably sensed on some level by both the audience and the authorities, as evidenced in the popular approval shown by the record viewing numbers on one hand, and by the often negative initial reception on the side of the more dogmatic nationalist reviewers. Indeed, "only after it [*How the War Began on My Island*] went over 100,000 viewers, many started revising their opinion about Brešan's film as non-serious, and perhaps even suspect making fun of the important theme of the Homeland War (which should perhaps be even prohibited), and became fervent defenders of this film." (Tomislav Kurelec, 2004: 70–1. I should add that I am also grateful to Kurelec for pointing out the connections between *How the War Began on My Island* and *comedia dell'arte*: "with the similar formal device of stylization and emphasizing of the individual characteristics of mutually very different characters, also underlying their comic quality with the frequent use of the close-ups in which excellent cameraman Živko Zalar uses wisely the distorting wide lens, *How the War Began on My Island* creates, just as *commedia dell' arte*, the representative gallery of the weird characters, whose interaction creates a funny, but also complex image of the times, and in Brešan's film it is Dalmatia at the beginning of the Homeland War. ... it is precisely the stage ... with whose lively diversity the islanders attempt to conquer the dogmatic spirit which rules the army." [Ibid., 120–1]. Kurelec sees this film as a successful combination of "the elements of Mediterranean type which come from *commedia dell' arte* with the elements of Central European mostly 'Švejkian' origin." [Ibid., 71].)

"imagined community,"[10] and again, this real place of home is shown as a smaller but more inclusive realm, able to include what the imagined concept of nation cannot, that is members of the other nation. The whole process of nationalism is also shown as a process of abstraction from the fullness of real lives into the flattening concepts and myths that literally take away a multitude of life's aspects. Brešan's film points away from a situation enforced by wars, in which people are reduced to their national identity, to a past marked by the reality of home with its emphasis on family, local community, and idiosyncratic individuals themselves. And lastly, by setting the story of the film in a small island town on the margins of the Croatian state, the film is able to create a space where the influences of the center and its ideology and discourses are weaker, and the personal eccentricity and poetry of individual lives can flourish.

The Past is Here to Stay: *Marshal Tito's Spirit*

"Protect brotherhood and unity as the pupil of your eye!"
("Čuvajte bratstvo i jedinstvo kao zjenicu oka svoga!",
Tito's famous saying, used in the film)

The fact that the title of this film in the Croatian original does not have any personal name attached to it, that it is reduced to the bare apposition ("Marshal"), which had to be complemented by a specific name to conjure up the same person for the English-speaking audience, testifies to the reality of there being only one Marshal for the Croatian audience—Tito. Born in 1892 in Kumrovec, Croatia, then part of Austro-Hungary, Josip Broz Tito was a leader of the Yugoslav anti-fascist partisan resistance during World War Two and a long-time president of Yugoslavia. He died in 1980. While the cult of Tito was institutionally sustained during the Yugoslav era, the positive and often admiring attitude towards Tito seems to be doing remarkably well on its own in the post-Yugoslav

---

[10] "Imagined community" is Benedict Anderson's much employed concept of a nation which draws attention to the conceptual nature of an allegedly natural national grouping.

Fig 8.2 Concert for the visitors of the island, *Marshal Tito's Spirit* (1999) (courtesy of Inter Film, Zagreb)

era, recreated and maintained by the people themselves throughout the whole territory of the Former Yugoslavia, as Mitja Velikonja's fascinating book *Titostalgia* amply demonstrates.[11]

Like Brešan's first film, *Marshal Tito's Spirit* is also a comedy. After the citizens of a small island town start witnessing repeated appearances of someone who very much looks like Tito in his older age, and is taken by some to be Tito's ghost and by others to be Tito himself, the island confronts the onset of a special kind of tourism—partisan veterans, now rather old themselves, come from all over Dalmatia looking for their supreme commander. They soon realize that "Tito" is actually being impersonated by a patient of the local mental clinic who indeed believes he is Tito and who does have an uncanny resemblance to the real president of the former Yugoslavia. Nevertheless they decide to proclaim that Tito is still alive; their goal is to use Tito's presence in an attempt to bring socialism back to the island, which would be the beginning of creating a socialist society in the whole of Croatia. The veterans, led by their former commander Marinko (Ilija Ivezić), make the

---

[11] Mitja Velikonja: *Titostalgia: A Study of Nostalgia for Josip Broz* (2009).

whole town look like it might have looked in the socialist era, with citizens getting appropriate roles as well. The entrepreneurial town mayor Luka (Ivo Gregurević) plays along for the material gains from this new kind of tourism, and the whole thing is investigated by a young policeman, Stipan (Dražen Kuhn), a native of the island, and his two local aides.

Like *How the War Began on My Island*, *Marshal Tito's Spirit* is again characterized by the Renaissance carnivalesque mode set in Mediterranean scenery full of sun and bright colors. This time, however, the role-playing encompasses the whole universe of the film rather than only an isolated character or only one line of the plot. Acting the role of someone else had been limited in Brešan's first film to one character, the austere art historian from Zagreb pretending to be an equally austere Yugoslav People's Army officer. By contrast, the play in *Marshal Tito's Spirit* envelops the whole island town with all its people. There are appropriate socialist slogans on the walls, parades celebrating labor, rituals of carrying the birthday *štafeta* (baton) to Tito, revolutionary speeches, a revolutionary court, recordings of Tito's speeches booming over loudspeakers, and the embodiment of Tito himself present in the authentic uniform perfectly delivering Tito's famous lines. The people don appropriate costumes (including a young pioneer-imitating uniform worn by the elderly townspeople carrying the *štafeta*, creating an effect both comic and grotesque), and act out their roles. The entrepreneurial mayor endorses his own role most enthusiastically, giving fluent speeches in the "socialist lingo": "comrades, socialism is built by workers, peasants, and the honest intelligentsia!" He steps out of his role only to outline the bright economic future of this new revolutionary ghost-hunting tourist trend: "... then we'll get the ghost of Honecker here, that's the German market, they have money, and then the ghost of Stalin, the ghost of Mao Tse-Tung ... A hundred and twenty million Russians and a billion Chinese, hey!!!" The lightness of the performative playfulness and the rules of comedy transform everything into a game, and ensure that even clashes are not violent: despite the presence of weapons and a few blows, no gun is fired and no one gets hurt.

Making this collective political performance into the focus of the film may imply that any form of political behavior can be genuine for some but largely a performance for the others. By highlighting the performative aspect of politics, *Marshal Tito's Spirit* also shows how those in power can make others act according to their screenplay, whether it be acting in support of a socialist Yugoslavia of "brotherhood and unity," or, for example, the nationalist fervor characterizing the new Croatia in the early 1990s. The performances may be scripted in the spirit of this or that era, but their underlying logic remains the same, and it is always rather hard to see whether someone's political behavior is a performance or the "real thing."

Though humorous in many aspects, *Marshal Tito's Spirit* as a whole strikes a much heavier note than *How the War Began on My Island*, and gives more of a direct social commentary. First, the fact that the main protagonists are veteran partisans of World War Two cannot fail to remind one of the then-current situation of these people, of what they did and still stand for, as well as of the situation in which the retired population at the time in general found itself. In the 1990s, under the watch of Tuđman's government, the legacy of the anti-fascist struggle in Croatia was on the whole suppressed and falsified. As Jelena Lovrić wrote: "In Croatian schools one could not find out basic facts about the nature of World War Two, nor about who the partisans were and who the *ustashas*."[12] Instead, "Tuđman's government flirted with '*ustashluk*,' de facto leading to its rehabilitation. Generations were formed with no idea of the historical facts, or with a twisted one ... For the whole decade the nation had its brain washed with suggestions that *ustashas* were the real and firmest Croats, the model of patriotism."[13]

---

[12] Jelena Lovrić: "Ustašama—nikad bolje. Crne košulje opet su u modi." *Globus* (Zagreb), 3 December 2004, p. 19.

[13] Lovrić (2004), 19. Vjekoslav Perica substantiates Lovrić's claims: "After 1992, in the newly independent Croatia, Tuđman allowed, and in some cases personally initiated, symbolic reminiscences of the NDH [*Nezavisna država Hrvatska*; Independent State of Croatia]. The key national institution—a national council or assembly known long ago under the common Slavic term *Sabor* (community), popular gathering, assembly)—adopted the unique *Ustaša* title *Hrvatski državni Sabor* (the Croatian State Assembly), which this institution had borne only from 1941 to 1945. Former Ustaše, returning from exile, appeared in public, and many were honored with high state offices and pensions. Streets in two Croatian cities were named after one of the top *Ustaša* leaders during the Second World War, Mile Budak, executed by communists and therefore, supposedly a hero. The Ustaša leader (*poglavnik*) Ante Pavelić, was commemorated in public meetings and in churches full of eminent

In the 1990s, partisan veterans of Croatia were not invited to schools and community centers to relate their World War Two experiences and help preserve the collective memory of their heroic fight unique in Europe—historian Robin Okey calls it "the resistance movement *par excellence* of the war"—in a manner similar to that in which, say, D-Day or other World War Two veterans in the US still relate their memories in public venues and are uniformly honored.[14] On the contrary, Croatian veterans had been humiliated and their legacy falsified, a legacy that includes the fact that "the communist-led partisans stood out consistently for ... the 'brotherhood and unity' of the Yugoslav peoples," and that even as early as "the time Tito declared a provisional government in autumn 1943, he had 275,000 people under arms,"[15] who,

---

individuals from the country's political, cultural, and business circles. [See dossier "Hrvatski fašizam," in *Feral Tribune*, No. 713 (17 May 1999), pp. 6–10.] Militant neo-*Ustaša* groups attacked opposition leaders, disrupted opposition rallies, and physically attacked union leaders and anti-fascists who commemorated the World War II Partisan resistance. ... More than 3,000 memorials dedicated to World War II antifascist resistance have been dynamited or otherwise damaged. According to the Croatian World War II veterans' association, which labored on rebuilding destroyed monuments, this symbolic destruction was not merely a spontaneous outburst of HDZ militancy but in some cases planned activity carried out by ruling party, state, and Church. [Radio Free Europe/Radio Liberty, *Newsline* (7 June 1997), online version at http://www.rferl.org.]." Vjekoslav Perica (2001), 60.

A commentator Vlado Vurušić reminds that Franjo Tuđman "already at the first conference of HDZ in 1990," said "how NDH was not only a crime but also an expression of a desire of Croatian people for their own state," a statement that could be seen as giving a green light to subsequent efforts to redeem or even glorify NDH, or to the situation in which, in Vurušić's words, "we shall even be denounced as not good enough Croatians if we point at the fact that NDH was, to put it mildly, one of the darkest periods of Croatian history." (Vlado Vurušić: "Tko je u škole pustio knjigu u kojoj se minorizira Jasenovac?" *Jutarnji list* (Zagreb), 15 December 2005, p. 18.) Although having "independent" in its name, NDH was not an independent entity but rather a Nazi puppet state "in which German and Italian commanders ... had more power than Croatian government," [Ibid.] and that relinquished large parts of Croatia to Italy and Hungary. For more on this period see Sabrina P. Ramet ed., *Nezavisna država Hrvatska [Independent State of Croatia]* (2009). Other excellent sources include Slavko Goldstein's *1941. Godina koja se vraća [1941. A Year that Keeps Returning]* (2007), and Ivo Banac's "The Fearful Asymmetry of War: The Causes and Consequences of Yugoslavia's Demise" (1992).

[14] Robin Okey: *Eastern Europe 1740–1985: Feudalism to Communism* (1986), 185.
[15] Okey (1986), 185.

increased in numbers to some 800,000 soldiers, liberated most of Yugoslavia by the end of the war. The 1990s witnessed the renaming of some 10,000 city squares and streets that bore names related to the anti-fascist struggle, one of the most famous cases being the renaming of Zagreb's *Square of the Victims of Fascism* (*Trg žrtava fašizma,* the place of the infamous *ustasha* headquarters during the war) into first *The Square of Croatian Rulers* and then *The Square of Croatian Greats* (the name *Square of the Victims of Fascism* was restored in 2000), the harassment of the people fighting for the preservation of these names and related collective memory, the lack of proper government protection of them, and the destruction of some 3,500 anti-fascist monuments by perpetrators who were not found or not prosecuted.[16]

Along with other retirees, veterans had been cheated out of their retirement funds in financial scams, and many of them had by the end of the 1990s become impoverished. These veterans also embody en entire generation that was at the height of its strength during and after World War Two, the generation that rebuilt a war-devastated country and created much of the country's resources after that war. According to the policy at the time, significant parts of the economic revenue did not go back to specific nationalized enterprises where this revenue was created, or into workers' salaries, but was rather directed into the development of collectively important projects such as ports, shipyards, railways, schools, and so on. This generation as a whole gave much of their work to the community, and in the 1990s this never paid labor, officially donated to the community and creating much of its collective goods, was privatized according to new laws, and transferred into the hands of a very few having ties with the ruling circles.

In short, the veterans in the film function as the rich symbols that bring to the screen many issues ailing Croatia of the 1990s: the suppression of something it should loudly proclaim (the history of the anti-fascist struggle unique in all of Europe), the massive embezzlement from all of the Croatian people but especially from

---

[16] The numbers cited in this sentence come from Paula Bobanović, "Mesić, Sanader i Račan brane Tita", in *Nacional* (Zagreb), no. 476 (28 December 2004), p. 21.

the senior population, and the criminal privatization of collective goods created and donated largely by this older population.

A second issue brought by the film revolves around the figure of Tito himself, a focal point of the film. The life-long president of Yugoslavia and a native of Croatia, Tito was esteemed on account of his leading the anti-fascist fight during World War Two, a break with Stalin in 1948, skillful maneuvering between the East and the West during the Cold War era, his founding of the Non-Aligned Movement with Egypt's Gamal abd al-Nasir and India's Jawaharlal Nehru, and his presiding over attempts to create a unique self-management form of economy and society. Although his legacy in post-Yugoslavia's Croatia has been viewed more critically, partly because of the legitimate reassessment of issues that were not dealt with during the Yugoslav era (e.g., the treatment of the political prisoners or the suppression of the 1971 Croatian Spring),[17] and more because of the 1990s Croatian government's agenda that portrayed everything related to Yugoslavia and Tito in a negative light, there are indications that Tito still seems to be by far the most popular and respected Croat of all times. In a survey by the weekly *Nacional*, he overwhelmingly led the popularity list: "Josip Broz Tito, a partisan commander and a long-time president of Yugoslavia, is the greatest Croat in history. This is the result of the largest public opinion survey to date."[18] While *Marshal Tito's*

---

[17] Regarding accusations leveled at Tito for the execution of the "people's enemies" at the end of the World War Two and under his watch, a Croatian historian Zorica Stipetić notes: "It is certain that Tito has his share of responsibility ... but I have to mention that documents that relativize this were published a number of times (e.g., in Ridley's book [Jasper Ridley's *Tito: A Biography* (London: Constable, 1994)], Prometej publication). Tito's telegram from Belgrade to the main headquarters of the Slovenian partisan army, dated 14 May 1945, prohibits in the most stern way the execution of the prisoners of the war and commands the transferal of the possible suspects to the military court." Zorica Stipetić, "An interview with a historian Zorica Stipetić." *Nacional*, 425 (6 January 2004), p. 52.

[18] "Tito najveći Hrvat u povijesti", in *Nacional*, 425 (6 January 2004), pp. 46–9. "[Tito's] realistic importance is most precisely clarified by [historian] Ivo Goldstein in an interview for *Nacional*, when he said that Tito was the only Croatian politician who was significant in the world arena, and who, connected with that, has decisively influenced the situation in the country." Ibid.

Assessing Tito's legacy related to the partisan fight in World War Two and Croatia, the themes forcefully brought into Brešan's film by its featuring of Tito's partisan veterans, historian Zorica Stipetić briefly summarizes:

Spirit employs Tito's famous instructions, such as "Protect brotherhood and unity as the pupil of your eye!", and "Let us work as if peace will last for a hundred years, let us prepare as if the war will happen tomorrow!", the film also remembers some of Tito's less known words as well, creating a more complex image of who the man was.

Third, the film draws attention to the 1990s' official lack of constructive dealing with the Yugoslav past, which, instead of being understood and used as a foundation on which to build, was either demonized or else simply discarded without ever having been rationally assessed. Much of the film takes place in an abandoned town museum which now houses discarded paraphernalia from the recent past—socialist-era statues and Yugoslav flags, symbols, pictures, slogans, even a bed in which Tito slept during his 1944 stay on the island of Vis—now chaotically thrown together and not marked or elaborated on in any way. The film brings this past back

---

Tito prepared the KPJ [Communist Party of Yugoslavia] for the resistance to the foreseen fascist aggression even at the time when the Soviet–German pact about mutual non-attack was still in power. That is why he was able, while all of Europe was on its knees in front of Hitler, to call the whole of Yugoslavia to rise up. During four years of the partisan warfare, Tito created, in opposition to both the Soviets and the British, the foundations for the federal organization of the country, for the affirmation of all peoples (the second meeting of AVNOJ in 1943), and for new forms of government: from the early partisan units and peasant self-protection he created a respectable regular army with more than 800,000 soldiers in four armies. ["AVNOJ," *Antifašističko Vijeće Narodnog Oslobođenja Jugoslavije*, means the "Antifascist Assembly of the People's Liberation of Yugoslavia"] Aside from the not important intervention of the Soviet Army on the North-East of Yugoslavia in the fall of 1944, that [indigenous] army had on its own liberated the whole country by the middle of May 1945 ... At the same time Tito annexed to the mainland Croatia Istria and part of the Adriatic coast which were given to Italy after the World War I, and he returned those parts of the country which were given to Italy, Hungary, and Bulgaria in the 1941 occupation. Today's Croatia is bordered with those AVNOJ's borders. This anti-fascist struggle ... saved Serbs in Croatia from the liquidation which was carried out practically and programmatically by the *ustashas*, and it also saved Croats from a potentially terrible Serb retaliation after the war. The long-time future of Croatia was assured precisely in that war, and we today are the inheritors of such a conclusion of the war. At any rate, it is precisely in Croatia where the People's Liberation Struggle [*NOB;* "*Narodnooslobodilačka borba*"] was the strongest and the best organized."

("An interview with a historian Zorica Stipetić.")

through its theatrical re-enactment, and allows us another look at this history by presenting us with a parodied impersonation of it. The island's re-enactment presents this past as a conglomerate of actions done by those who did things for their own benefit while "performing," or merely paying lip service to the greater good, but also by those who genuinely desired and attempted to achieve this greater community good with their actions and work. Altogether, *Marshal Tito's Spirit* articulates the need for a new and critical evaluation of the past, and comes across as sympathetic with it yet not uncritically taken in by it.

Finally, the film articulates a strong indictment of Croatia in the last decade of the twentieth century, with the mayor being the embodiment of the new government and what it did in the name of "national interests." In the words of Marinko, the mayor "bought half of the town for two *kunas*," which is a reference to the practice of "privatization" or the transferal of social goods to private hands, benefiting a small circle of people close to the governing circles and resulting in overall economic deterioration rather than improvement. The term "privatization" had become synonymous in the latter 1990s with the legalized theft of collective and collectively achieved goods. The mayor in the film has thus been able to buy his city's museum, hotel, and so on, for next to nothing. As he himself puts it: "oh well, it wasn't expensive ... if it had been expensive I wouldn't have bought it." The new "special forces" sent to the island from the capital, Zagreb, a young man and woman dressed in black, slim and "cool," with sun glasses and cell phones, are also representatives of the new times, a clear reference to the Western role models which Croats are supposed to emulate, and they are shown without much sympathy, as flat and boring characters who are unlikable, cold-blooded, and lifeless—which in the universe of Brešan's first two films may be the worst trait of all. They bring to mind vampires with their hyper-white skin and their black clothes in contrast to the colourful, tanned Dalmatian folk of all shapes, and the efficiency they visually symbolize according to the codes of contemporary Hollywood-originated mass iconography (thin, "perfect" bodies, in great shape, cold and to the point) dissolves rather rapidly when confronted with aging partisan veterans.

Marshal Tito's Spirit enacts a theatrical clash between past and present, with the past inevitably losing, yet doing so in a grand gesture which inspires wonder. In the final sequence of the film the man impersonating Tito gets on a small boat, alone, and the boat drifts away on the open sea with the "Marshal" standing on it firmly and looking into the horizon and the setting sun, never turning back to look toward the coast. With "Tito" standing and giving himself to the sea, this scene enacts departure and death, as well as fearlessness in front of it. The present returns to normalcy, with veterans refusing to go into the sea after their supreme commander, and with their commander Marinko, who did start going after "Tito" and is waist-high in the water, himself stopping and saluting him. The policeman throws his hat in the air and then he and a young woman teacher, who happens to be "Tito's" daughter, embrace each other, replaying the motive of the assertion of life with its genuine human relations, which literally turns its back to politics—locked in a long kiss, the two do not even notice that the small boat with Tito is slowly drifting away. The final scene of the film, however, is a very brief one touching on the profound impact, yet to be fully realized and assessed, which the real Tito has had on his own posterity, and the present and future of Croatia. The policeman's deputies, two young island men who have come to maturity in the post-Tito and post-Yugoslav era, and who are throughout the film seen mostly as being either high on grass or else comically incompetent, look at the Marshal's final disappearance with an unusually alert and astonished gaze. After a moment of reflection, one says: "Well, it was honorable living with Tito" (*"Pa bilo je časno živjeti s Titom,"* a re-phrase of the famous Tito-era slogan "it *is* honorable to live with Tito"), and the other one responds curtly "Tito is the law" (*"Tito je zakon"*), using slang ("this or that is the law") for something that is thoroughly fundamental and beyond question.

Witnesses

"I said that [Croatia] must deal with the system of evil in its own midst."

Vinko Brešan[19]

---

[19] Dean Sinovčić, "Stav o hrvatskim zločinima ponovit ću i u Beogradu" [An interview with Vinko Brešan], in *Nacional* (17 February 2004), pp. 70–2.

Based on Jurica Pavičić's novel *Plaster Sheep*, discussed in the previous chapter, the story of *Witnesses* takes place in 1992 in the Croatian city of Karlovac. The film begins with the unintended murder of a Serbian civilian perpetrated by three Croatian soldiers who had planned to bomb the man's house—which was supposed to be empty—and intimidate rather than kill him. The center of the story's suspense is the destiny of the slain man's young daughter, who witnessed the murder and has now been abducted by the three soldiers who are trying to decide what to do with her.

The narrative procedure employed in this film resembles that used in films such as David Lynch's *Mullholand Drive* or Christopher Nolan's *Memento*, and also brings to mind procedures of some older movies such as Francis Ford Coppola's *The Conversation* or Antonioni's *Blow-up*. *Witnesses* is not built from a series of sequences that appear only once during the film and progress chronologically. Rather, a small number of sequences are repeated in various versions, each time returning a certain part of the story to its beginning point, and each time adding or changing our view of some crucial piece of information by, for instance, being shot from a different place which allows a different view of the events happening, or by including new material before or after the already-seen sequence. An example of this procedure involves the return from the front to the city of Krešo, a brother of one of the three soldiers involved in the murder, and one of the film's central characters. Krešo's girlfriend Lidija, a journalist who suspects that the slain man's daughter witnessed the murder and was probably kidnapped or killed, and who is now trying to unearth the story and help the girl, looks out from her window to see Krešo standing behind a car, which blocks the view of his lower body. She ecstatically runs down the stairs to meet him. The second time this sequence appears it lasts a moment longer: the car pulls away, and we now see that Krešo has a missing leg and crutches, which at that point comes as a complete surprise to both Lidija and the audience.

Witnesses plays masterfully with the distinction between a story, a chronological development of a story in a real time, and *sujet*, the way a narrative art form relates this story, sometimes cutting it into constituent parts and then re-assembling these parts in non-chronological ways. Chronologically, the story of *Witnesses* does not start with the murder of a civilian, but at some point before the murder,

Fig 8.3 The three soldiers, *Witnesses* (2003) (courtesy of Inter Film, Zagreb)

a point which led to this murder. The story then goes onto the murder and continues after it, to the resolution of the kidnapped girl's destiny. In the film, however, the sequences from the past and from the long-evolving present are mixed, and one is able to understand only gradually what sequences came before and what after; what happened in the past and what is happening now; and thus also, most importantly, what events can be seen as causes of other ones and what events as consequences. We see a repeated sequence, for instance, in which the mother of Krešo and his younger brother sits in a room of her house, in whose garage the little girl is hidden. We see only a close-up of her face in semi-darkness, and hear shots fired outside the house. Given that we don't know until the very end of the film when this shooting happens, we can only guess: if it happens at the end, it may mean that the girl witness is indeed being killed; if before, then who is shooting at whom? When? And why?

Witnesses activates the potentials of the Brechtian *Entfremdung* effect which calls for a certain distancing from, and an analytical appreciation of, what is happening before our eyes in order to arrive at some insights, instead of a total immersion with the material along the lines of most common contemporary Hollywood-influenced cinema of empathy and catharsis. While we are asked to construct both the present story (the unintended murder of a man, kidnapping of his daughter, and what comes after), and the past one (events at the battle front in which the involved soldiers participated before coming back to their city for a short break in which this all happens), our practice of doing so becomes also an ethical practice of speculating about the characters, their deeds and their motives, and about the more general individuals' behavior in times of crisis and violence. *Witnesses* draws us into a guessing game, judgments and—most importantly—successive radical revisions of those judgments and attendant facing up to our own presuppositions which shaped those previous judgments, now shown to be wrong. Here we make ethical judgments about depicted individuals but also, and more importantly, about our own thinking and behavior, and we make these reflections during the movie but also—hopefully—in the aftermath of the viewing itself. *Witnesses*, in other words, invites and informs the practicing of our ethical judgments about the events and people's behavior shown in the film as well as, of course, about related things in the "real" world.

The story is built from puzzle pieces whose ever-new constellations change our understanding of what we actually see and how we comprehend and judge that which we are seeing. Through the course of the film we are constructing a chain of past events which led to the murder of a Serbian civilian; and it is this murder that opens the film. There is a repeated scene in which the three soldiers sit in a bar, drink, and talk about a local Serbian merchant who owns not just a house but "rather a villa, from whose windows he watches funerals [presumably of Croatian soldiers and civilian victims] like cartoons," as Krešo's brother puts it. The first time we see this scene it is followed by another one in which the three soldiers, with their car lights off, drive to the Serbian merchant's house to destroy it. The connection seems a clear one between the hate talk and the consequent violence. Later on we see an event which presumably happened in the more distant past, in which the three soldiers are seen clearing enemy territory and killing a man who runs out of one house shooting at them, along with a woman who ran in front of this man (perhaps pushed by him), and was shouting "Don't shoot! I am a Croat, a Croat!", and in which action the father of Krešo and of his brother, the father who was himself the soldier of the Croatian Army and in the same unit as the three soldiers, gets killed. We see now the murder, started by Krešo's brother's words, as a more personal one, a misplaced revenge for the death of a father. Later still, however, we revise this judgment as well. We see again the conversation in the bar sequence, but now we see and hear the part of it which directly preceded the three soldiers' discussion of the Serbian merchant. In this previous part of the conversation they ask themselves whether the woman whom they killed may really have been a Croat, and if so, what she was doing in "enemy territory" (under Serbian military control). Krešo's brother says something like "Why would she not be there? That was where her house was, everything she had, where would she go?" and then makes a comparison with their own local "enemy citizen," a Serbian merchant in a Croatian territory city, about whom he says something like "Well, see this Vasić of ours, he also stays where his house is ..."

But then Krešo's brother makes a crucial turn in his speech, and jumps from a comparison asserting some commonality in human behavior (people stay where their homes are), and thus some commonality between a Croat woman and a Serbian man staying in newly "enemy" territories, to the hate speech which again completely alienates the Serbian merchant, speech in which Krešo's brother proceeds to say that it is not a house but rather a villa that Vasić has ("what—'house!'—villa!"), from whose windows "he watches funerals like cartoons." This turn in speech can now be seen as the fatal beginning or main cause of the soldiers' later hate crime. In other words, this particular speech is more of a cause of this crime than any real event, including Krešo and his brother's loss of their father, given that his brother could respond to this loss in a number of ways other than with a speech attributing the guilt to an unconnected local person.

It is only at this point that we realize that the three soldiers' conversation, which preceded the murder and kidnapping, is not only about the recently killed father, but also about their own unintended killing of a civilian woman in the same action. Now we see this conversation as more complex, struggling with the contradictory position of being both persecutor and victim. This position of psychological and ethical impasse makes a fertile environment in which one person can seize the conversation (which could have gone in some other direction), and lead it away from uncharted and hard-to-bear intellectual and emotional terrain onto the familiar and thus comforting terrain of a speech which replicates on a private level with known acquaintances the nationalist demonization of a whole people of "enemy ethnicity," and leads to another unplanned, haphazard murder of yet another civilian. Krešo's brother responds to his intimate crisis brought by the war—becoming a victim and a murderer in the same moment—with what is "out there," the nationalist talk pushed on the public by the government and the government-orchestrated media, and adds his own creative spin to this pre-given talk.

Krešo's younger brother, as it turns out, has a history of having been a "trouble-maker." We learn of his having been a problem child, and in a scene from the war where he, Krešo, and their fellow soldiers are seen guarding two captured enemy soldiers in an open field, he starts urinating on them and does it until Krešo notices and stops him. In a continuation of this scene, Krešo's brother walks up to a small roadside shrine with some sheep made of plaster placed in it and reaches out to touch them; at that moment one of the prisoners yells "Don't touch that! We mined it!", and he withdraws his hand quickly. The next time this sequence appears is towards the end of the film, when it goes further and we see its conclusion. Krešo's brother is now idly lying on the grass some distance from the shrine, looking bored. He says: "I bet I'll manage to hit the sheep!", and right away, without giving anyone a chance to respond, throws a stone at the altar. An explosion follows and as the smoke clears Krešo's brother yells: "I got it!" The camera closes in on Krešo, who is sitting grotesquely on the grass and looking at his leg, folded unnaturally beside him.

It was not the enemy soldiers who mined the sheep that ultimately claimed Krešo's leg, but rather his own brother's destructive imagination and impulsiveness, in a similar way in which a Serbian civilian is not killed because of some other more apparent reasons, but primarily because of Krešo's brother's words which directed the impasse and despair the three soldiers found themselves in. When Krešo comes home after the rehabilitation and hears his girlfriend Lidija telling him about the murder and possible kidnapping of a child, he is at first unwilling to help, but soon after he finds out that he cannot do otherwise, given his own internal make-up, than try to help Lidija. He gradually discovers that his brother is involved and that his mother may be hiding the kidnapped girl. Krešo's battle for the girl's life is now not against the enemy at the front, but rather against his own brother and mother.

> *Whoever works in film and has managed to push the line of freedom, be it political, artistic, or some other type of freedom, does good things. I always have the need to push this line, although, of course, I can't tell how much I have really succeeded. Now, whoever has this kind of need has to accept the fact that pushing the limits creates resistance on the other side. This is natural. I no longer get upset about this. Perhaps when I was younger, I would have gotten worked up, but now I am aware of these social moments. This is, after all, my decision. The point is that you push the limits, then there is a fuss over it, but it has happened and there is no going back. That is a good thing all around.*[20]

The script of *Witnesses* is a result of collaboration between Vinko Brešan, Jurica Pavičić, and cinematographer Živko Zalar. Their script changed many aspects of Pavičić's original novel, *Plaster Sheep*. The novel takes place in the coastal city of Split, while the film is set in the city of Karlovac: aside from Karlovac being on the border of the Croatian *Krajina* territory (occupied in the early 1990s), the move away from the coast also signals a move away from both the atmosphere and the preoccupations of Brešan's first two movies, comedies set in the picturesque setting of the Adriatic islands. Also, the main character Krešo is an unambiguously positive character in the film, who is trying to save the child witness from being killed, whereas he is a much more complex character in the novel, only gradually emerging from self-pity and guilt. But most importantly, the film's script centers on the narrower social microcosm—eventually reduced to just one family—affected by the war, rather than on the wider social *milieu*. The number of characters is reduced from a large number interacting in Pavičić's novel to a smaller number of characters who are more tightly connected,

---

[20] Vidan and Crnković (2011).

thus switching the modus from the novelistic expansiveness and complexity (though that of a successful and suspenseful thriller), into a chamber piece reduced to bare essentials, resembling a Greek drama in the way in which the main conflicts happen among members of a single family. In the novel, it is not anyone from his own family whom Krešo has to confront. But in the film it is Krešo's own brother who participates in the killing of the Serbian civilian and kidnaps his daughter, following the death in the war of his and Krešo's father. Fighting for the child witness's life, Krešo is thus in conflict with his own brother as well as his mother, who would do anything to save her younger son from the consequences of his own actions and thus herself eventually endorses the killing of the girl. The journalist Lidija, who is instrumental in saving the girl, is Krešo's sister in the novel but his girlfriend in the film, and this change is consistent with the film's emerging division in which the "natural" alliances of the given family break up and the main divide appears between Krešo on one hand and his brother and mother on the other. The new alliances that appear in the film are based on profound ethical commonality rather than on belonging—or not—to the same family.

At the end of the film, Krešo and Lidija manage to save the child and drive to the Adriatic coast; we see them from behind in a long shot and long take, standing and looking at the sea, and at that moment the little girl, whom we did not see until the very end of the movie, raises her hand to take Krešo's hand while still looking at the sea, thus forming, as it were, a new family based not on blood ties but rather on basic humanity and great courage.[21]

---

[21] A few critics perceived this ending as stereotypical or kitschy, given that the scene that is already emotionally charged, with the little girl (whom we see for the first time only a few minutes prior to this ending) giving her hand to Krešo, is also accompanied with exultant music and, for the first time in this rain-drenched gray film, with reddish and golden lights of the rising sun. This scene, however, comes across as rather pitch-perfect to me, because it is not intimidated out of its own existence by fixed rules of what is supposed to be kitschy and what not in each and every circumstance, but is instead following the logic of this particular film which, after all the meandering and complex plotting, and all its dark and shadows-textured atmosphere, ends best with the straightforward and differently lit moment.

Also, it could be noted that *Witnesses* was the target of an intense negative media campaign by the right-wing *Croatian Party of Rights* (*Hrvatska Stranka Prava*), which accused the film of being "anti-Croatian." While this was in some

Final Reflections: It Will Not End Here

I make the viewer examine his position inasmuch as I ask myself to do the same. This is the only path that can lead us to answers or potential answers. Of course, here we come back again to the ethical component. For me it is essential, but at the same time I don't set out to make a film by thinking how to convey this or that ethical dimension. I've never worked that way. The script either contains this dimension or it doesn't, there's no help there. If you as a spectator recognize it in my film, this will make me enormously happy.[22]

Brešan's last film to date, *Will Not End Here*, revolves around the relationship between a Croatian Croat man and a Croatian Serb woman which starts with the two being on opposite sides of the gun during Croatia's Homeland War, and ends with their falling in love. The film is an engrossing exploration of the ways in which people (especially the woman in the story) become attached to each other and find themselves through this attachment, as well as draw strength and courage from it to fight the powerful adversarial forces. Including elements of a war drama, a contemporary thriller, and a dark comedy, this film has a number of excellent and thought-provoking aspects.

Vinko Brešan's films promote the values of humanity and laughter, of individual idiosyncrasies not homogenized by the

---

ways to be expected given the still highly nationalistic tone of public debate and discourse in the early 2000s, reasons for hope can be found in the public response to this campaign by the Croatian Association of the Demilitarized Defenders of the Homeland War (*Hrvatska udruga razvojačenih branitelja Domovinskog rata* or HURBDR). In their press conference of 14 April 2004, in Šibenik, the leading figures of that Association said that "[t]he film *Witnesses* is a masterpiece of Croatian film" ("Brešanovi *Svjedoci* su remek djelo" ["Brešan's *Witnesses* are a masterpiece"], in *Novi list* (Rijeka), 15 April 2004), and strongly criticised HSP for its aggressive campaign against that movie. The president of the Association, Vladimir Gojanović, perceptively characterized *Svjedoci* as a film that shows objectively two sides of Croatian society, "one terrible one, and the other which represents the true value of ... the common struggle of citizens and defenders for just, ethical, and spiritually richer society." (Ibid.) He also said: "We tell to all defenders and citizens ... to see the film with a pure heart and without prejudices." (Ibid.)
[22] Vidan and Crnković (2011).

Fig 8.4 Đuro, *Will Not End Here* (2008) (courtesy of Inter Film, Zagreb)

collectivity of nationalist passions or political projects. They re-evaluate the past in a way subversive to the dominant ideologies, and address the more basic need to really see the past for what it was, rather than just use it in this or that way in obeisance to the current political climate. They address problems of the post-socialist transition, privatization, and the concealment of private interests with national rhetoric, and their relevance extends beyond Croatia and the post-Yugoslav region. But Brešan's cinema also promotes an allegiance to humanistic values and the literal tearing apart—if necessary—from "one's own people" and even one's very own family in assertion of this basic humanism. The assertion of universal ethics and humanity over the exclusiveness of the particular group or affiliation is shown in Brešan's films as the *sine qua non* of a healthy individual and society. When, in *Witnesses*, Krešo's younger brother asks Krešo: "You are doing it all because of Lidija, right?", asserting again the logic of tribal and emotional allegiances, Krešo answers: "You still don't understand anything," and this answer can be seen as a direct challenge to the part of the audience that may still "not understand anything," and that should ask itself why Krešo did what he did, and what all of it has to do with them.

Brešan's films assert both the broadly termed "Renaissance" values of individualism, body comedy, satire of ideologies and dogmas, as well as the "Enlightenment" values of one's own critical thinking with one's own head, and of perceiving the human being as the goal of any political practice rather than merely the means of it. These films imagine in front of us, and in given conditions, the world in which identity and practice are not based on one's own allegedly pre-given ties and environment, but rather on one's difficult growing into one's own individual distinction and ethical clarity and courage. In addition to being illuminating and inspiring, these internationally awarded films are also a genuine pleasure to watch, and are steadily increasing Brešan's stature as one of the most renowned film-makers from the territories of the Yugoslav successor states.

9

I am You and You are Me
On Liberating Anti-Nationalism

And thus I would like to send a message to those who worry about my soul, that I do not need any indulgence of theirs for the sin of writing in the language in which I write... because this is my language! And if we do not understand each other "to the end and to the bottom"... this is not because these gentlemen of permits and decrees do not understand what I say and write, but because we have misunderstandings of a different nature.

DANILO KIŠ, *THE ANATOMY LESSON*[1]

To Whose Music do They Dance: the "Underground" Presence of Serbian Culture in Croatia in the 1990s

In the latter part of the 1990s, at time of hostile relations between Croatia and Serbia, the period roughly following the wars in

---

[1] Danilo Kiš, *Čas anatomije* [*The Anatomy Lesson*], (1978), 46. Translated by Gordana P. Crnković.

Slovenia, Croatia, and Bosnia and Herzegovina (1991–5) and before NATO's Spring 1999 bombing of Serbia, there was a solid "underground" presence of Serbian culture in Croatia. This chapter looks at three specific instances of how Serbian culture existed and functioned within Croatian culture of the time: Đorđe Balašević's music, Danilo Kiš's writings, and Srđan Dragojević's 1998 film *The Wounds*.

At a party in the early summer of 1995, which took place in a small apartment in the Croatian capital of Zagreb and was attended mostly by a student crowd in their 20s, I was astonished to see just what kind of music these young people enjoyed. To begin with, it was the rock music of the early 1980s, to which my generation, some 10 years older than the crowd gathered at this specific party, had listened a decade-and-a-half ago, at the time of the existence of the Socialist Federative Republic of Yugoslavia. But the fact that this was "retro" music was not shocking in this age of universal retro-trends in pop culture—the really intriguing aspect of the Zagreb party was that the music was mostly by Serbian bands from the early 1980s. We listened to the group *Idoli* [*The Idols*] and its songs "*The Little Ones*" ["*Maljčiki*"], "*Amerika*," and "*I rarely see you with girls*" ["*Retko te viđam sa devojkama*"], to *Šarlo Akrobata* [*Charles the Acrobat*] and its "*She is waking up*" ["*Ona se budi*"] and "*No one like me*" ["*Niko kao ja*"], to *Disciplina kičme* [*Discipline of the Spine*], and *Pekinška patka* [*Beijing Duck*]. People at the party did not only listen to these songs, they sang along as they were played, knowing their lyrics by heart—and they seemed to genuinely like them.

I was perplexed and intrigued: how was it possible that these young people knew these old Serbian rock songs so well, given the official Croatian environment—at the time—of rigid cultural nationalism and anti-Serbian practices in which they grew up, the cultural nationalism that has accompanied the creation of an independent Croatia and that has, since 1991, literally moved Serbian books to the back rooms or basements of the libraries (or their dumpsters in some cases), erased Serbian authors from the school curricula, and banished Serbian music from the TV and radio airwaves? Where did these young people hear these songs? What, if anything, did these songs mean to them?

Official Croatia of the 1990s did a lot to distinguish Croatian culture from the Serbian one with which it had been connected during the Yugoslav era. The culture of Serbia was often simply defined as the complete opposite, the "other" of Croatian culture: "*they* are Eastern, Oriental, Byzantium, primitive, rural, backwards, violent, while *we* are Western, European, advanced, urban, democratic, and peaceful." What was previously termed in Croatia the Croato-Serbian language (which had officially been called in Croatia in its last renaming *"hrvatski ili srpski,"* "Croatian or Serbian") was now meticulously separated into two languages, Croatian and Serbian, and dictionaries of the differences between the two languages were published. And yet, as I spent more time in Croatia in the succeeding years, I noticed numerous other instances of the underground—or not visible on the surface of things—but vibrant popular presence of the proscribed and demonized Serbian culture in the Croatian cultural space. It was hard to remain insensitive to this "underground" presence in its many aspects—literature, popular music, film, theater, even slang. One could walk through the very center of Zagreb on New Year's Eve 1999, for example, and see, in a small and temporarily-erected compact disk shop called *A Crumb* (*Mrvica*), discreetly displayed collections of Serbian rock—*The Best of Momčilo Bajagić Bajaga, Riblja Čorba, Ekatarina velika*. According to the salesman, all these CDs were much sought after and sold in large quantities, despite a rather forbidding price.

In the fall of 1998, an inconspicuous poster that appeared in all the major Croatian cities announced a concert by Vojvodina (the autonomous province in Serbia) singer-song writer Đorđe Balašević, one of the most prominent ballad-singers of the former Yugoslavia, which would take place in Ljubljana's Tivoli Hall on 9 December of that year. I found out that going to Balašević's concert in Ljubljana was a yearly ritual for many Croatians. Given that Balašević could not perform in Croatia (allegedly because of the government's security organs' inability to guarantee his safety), people from Croatia would go to see him in Ljubljana, the Slovenian capital, approximately a two-hour drive from Zagreb. It was impossible to get the facts of how many people from Croatia attended the December 1998 concert, but, having been there myself, I can attest that in the 7,000-seat Tivoli Hall he played to standing room only—and it was filled mainly by Croatians. The city of Zagreb buzzed for days before and after the concert actually took place; the rumor had it that at least nine buses full of people took off from only one of several gathering places in Zagreb. (The tickets for the concert, as well as the organized transportation, were inconspicuously but efficiently available in Zagreb itself.) The border between Croatia and Slovenia was packed with private vehicles and buses headed for Slovenia, and it was also stalled for hours at one border crossing thanks to the generous intervention of Croatian border officials, who of course knew where the entire crowd was going (it was a workday evening, when the usual excuses of going to Slovenia for shopping or skiing did not make much sense), and who expressed their (and/or the official Croatian) disapproval of this excursion by body-searching people, questioning them, and taking ample time to go thoroughly through their passports.

The highly enthusiastic and mostly Croatian audience at the concert spanned generations—one could see 20-year-old students, teenage neo-punks, and middle-aged professionals with their not-yet-teen children. All of them joined amiably in creating a massive chorus that sang, word for word, almost all of Balašević's songs together with him. The concert itself lasted some five hours, from 8 p.m. to 1 a.m., and Balašević did not once leave the stage. He opened the concert by greeting the Slovenian and Croatian cities one by one; when he said the names of specific Croatian cities, distinct parts of the audience responded, showing the high concentration of people from that particular city bussed in in huge numbers, seated or standing together. Balašević greeted Split (huge response), Rijeka (huge response), Osijek (huge response). When he came to Zagreb, the Croatian capital and the country's biggest city, Balašević had to break his greetings of the whole city into cheers to separate districts of the city: *"Zdravo Peščenica," "Zdravo Medveščak," "Zdravo Dubrava"* ("Hello Peščenica," "Hello Medveščak," "Hello Dubrava").

It was fortunate that the sound system at the concert was as good as it was so one could actually hear Balašević, because the audience, as I mentioned, sang all of his songs together with him. How come, I wondered, that these 20-year-olds and even younger people knew these songs, given that they were all of four or five years old—or not yet born even—when Balašević had released the first hits with which my generation grew up, hits such as "Life is the Sea" (*"Život je more"*), "The Beautiful Priest's Daughter"

("*Lepa protina kći*"), "Forgive me, Catherine" ("*Oprosti mi, Katrin*"), or "The First Love" ("*Prva ljubav*")? How was it possible that these people knew Balašević's songs so well—and obviously loved them—when they grew up after the break-up of the former Yugoslavia, in a nationalist Croatia of the 1990s which had effectively removed all things associated with Serbian culture, and which did not have Balašević's records in the stores or Balašević's concerts in its concert halls? And what did Balašević and his music, and all those other many things by other Serbian artists, writers, filmmakers, and so on, mean to these Croatian people?

Before trying to answer this question, let me mention some of the many other Serbian things living their underground—or at least very quiet—existence in Croatia of the 1990s. Examples abound. The film *The Wounds* (*Rane*, 1998) was the first Serbian film to be officially presented in a Croatian cinema after a years-long hiatus. It played in the movie theater *Kinoteka* in the spring of 1999, was very well attended despite the fact that it had received almost no publicity, and the video version of that film, which became available in Croatia soon after the film played in theaters, became a kind of a cult film for many Croatian young people.[2] The predominantly young audience at *Kinoteka* seemed to genuinely enjoy the raw humor of *The Wounds* and its engaging, fast-paced rhythm, unexpected plot turns, lively dialogues, inspired directing, and excellent acting. They laughed at the presence of Croatian subtitles: the theater, however, had little choice in wanting to avoid any possible problems with the powers-that-be that could prevent the showing of this film, and given that Croatian and Serbian were proclaimed to be two languages, Kinoteka had provided Croatian subtitles of this Serbian-language movie. However, on account of the fact that the Serbian and Croatian languages simply happen to have a hugely overlapping vocabulary and grammar, subtitles often grotesquely translated one set of words with the exact same set of words ("*Kako si?*" ["How are you?"] into "*Kako si?*", or "*Lud je*" ["He's crazy"] into "*Lud je*"). One member of the audience, a girl in her early 20s, shouted

---

[2] The film opened "just days prior to the NATO bombing of Yugoslavia (consisting then of Serbia and Montenegro) in 1999," and the director "Srđan Dragojević ... was invited to be a guest at Zagreb's *Kinoteka*" for this screening. Aida Vidan, "In Contrast: Croatian Film Today" (2011), available online at http://www.kinokultura.com/specials/11/intro-vidan.shtml (accessed 5 November 2011).

excitedly to her friend on the other side of the cinema hall: "Oh well, I came to see this wonder [*čudo*] with subtitles!"

One could also witness, in the city of Zagreb, the quiet proliferation of video recordings of Belgrade performances of plays by Serbian playwright Dušan Kovačević, known internationally as the writer of Emir Kusturica's movie *Underground*. I saw a recording of the Belgrade theater performance of his *Radovan III*, and I happened to have been accompanied at this particular viewing by yet another set of curious Zagreb 20-year-olds, all of them having had very little (if any) official Croatian media, or school-related exposure to Serbian culture. And when I looked for a book by Serbian and Yugoslav author Danilo Kiš in one of the city's major libraries, thinking that it would be easy to get that book "now," in the mid-1990s, when Kiš was not read in the school curriculum and when any public mention of him was rather scarce, I was surprised to find that I could not borrow his book for quite a while, and that I would actually have to put my name on the waiting list to get that book in a few months' time. The librarian explained to me that Kiš in particular was in great demand, as were some other Serbian writers such as Borislav Pekić.

Even the speech of the "coolest of the cool," as the students of Zagreb's College of Arts and Letters (*Filozofski fakultet*) like to think of themselves, sometimes playfully utilized the Serbian language within their own particular slang. I was astonished when, walking through the university in 1999, I heard a young man laughingly say to his friends: "*Ajde da se nađemo da malo pročaskamo o tom problemčiću!*" ("Let us get together to chat a bit about that little problem"). The word choice ("*časkati*"), grammatical structure (*da* + present instead of the infinitive), delivery (slower than Zagreb's speech), accentuated difference between the so-called hard č and soft ć (*pročaskamo, problemčiću*), and emphasized soft đ, all instantly marked this exclamation as part of the Serbian language—parodied and playfully used, no doubt, but definitely not just laughed at, which could have been the case in the 1980s or early 1990s. The slang, in short, was instantly recognizable. But what was less clear was the purpose—if any—of such inclusion of the Serbian language in this "cool" Zagreb speech.

Indeed, how can one interpret such a prominent presence of Serbian culture in Croatian popular culture? Exposed as they were to the intense vilification of the entire Serbian nation and everything it does, what did it mean to have all those Croatians dance to Serbian pop music, go to concerts of Serbian rock-stars, read books by great Serb literati, watch Serbian movies and plays, and incorporate the Serbian language into their own slang? Though absent from the Croatian media—the government's and the opposition's alike—Serbian culture was undeniably present in the very life of the Croatian culture of the second half of the 1990s. Why was that the case?

The Missing Parts of Me

Having mentioned the Ljubljana concert of Đorđe Balašević in 1998, we may start with a consideration of what he and his music may give or represent to the Croatian audience. Born in 1953, Balašević has been a prolific author of pop songs for decades, one whose popularity, established during the Yugoslav era, has remained high throughout the now politically rearranged region. His songs have catchy melodies and simple, unabashedly emotional lyrics, but are also often characterized by refreshing humor and self-irony. They have an appealing warmth that help make them an integral part of the audience's lives. "Count on Us" (*"Računajte na nas"*) was a mega-hit in 1970s, "Forgive me, Catherine" (*"Oprosti mi, Katrin"*) and a score of his other songs have been a staple of Adriatic beaches, where young people entertain themselves by singing their favorite songs, and anecdotal evidence tells of people who record for personal use one or the other of Balašević's most successful songs containing some inimitable "life wisdom" (such as, notably, "Life is the Sea" [*"Život je more"*]) at the beginning, middle, and end of a single side of a cassette, so as to hear it in regular intervals without having to search for it.

The persona of the "I" created in Balašević's songs is that of a non-materialistic wanderer and dreamer who lives peacefully and quietly, "sometimes play[s] cards or write[s] a verse" (*"ponekad bacim kartu ili napišem stih"*), and still "steals days from God" (*"ja još kradem dane bogu"*), that is, does not do something purposeful or useful, and in general prefers romantic reveries over rational or pragmatic behavior. The majority of his songs are in the minor key, and they sometimes employ Roma, Hungarian, or Russian melodies in their rhythms and orchestration. The space invoked in these songs is not that of an urban metropolis, but that of a small, quiet, and slow Vojvodina province or village, and often-times that of nature: Balašević sings about rivers, fields of wheat, tall grass, the ponds and lakes of Vojvodina's landscape and of one's idealized childhood ("when I was very young // some swamp birds I hunted" ["*kad sam bio sasvim mlad // neke barske ptice sam lovio tad*"]) or romanticized past. Balašević's own stage image is completely unproduced: he really looks like someone who just stepped into a performance straight from the car or a walk by the river, a middle-age man in everyday casual clothes that are not particularly flattering and that genuinely look like they never got even the smallest share of his attention.

If we make a short catalogue of the above-mentioned characteristics of Balašević's music and performance—the neo-Romantic persona of a nostalgic dreamer, much use of nature symbolism and nature, the common integration of "Eastern" melodies, and Balašević's stage image, we see that these characteristics are largely missing from contemporary Croatian popular music. There has simply been no musician of Balašević's type in that music—the older generation of Croatian authors of ballads, such as Arsen Dedić and Ibrica Jusić, for example, are very different. There is no one so unabashedly romantic and sentimental, so straightforwardly emotional, as Balašević. His music clearly provides something which is missing and is *missed* by many Croatians, and which evokes a positive response when recognized.

One could argue that Balašević's music brings back or contains many of the aspects which had been present in Croatian culture during the Yugoslav period, and which were subsequently purged from Croatia in the 1990s with the wholesale expulsion of cultural elements that were proclaimed to be Serbian, or Yugoslav. The dreaming, romantic, nostalgic "I" persona of the songs, for example, was a trademark of much of "Eastern" rock made in Bosnia and Herzegovina and Serbia (e.g., in the music of groups such as Sarajevo's *White Button* (*Bijelo dugme*), for a long time the most popular band in the former Yugoslavia), as was the use of Eastern (Roma, Russian, Hungarian) melodies and folk melodies in general, or the employment of natural imagery in lyrics. Croatian and Slovenian rock, on the contrary, was roughly speaking traditionally much less romantic, "folksy", and melodious, and much more dissonant and "expressionist" (e.g., Zagreb's *Azra*), playful and humorous (e.g., Slovenian *Buldožer*), or experimental, conceptual, and political (most notable here is Ljubljana's *Laibach*, especially during the 1980s when the group was an integral part of the *Neue Slowenische Kunst* movement rather than "just" another rock band). A Croatian listener during the Yugoslav era could have liked Serbian rock or could have found a good part of it too kitschy and sappy, but in either case this Serbian rock (and Bosnian, Slovenian, or Macedonian—e.g., Skopje's excellent *Bread and Salt [Leb i sol]*), was a comfortable part of one's overall soundscape which rather naturally included and combined domestic rock from all over socialist Yugoslavia alongside the canonical imports from Great Britain and the United States.

This Croatian soundscape and the wider cultural terrain were in the 1990s impoverished and diminished by the systematic practices of exclusion and expulsion of what was proclaimed to be "non-Croatian" elements. During the Yugoslav period, for example, the music of Belgrade's group *Idols* (*Idoli*) or of Momčilo Bajagić Bajaga was rather popular in Croatia, and quite unproblematically integrated into the Croatian cultural sphere or, more precisely, into the cultural *milieu* of any individual Croatian interested in contemporary rock music. It was of course known that this music happened to be Serbian (in the sense of having been made in Serbia), but its having been Serbian both did not matter too much and perhaps even added the flair of something slightly exotic and therefore intriguing and attractive. This music was different (some difference in language and in slang, often different overall atmosphere) and yet familiar because of many shared cultural concerns, and easily understandable because of the greatly overlapping language(s).

But what used to be experienced during the Yugoslav era as an element of the Croatian cultural space (because it had its place and relevance in that space), even though it may have originated in Serbia and was acknowledged as "Serbian," was in the 1990s officially proclaimed to be Serbian as opposed to Croatian, or Serbian and therefore *not* Croatian, and was aggressively purged from Croatian culture. The Croatian culture was thus pushed into losing its hybrid, cross-cultural identity characterized by the lively interaction of different cultural spheres on account of the claim that this hybrid identity actually enacts or aids the subordination of Croatian's *own* national culture to either a Serbian one, seen as having clear hegemonic aspirations, or else a "Yugoslav" one, seen as either artificial or else just a cover-up for Serbian dominance. The problem, however, lay in the fact that it was much easier to remove "inappropriate" materials (e.g., Serbian literary works from the school curriculum or Serbian musicians from Croatian stages), than to find an adequate replacement for them within the sphere recognized as Croatia's "own" culture. Finding replacements for discarded things became especially difficult when the official policies of cultural purging went on to include (or rather exclude) not only things created outside of Croatia, but also those which were by origin "Croatian" but tainted with what was officially proclaimed to be "non-Croatian" sentiments, such as politically oppositional or ideologically unacceptable works, or else clearly regional and not sufficiently "national" publications or points of view. The list of the cultural elements and aspects that were proscribed and not to be used any more grew large, and the nett result was that Croatian culture became severely impoverished in numerous ways.

Given this situation, one could argue that Balašević's music and other things Serbian were popular in 1990s Croatia not so much because they were "Serbian," but because they articulated missing elements of the impoverished Croatian culture itself. These Serbian cultural elements functioned as, so to speak, ready-made missing parts of the Croatian culture which could not readily "help itself" with the heavily promoted "European" German, French, or Austrian cultural elements (given the simple reason of linguistic, contextual, historical, and myriad other incompatibilities), but could easily understand, communicate with, and appropriate elements from Serbian culture.

At the beginning of this chapter I mentioned the rigid official differentiation between the Croatian and Serbian languages, and the creation of the dictionaries of differences between the two. In Tuđman's Croatia, one could not easily come across the Serbian language, which is characterized by, among other things, the use of *ekavica* where official standard Croatian uses *ijekavica* (that is, "*e*" instead of "*ije*" in words such as *mleko* [Croatian *mlijeko*, milk], or *belo* [Croatian *bijelo*, white], etc.), and some different lexic (e.g., *hleb* instead of Croatian *kruh* [bread]).[3] But the songwriter Đorđe

---

[3]While *ijekavica* is the official variant of Croatian language, the situation on the ground and among the language's users is rather "messy." The Croatian capital,

Balašević, with his considerable poetic talent, manages to show much of the beauty of the Serbian language in his lyrics: his long "e" can actually sound much gentler and softer than "ije" would in this stanza from his song "I don't like January" ("*Ne volim januar*"):

Ne volim januar
ni *bele* zimske vragove
u svakom *snegu* vidim iste tragove

[I don't like January
nor white winter devils
in every snow I see the same footprints][4]

This long "*e*" lends itself here better to being sung than "*ije*" would; one can hold a long note on the "*e*" and cannot on "*ije*". The Serbian and in some cases Bosnian words such as *ker* [dog], *džabe*, *divaniti*, *čiča* [uncle; older man], and *sokak* [narrow alley], bring with themselves a slightly different meaning from their Croatian counterparts, and seem to be better understood and employed as complements rather than alternatives to Croatian lexic: *divaniti* is not quite the same as *pričati*, *govoriti*, or *razgovarati* [talk, converse], *džabe* not the same as *uzalud* [futile, not producing a result]. In addition to other particular aspects (mentioned above) which Balašević's songs may bring to Croatian popular culture, the widening and enrichment of the Croatian language itself, which has been reduced by the extraction of numerous "non-authentic" words, is not the least important one.

Zagreb, for instance, has a lot of *ekavica* on its streets and in oral and unofficial language use, primarily because of the influence of the *kajkavian* dialect of northern Croatia. The famous song about Zagreb is called "*Beli Zagreb grad*" ("The White Zagreb Town"), not "*Bijeli Zagreb grad*."
[4]Balašević's recent live performance of this song in Arena Hall, Zagreb, on 18 December 2010, can be seen online at http://www.youtube.com/watch?v=FPFpGL F5B48&feature=related (accessed 5 November 2011). A better quality live version is available online at http://www.youtube.com/watch?v=gPWfBQ3mp-U (accessed 5 November 2011).

"It is Glorious to Die for One's Homeland": Croatian Victims and Serbian Writers

The popularity of writer Danilo Kiš can be seen as yet another example of Serbian artefacts' enlargement of Croatian cultural vocabulary. Though cultural anti-nationalism in Croatia primarily existed on the "ground" level of the people themselves and was usually not present in the media (with the exception of some oppositional media which, for example, had a policy of including contributors from Serbia), the appreciation of Danilo Kiš often made its way into oppositional journalism. Kiš's work was often mentioned in regard to one or other of his more well-known pronouncements against aggressive or chauvinistic nationalism, and it was marked in the minds of many older-generation readers by the memory of the writer's own heavily paid public fight against his critics.

An interesting example of the placing of Kiš within the oppositional Croatian discourse is an article by Heni Erceg, "It is Glorious to Die for One's Homeland" (*"Časno je za domovinu umrijeti"*), published in *Feral Tribune*, where Erceg uses Kiš's story with the same title as an implied frame of reference which explodes in a manifold way the scope of her own article. The title itself brims with connotations, as it is a rendition of Horace's verse *"Dulce et decorum est pro patria mori"* ("It is sweet and honorable to die for one's country") and also brings to mind Wilfred Owen's poem of the same title, ending with:

> If you could hear, at every jolt, the blood
> Come gargling from the froth-corrupted lungs,
> Obscene as cancer, bitter as the cud
> Of vile, incurable sores on innocent tongues, –
> My friend, you would not tell with such high zest
> To children ardent for some desperate glory,
> The old Lie: Dulce et decorum est
> Pro patria mori.[5]

---

[5] Wilfred Owen, "Dulce Et Decorum Est" (1963), 55.

Heni Erceg's article is a text about the death of a Croatian army soldier named Silvio Jozić. The text shows that the death of this particular soldier cannot be attributed to the actions of the enemy on the battlefield, but rather to the carelessness and ignorance of Jozić's own superiors, who were later rewarded rather than punished for a series of military and moral failures. Erceg's text is a collage: a photograph of Nada Majstorović, the mother of the slain soldier, an emaciated woman in black whose facial expression while talking, as well as her hand gestures, seems to indicate that she is desperately trying to communicate something; the official notification of the death of Silvio Jozić, issued from military headquarters; a letter which Mrs. Majstorović received as a response to her request for additional information about her son's death, informing her that she could get that information only if the civil court requests it in her name; and the text of Heni Erceg's article. Most of this text is in italics, which note the direct speech of Nada Majstorović, which is not interrupted by the journalist's questions or comments. Heni Erceg marks the places of her cutting of Majstorović's speech by three dots. Aside from being shortened, Majstorović's talk appears completely unedited.

Heni Erceg constructs her writing as the silent listening to another woman. She does not write a single word of her own until the very last column—it is the other woman's voice that fills her article. The journalist uses her public space by giving it to those who are silenced by the nationalist discourse. Erceg's few concluding remarks point out that the title of her story, "*Časno je za domovinu umrijeti*" ["It is Glorious to Die for One's Homeland"] is actually only a Croatian rendition of the more Serbian sentence, "*Slavno je za otadžbinu mreti,*"[6] which is the title of a story by Danilo Kiš:

> The confession of Nada Majstorović, the mother of a killed Croatian soldier, her sadness and her revolt appear futile today and here. Because futile stories—when told—turn attention to the hidden part of the war, that bitter residuum which is to remain hidden under the refreshing heroic epic which the survivors have to drink up together, and in which every

---

[6]The phrase itself is a rendition of Horace's "*Dulce et decorum est pro patria mori.*" (*Odes*, III.2.13.)

individual drop loses both its taste and its importance. As it is probably futile to attempt to draw one individual confession out of silence ... In one of his stories Danilo Kiš wrote: "History is written by the victors. Legends are woven by the people. Writers fantasize. Only death is certain." The story's title is: "To Die for One's Country is Glorious."[7]

Included in Kiš's collection of stories *The Encyclopedia of the Dead*, "It is Glorious to Die for One's Homeland" tells of the brave death on the gallows of young Hungarian Count Esterhazy, who either "died a brave and noble death, fully conscious of the certainty thereof," or else was simply tricked by his mother into behaving bravely (because he thought he was going to be pardoned at the last moment), in which case "the whole thing was merely a clever bit of play-acting directed by a proud mother."[8] Kiš's story indicates that the appearance of a heroic death might hide a very different reality: the rules of theater may shape the politics of death. Deception figures prominently in Erceg's article as well. Theatrical government officials take the central stage and storm out the "'heroic epopea' about the defense of the country," pointing at the dead bodies on the ground and interpreting these silent bodies, speaking in their name. This façade of national defiance and bravery erases from the collective consciousness those deaths that are shameful and un-needed. The task of an oppositional journalist is to write a text which functions as a missing sign or presence of this absent dead body.

Furthermore, Erceg displays the possibility of saying something very much "hers" through the words of someone whom the nationalist discourse proscribes as being very much "theirs" (*Serbian* Danilo Kiš), thus again showing how readymade Serbian cultural artefacts, previously a part of the shared Yugoslav cultural sphere and considered both Yugoslav and Serbian, can express a Croatian situation in an economic way. Erceg's inclusion of Kiš also emphasizes, to spell it out, that "their" (Serbian) writer is mine or is nothing less than I myself (if my own speech is me), and that

---

[7] *Feral Tribune*, No. 464 (8 August 1994), p. 16. Erceg is quoting Kiš's text in its original Serbian language. I am using Michael Henry Heim's translation. See Danilo Kiš, *The Encyclopedia of the Dead* (1991), 131.
[8] Kiš (1991), 131.

I am not identical with the "we" of the homogenous nation as proscribed by the powers-that-be.[9]

The Film *The Wounds* and Balašević's Positive Alternative

Another example of Serbian art articulating features of the Croatian situation, this time in the form of a feature film, can be seen in the

---

[9] By her reference to Kiš, Erceg unlocks, or brings to the forefront of many Croatian readers' minds, the whole mental file with the title "Danilo Kiš." Aside from Kiš's fictional work, that file contains his reflections on the theme of nationalism, the relation between nationalist politics and kitsch in ideologically or interest-driven arts, the way in which nationalism recreates the minutiae of everyday life in its own image, and so on. The file "Danilo Kiš" also contains a memory of the biggest literary and cultural scandal in post-World War Two Yugoslavia. Following the publication of his master-piece *A Tomb for Boris Davidovich* (*Grobnica za Borisa Davidoviča*, 1976), a collection of stories having as their theme the fate of revolutionaries from across Europe (none of them Yugoslav, many of them Jewish) in Stalinist purges, a smear campaign was orchestrated in Yugoslav literary circles, accusing Kiš of plagiarism. In effect, this campaign was "[aiming] to ... dismiss him [Kiš] for his lack of national consciousness and insufficient affinity for the traditions of his milieu" (Dragan Klaić, "'Danilo Kiš': The Theatrical Connection" (1994), 204), or, in other words, for his lack of proper national(ist) consciousness. Kiš wrote a whole book in response, the scathing *The Anatomy Lesson* [*Čas anatomije*, 1978], many aspects of which deal with nationalist culture, ideologies, and mind sets. A huge polemic ensued among the "cultural workers" (as they were called at that time) from the former Yugoslavia, who divided themselves between those for and those against Kiš.

The recollection of a scandal associated with Kiš also includes the memory of a loss and tragic ending. Kiš left Yugoslavia and relocated to France, where he died rather young from a terminal illness. Some attributed his becoming sick in the first place to perhaps irreparable wounds which Kiš, proud as he was, incurred while fighting the infinitely inferior but numerous, loud, and established opponents who charged him with plagiarism. In the eyes of the world at large—gullible, distracted, scantily informed, and even less interested—one can never wash oneself free of that kind of accusation, and this realization perhaps hurt Kiš deeply despite his own better judgment. As he himself wrote, "in the merciless battle of equal opponents ... no one comes out unharmed" (Danilo Kiš, *A Tomb for Boris Davidovich* (1980), 27). Heni Erceg's article, both drawing Kiš into the sphere of her text and enlarging that sphere by the implication of Kiš, talks about present-day Croatian nationalism and its lies and victims—a killed young poet and translator Silvio Jozić—by reminding the reader of another translator and writer, Danilo Kiš.

reception in Croatia of the Serbian film *The Wounds*. This film is not only an open-eyed statement of what Serbian society had become under Milošević's rule, but also the successful coming-of-age story of two Belgrade adolescents, Pinki and Švaba (Dušan Pekić, Milan Marić), as told by one of them. Pinki and Švaba graduate from admiring the neighborhood thug (Dragan Bjelogrlić) and the things he does to inheriting his trade. *The Wounds* is of course not a "realistic" portrayal of Serbian society, but it embodies in its plot, images, characters, and language some of characteristics of Serbian society during Milošević's era, such as that of thieves and gangsters being called heroes. The main criminal, for instance, repeatedly goes to "liberate the Serbian town of Vukovar," from which he brings back truckloads of loot. The grand war of "liberation and national cause" is plainly shown as just a façade for the basest criminal activity, and for plunder and pleasure in the destruction of things and in the killing of civilians. *The Wounds* also externalizes in some humorous but also eye-opening scenes the swift and radical change of idols, from the icon of "brotherhood and unity," Yugoslavia's President Josip Broz Tito, to the icon of nationalism and national paranoia who enabled the unprecedented aggression, Serbian president Slobodan Milošević. The film's thematic and structural features, though relating to Serbian society of the 1990s, could also be recognizable in Croatian society at the turn of the century, where they existed in a watered-down, weaker version and were not so widespread, yet still there they were and had to be recognized and confronted. In Croatia, too, some criminal characters had at one period been proclaimed or were allowed to be seen as national heroes. The collective icons were officially changed there with great speed as well. Yugoslav president Tito, from the Croatian region of *Hrvatsko Zagorje*, was replaced by Franjo Tuđman, the first president of Croatia, who came from the same region.[10] The rhetoric of socialism was replaced with the rhetoric of nationalism, and the action of the liberation of the occupied Croatian territories (the 1995 *Storm [Oluja]*) was used by some as a cover up for looting and the killing of Serbian civilians. Overall, of course, the situation in Croatia differed in many aspects from that in Serbia. Also, the scale of the negative

---

[10] *Hrvatsko Zagorje* is the region of Croatia north of Zagreb.

Fig 9.1 Pinki, *The Wounds* (1998)

things that were similar in the two countries was different: while Croatia in the 1990s had an authoritarian regime that intimidated opponents, Serbia had a criminal regime which liquidated its most outspoken critics. Still, these similarities between the situations in the two countries could provide one of the reasons why the film *The Wounds* was so well received in Croatia.

If *The Wounds* spells out all the negative aspects of nationalism, shown in the context of Serbia but recognized in Croatia, Balašević creates a positive alternative to pathological nationalism in much of his music. Many of Balašević's songs go against the nationalist premise that those who are from another nation are indeed the "others", different and dangerous people to be cut off and avoided. Individuals in Balašević's songs connect just fine across national borders, and the boundaries prove illusory. The bodies and dreams communicate without problems. The loved women in Balašević's songs are of various nationalities, and the romantic male "I" of the songs remembers having loved a "Šokica … whose eyes still enchant with the same luster" (*Šokica* being a Croatian woman) in "The Verse on the Asphalt" ("*Stih na asfaltu*"), the Bosnian woman from

Banja Luka whom the singer loved while he was on his military tour of duty in Banja Luka at the time of the former Yugoslavia in "The Return" ("*Povratak*"), a Hungarian woman in "I Can't Speak Hungarian" ("*Ne umem mađarski*"), a French one in "Forgive Me, Catherine" ("*Oprosti mi, Katrin*"), and so on. Romantic attachment and sexual attraction do not observe national boundaries. On the contrary, the specific cultural *milieu* which each of these women carries with her or around her in Balašević's songs—as present in the verses depicting the city of Zagreb in the "The Verse on the Asphalt"—only enchants her individual beauty, much like an idiosyncratic style of dress which is worn naturally and gives distinction, something specific which delights with its difference.

In the song "*Sevdalinka*" (*sevdalinka* being the genre of Sarajevo's urban folk music), the whole country becomes a person one relates to—Bosnia is personified in a figure of a young, tearful shepherdess who "said her name was Bosnia // a strange name for a girl." In this song Balašević spells out again his credo, which asserts that the essence of a human being is precisely his/her internal connectedness or relatedness with the others that cannot be deterred by such crude divisions as national ones. He sings:

Nekom Drina teče desno
nekom Drina lijevo teče
sve da teče u dubinu
na dve pole svet da seče
znam tajni gaz, moje lane
most se pruži gde ja stanem
sve da vuku me konji vrani
nema meni jedne strane
dok si ti na drugoj strani.

[To some people Drina flows to the right
to some people to the left
but even if it were flowing into the depths
cutting the world into two halves
I know a secret crossing, my fawn,
the bridge lies itself down where I stand
even if I were pulled by black horses
there is no one side to me
while you are on the other side.]

(The river Drina defines the border between Bosnia on the west and Serbia on the east).

It is the person's own most intimate part, aspect, or side that is missing when "you are on the other side." And "their worries worry me," regardless of the fact that *they* are Bosnians and *I* a Serb, because the two—they and I—are not at all radically separated as the aggressive nationalist rhetoric would have us think. On the contrary, they and I are connected in complex ways through some old ties of not only friendship ("the friends are mentioned hundred times in a prayer"), but also of shared dreams and shared identity: "Once we got to be brothers by looking at each other // guessing that we dreamt the same // and it mattered none to God // whether we crossed ourselves or bowed" (*"Nekad smo se bratimili po pogledu // sluteći da isto sanjamo // i bogu je prosto bilo // krstimo se ili klanjamo"*). The basis for connection with the others is "the apprehension of the common dreams," which emerges when the two people look at each other and recognize in each other a kindred soul. What matters is this kind of substantial kinship, and what emphatically does *not* matter, even to God, is whether one bows as a Muslim at prayer or crosses oneself as a Christian at prayer, i.e., whether one is a Muslim or a Christian.

Balašević's songs, in short, subvert the nationalist discourse and ideology primarily by creating a different, non-nationalist vocabulary of human relations and identity.[11] The songs invoke people who do not bind along national affiliations but along personal affinities. The loss of lovers and friends, parts of language and culture, ways of relating, and places associated with now adversarial nations is always experienced as a loss: Balašević sings "If I could just pass through Ilica [Zagreb's main street] one more time ..." At the same time, that which is lost is brought back and retrieved precisely through the lyrics' detailed memory of it. Lost Zagreb, for example, includes the streets Ilica and Vlaška, the statue of a "fiery count" (of *"strašnog bana"*), referring to the

---

[11] Balašević's emphasis on the positive side does not mean that he does not have critical songs in his opus. On the contrary, the first part of his album, *The Nineties* (*Devedesete*), for instance, has much criticism relating to what Serbia had become in the 1990s. The songs such as "The Nineties," "Balkan Tango," and "Pero the Stupid One" are all more or less ironic or humorous indictments of nationalism in general and Serbian nationalism in particular.

statue of Count Josip Jelačić marking Zagreb's central square, the national drink *gemišt*, the old term *Šokica* repeated in a refrain, which sounds like a pure word of endearment in comparison with the 1990s violently sexist and racist marking of Croatian women in the Serbian language. The employed musical genres exhibit an irreverent, not nationally bound variety: the mix includes Argentine tango, Sarajevan sevdalinka, Hungarian chardash, and so on.

One can argue that another reason for Balašević's popularity with the Croatian public lies in his songs' creation of a generic vocabulary, so to speak, of anti-nationalism, a vocabulary and attitude repressed in Tuđman's Croatia. Balašević's popularity in Croatia is also often ascribed to the sentiment of Yugo-nostalgia, or nostalgia related to the former Yugoslavia. But if there is any nostalgia, it seems that it relates primarily to the many lost facets of everyday life that existed in the past and have disappeared in the present, rather than specifically to the political entity of the previous country. What people seem to mourn together with Balašević is the loss of the sentiment which they had before, when they felt more "at one with the world," the loss of the passports with which they could travel anywhere, or "flags which were sown by the needles of the record-players" rather than by national inclusions and exclusions, and the loss of what in some aspects were safer and better lives. Balašević's songs, therefore, may function as a needed catalyst for recognition and re-appropriation of that lost past.

Balašević's music, Danilo Kiš's writings, films such as *The Wounds*, and many other Serbian artefacts had their intense life in Croatian culture of the late 1990s because they provided this culture with the aspects that it needed, and because they enlarged considerably the newly-impoverished Croatian cultural vocabulary. Serbian things were thus popular not because they were Serbian but because they were or had become *Croatian*—needed by the Croatian culture and easily integrated into it. It is impossible to say how much presence Serbian culture really had in Croatia in the 1990s, given the fact that its reception existed largely outside representation by the media or academic attention. But it is safe to say that it was there in a rather strong and varied fashion, and present much more than previously supposed.

The situation in Croatian culture changed at the turn of the century, paralleling the change in the governing political structures. Presentation and public consumption of Serbian artefacts or cultural things became much more widespread, came "above ground," and also became much less controversial and followed by significant media attention. Well-known Serbian playwright Biljana Srbljanović's play *Family Stories* was performed in Rijeka in 2000 before a full house, for instance, and received rave reviews. This and other similar events were at the time perceived by Croatian cultural commentators as exciting new encounters between Serbian and Croatian culture after a 10-year hiatus in which Croatians knew nothing about things Serbian. But that was obviously not the case: the more visible presence of Serbian culture in Croatia after the year 2000 should be more properly seen as the surfacing of underground trends which had been there all along during the era of "high nationalism," and not as the appearance of something entirely new. And the whole Croatian culture, as well as the relationship between Croatian and Serbian culture in the recent two decades, should be reconsidered accordingly.

10

Pleasant Distractions
The Danger of Close-ups and Maja Weiss's *The Border Guard*

I do not divide people by nationality but, if I have to, into "Beatles" and "Stones," or into the good ones and the bad ones.

BRANKO ĐURIĆ ĐURO[1]

Slovenian film recently celebrated one hundred years of existence (1905–2005), and, in honor of that occasion, a number of Slovenian films, many of them the most recent ones, were made available to numerous cinema venues and universities within the country and abroad. I was very eager to see all of these new films. After seeing them, I was rather surprised. In their own various ways, all of these newest films dealt with the issues of transition and of the manifold and profound changes that were happening in Slovenia after the break-up of Yugoslavia in 1991, and the

---

[1] Branko Đurić Đuro, a quote from the promotion material for the film *Cheese and Jam* (*Kajmak in marmelada*, 2003), which he directed and in which he plays the main role. Đurić Đuro relocated from his native Bosnia to Slovenia in the 1990s. This material was made for the week of the *International Promotion of Slovene Films*, 21–4 November 2005, organized by the Center for Slovene as a Second/Foreign Language.

replacement of the socialist federative country with the capitalist democracy on its way to becoming an EU member in 2004. Yet the realities or the aspects of realities that were articulated by those films included those that were somehow not the ones I would have expected. This situation, of course, was both puzzling and gratifying, as it challenged my own understanding of the transition in Slovenia, especially with regard to the changes concerning women and the changes *of* women, as seen through the lenses of these films.

New Borders, New Bad, and New Good

Upon its release, *The Border Guard* (*Varuh meje*, Slovenia, 2002),[2] directed and co-written by Maja Weiss, provoked considerable international attention. On one hand, the film earned a prize for the most innovative film at the Berlin Film Festival and a very enthusiastic *New York Times* review; on the other hand it was received with animosity at the Melbourne Queer Film Festival. Described as a "lesbian-exploitation road movie, except the road is the river separating the relatively affluent Slovenia from war-stricken Croatia,"[3] *The Border Guard* programmatically addresses a number of major crossroads in contemporary Slovenia.

The film's plot revolves around a kayaking trip down the river Kolpa, a natural border between Slovenia and Croatia, undertaken during the summer vacation by three young women students in the capital city Ljubljana, Žana (Pia Zemljič), Alja (Tanja Potočnik), and Simona (Iva Krajnc). Friction grows between aggressive, entrepreneurial and daring Žana, who wants to become sexually intimate with Alja, and Simona, Žana's timid and traditional opposite, who is becoming increasingly isolated yet also vies for Alja's attention and support. Alja, a native of a small town nearby where the trip starts, is a shifting symbolic middle, unhappy with her relationship with boyfriend *Medo* ("the Bear," Goražd Žilavec) at the beginning

---

[2]The film is distributed under the title "Guardian of the Frontier."
[3]Annie Wagner, "Slovenia Makes Movies," *The Stranger* (Seattle), 18 November 2004, 95.

Fig 10.1 Simona, Alja, and Žana, *The Border Guard* (2002)

of the trip, but not satisfied either with an alternative (being with Žana) that she tries later. The setting of the trip in an environment of wilderness that is unfamiliar and threatening to these very urban girls, the bits of plot indicating a possible murder mystery—a woman's shoe is found in the river; a woman has been missing—and repeated encounters with a mysterious man, all contribute to the film's suspenseful atmosphere, as do cinematic elements such as repeated use of the camera's point of view implying a hidden silent observer who is following and watching the girls from somewhere on the river bank, but cannot be seen, and the use of soundtrack.

From the start, *The Border Guard* is built on the productive tension between the two processes: on one hand, there is the articulation of the many aspects of both discursive and material practices of nationalist exclusion, including the programmatic creation of such practices and their aggressive public promotion and government enforcement, but also the film's own ironic commentary on nationalism's phobias and speech. On the other hand, there is the experiential reality of the three main characters that increasingly, though also predictably, develops in a different direction from that posited by the nationalist framing of the world.[4]

---

[4] A distinction and difference between discourses and ideologies, and experiences, posited here, is inspired by Russell Berman's work in his *Enlightenment or Empire:*

In the film's multi-faceted articulation of nationalism, the discursive construction of the neighboring Croatians as dangerous savages, for instance, is repeatedly and often ironically quoted. Simona's mentioning of Croatia ("And that there [on the other side of the river] is Croatia, right?"), is accompanied with the noticeable onset of tense music and the camera's sudden move into the stalking position behind the characters, and Žana's lines about "those crazy Croats, war veterans ... [who] cannot stop killing," in relation to the possible murder of the missing woman, are obviously ironic quotes of the seemingly often heard or implied statements of that type, existing in the public space. But then such ironical dismissal of nationalist discourse is in turn opposed, and eventually apparently overrun, by the "dead serious" xenophobic nationalism embodied in the "border guard" (Jonas Žnidaršič). Both his speech and his material practices define and enforce the national space of Slovenia as well as the realm of those, "the real Slovenes," who are the only ones belonging and entitled to this space which is, according to the "border guard," endangered by external as well as internal "foreigners" of all kinds.[5]

When it comes to the realities actually experienced by the three women, different things—unuttered, silenced, or directly opposite

---

Colonial Discourse in German Culture (1998). Berman writes, for example, that "in the wake of ... the enormous influence of the historiographical work of Foucault, the major tendency within the cultural studies scholarship involves the tracing of discourses understood to constitute the experience of subjects. Indeed, subjectivity altogether—not the particular versions but the fundamental possibility of subjectivity—is treated as a consequence of discursive structures.

This consistently discourse-theoretical cultural studies is, however, deeply problematic, representing ultimately a return to an idealistic historiography, in that it asserts an overriding zeitgeist or episteme (to use Foucault's term) and then fits the historical data into prescribed frameworks. It thereby loses the sense of an objective historical past as well as the concrete subjectivity of human experience in particular contexts." Berman (1998), 14.

[5]The casting of Jonas Žnidaršič in the role of the "border guard" itself brings an ironical commentary to his performance: Žnidaršič is well known to the Slovenian audience as a leftist and liberal celebrity, often making fun of the xenophobic features of contemporary Slovenian society, and his excellent and clearly "over the top" performance as the "border guard" may thus be seen as an intentional parody, being a part of the film's own ironical take on nationalism. (However, awareness of Žnidaršič's off-screen persona is limited to Slovenian viewers only, so this particular irony is lost to the international audience.)

to the nationalist discourse—start to happen. The women cross the river Kolpa and enter Croatia, where Alja and Žana forge probably the most positive relationship of the entire film with a gay Croatian man whom they meet in the border village. The commonality of artistic interests (the Croatian man is an actor, Alja would like to become a novelist, and Žana is a photographer), as well as the relationship of support that quickly develops between an older man who is established and comfortable both in his profession and his sexuality (a well-known actor, having a comfortable gay relationship), and the two girls flirting with both becoming artists and having a lesbian relationship, strongly wins over any presupposed national divisiveness. As their trip resumes, it becomes increasingly clear that while the danger to them, the three Slovenian women, is indeed more than real, it does not come from the "crazy Croats" or illegal immigrants, but rather from the "inside," from the self-proclaimed guardian of the border who will follow, berate, and eventually attack them, all the time behaving quite in accordance with his own concept of the protection of the ideal Slovenian space and identity—non-liberal, rigid, patriarchal and exclusive, and defended from the "progress [which] is destroying the world."

There are several increasingly violent encounters between the three women and this mysterious and threatening man, the symbolic *varuh meje* ("border guard") of the title, who embodies as well as unites within himself a number of new borders erected in Slovenia. He is at once a government official who supervises the police in capturing illegal Chinese immigrants crossing the river from Croatia into Slovenia, a hunter and a fisherman, assertively plucking fish from the river and shooting at a deer, and an outspoken guardian of proper "Slovenian" characteristics, which he defines as unequivocally traditional and patriarchal. He admonishes Žana and Alja for their "un-natural" masculine behavior (pointedly excepting the feminine Simona), behaves in a commandeering and aggressive way towards them, and as a candidate for a local *župan* (regional official) appears at an evening fair and gives a very clear speech on where he stands. Stating that "we have to protect not only the borders of our beautiful country against foreigners who want to come here, but [we also have to protect] the border of that which is good against that which is bad", he goes on to assert that "foreigners are not just coming across the border from other countries, but ... they come here from our own big cities."

> [They] come here without respect for our values ... [for] traditional family ... progress is destroying the world; we are not afraid to say "the family is sacred," we are not afraid to say that girls have to be mothers, and mothers should stay at home ... that homosexuality is unnatural ... girls should not behave like boys ... and boys should not look like girls; there is a very clear border between that which is good and that which is bad; in the same way in which we defend our country against foreigners, we have to defend the border between good and bad ...

Creating an image of a country under attack by both external and internal "foreigners," this speech shifts the area of public focus and concerns from pressing transition issues such as the changing economy or social safety net to matters of gender and sexuality. National defense is equated with the defense of ways of behavior proclaimed as "natural" ("girls have to be mothers/stay at home/not behave like boys;" "homosexuality is un-natural"), and the stunning natural environment of the region, the home of the people living here, is used in support of this new division: the "un-natural" big cities versus the "natural" traditional values. The "border guard's" speech both creates the emotionally heightened atmosphere of fear and nationalist xenophobia, and then projects this tone onto the terrain of gender and sexuality. This speech is the film's clear metonymic articulation of the organized move on the side of conservative Slovenian parties and social elements to displace the overwhelming problems of transition with gender and sexuality issues, and thus to go from a terrain where they could (or wanted to) do comparatively little, to one where they thought they could exercise a lot more control.[6]

---

[6]With regard to one of the most explosive of the women-related issues, abortion, for example, Vlasta Jalušič wrote: "[T]he logic behind the anti-abortion rights campaign was to create a 'real,' 'big problem' behind which all other problems such as social policy, employment, the impact of market, political representation, and so on, could be hidden." Vlasta Jalušič, "Women in Post-Socialist Slovenia" (1999), 122.

Both in his actions and his speech, the "border guard" embodies a potent fusion of nationalist, gender, and sexuality re-figurations that have appeared in post-independence Slovenian culture and politics, separating outsiders (foreigners, "non-traditional" women, homosexuals), from "real Slovenes." Young women like Alja and Žana are un-natural and "foreigners" themselves because they inhabit the big cities with no "respect for our values," because they study rather than stay at home, and because they experiment with their sexuality. As such, they are proclaimed to be not "real Slovenes," and can thus be a target of nationalist exclusion or even pointed aggression, symbolically equated with Chinese immigrants caught at the border, or with animals hunted by the "border guard." The animosity towards exploratory, transgressional, or simply non-traditional gender practices gains a manifold intensity when constructed as the rightful defense against women who are, above all, not real Slovenes, who are weakening or even outright threatening Slovenia, and against whom Slovenia should be protected. And the conflagration of gender and sexuality issues with the national(istic) ones gains potency on account of the importance of the national issues in post-Yugoslav Slovenia.[7]

The Close-Up Vision

The "border guard's" speech is followed that same night by an attempt to rape the three girls, perpetrated by himself and his two aides. This attempt may have been real or fictional (about which more later). The "border guard's" speech and his aggression towards women form the symbolic center of the film. The identification of national danger and national enemies, as well as

---

[7] After its independence from Yugoslavia in 1991, the country went about defining its independently *Slovenian* identity as different from the one it had as a part of Yugoslavia. This task of identity-building gained even more pertinence because of the fact that, among all rather small post-Yugoslav successor states, Slovenia is one of the smallest, with a language not shared by its neighbors, to the west and north bordered by Italy and Austria, non-Slavic countries with historically hegemonic cultures (Austria in particular being the site of past Germanic dominance in the region, as the center of the Habsburg Empire and Austro-Hungary, under which Slovenia itself spent a number of centuries).

the assertion of the needed action (protect the country against "foreigners," maintain "the border between good and bad"), are shown as clearly leading to the rape scene: rape justified as being, in fact, a protection of the country and of "good." Once unleashed, aggression is also characterized by the convenient widening of the target population: not only atypical and dangerous women like Alja and Žana are a good target for the nationalist "defense," but all women become so as Simona is threatened as much as the other two women.

Up to this point (the moment of the "border guard's" speech and the rape attempt), the film strongly emphasizes the three women's utmost lack of awareness of the potential danger, and their literal inability to see it. Efficient seeing in the film is not done by them, but instead by the point-of-view shots taken from the vantage point of a hidden observer and, as it becomes increasingly clear, a hidden predator. He sees without being seen, plots without being known, and always encounters the unsuspecting women in his own time. The three women, on the contrary, cannot see through the impenetrable banks of the river, and the motif of their being unable to see in general recurs over and over again: it is hard for them to see clearly the man behind the cross in the forest, or who shoots and where the shooting is coming from, or who left a fishing line that leads to them and why. They see only the grotesque and terrifying shadows of their attackers through the sides of their tent, and all of the film which Žana develops ends up being blank. A symbolic division appears between the "border guard" who views the world with "long shots," so to speak, takes in the wider area with his gaze, always sees the three women (even when they try to hide amongst the throngs of other people at the fair), and claims a wider political influence and power, and the women who occasionally try to see a wider area (Žana with her camera) but repeatedly fail in doing so, and eventually seem to be able to both see and want to see only in "close ups." Alja and Žana thus gradually become each other's main object of seeing. Sitting by the fire at night, they are separated from the rest of the environment by the complete darkness that surrounds them, and they look at and see only each other in alternating close ups of their faces. This short-range focus seems to take over their ability and desire to see farther, and observe a wider community and space where they find themselves. When they chance upon the villagers' fair at night, Žana will appear as if she literally does not clearly see the folk dance in front of her, behaving in an inappropriate and seemingly disrespectful manner, dancing her wild dance next to the orderly circle of the folk dancers.

The three girls' conversations also focus solely on the private space; they talk about their potential futures, or about their fathers and their present and past boyfriends or lovers. Their inability to see any wider context correlates with their apparently genuine lack of interest in or knowledge of the variety of such "wider" spaces: the natural environment which they entered (they are ignorant about both nature itself and the ways of behaving outdoors), the people who actually live in that area, the people who momentarily enter and are then forcefully expelled from that area (Žana takes pictures of the capturing of the group of presumably Chinese people trying to cross the border, but neither she nor the other two girls ever show much concern for those people), or the political landscape of Slovenia which may be literally changing under their feet, so to speak, and forming new connections amongst that nature, the area's "real Slovenes," the briefly glimpsed "intruders," and the three women themselves.

The "border guard's" speech articulates and naturalizes conservative policies regarding gender and sexuality, and forcefully asserts them as truly "Slovenian" ones. The ensuing rape scene forms the second half of the symbolic center of the film, but it also creates a cognitive breakthrough of the film. Up to the point of the rape scene, the film could be perceived as highlighting and emphasizing a dangerous—but also conceptually recognizable—conflagration of nationalist, gender, and sexuality borders, as well as the women's "close-up" vision that precludes a more effective seizing of and dealing with this situation. But the rape scene ushers in a challenging finale to the film that gives an additional aspect to all that we have seen so far, and supplements the existing conceptual articulations of this situation.

Betrayal and Defeat

Part of the productive potential of the rape scene lies in its sheer ambiguity, in the fact that it is not clear what actually happened. This ambiguity is a result of the film's mixing of reality and fantasy in ways that are intentionally open-ended, with the lack of keys as to the final "reality" of what happened, and with a poignant refusal to provide the decoding pointers as to the reality or fantasy of what is presented in the scene.

After the three girls leave the fair and return to their tent, three men come along and threaten the terrified girls with rape, say they would settle for only one of them, upon which Simona volunteers to be the one, gets out of the tent, and is suddenly seen from the outside as the enchanting mythical "bride of the forest," a figure presumably of local folklore. Clad in a traditional costume, she goes to a clearing in the forest with a bath-tub full of flowers, takes off her clothes, and willingly receives the "border guard," starting a sexual encounter that will end with a phantasmagoric scene and her screaming emergence from the water. Left alone in the tent, Žana and Alja make love for the first time and fall asleep. In the morning, Alja's boy-friend Medo comes to pick the three girls up and sees Alja in an embrace with Žana. The four go back to the border city, where all of the young women's respective narratives of what happened to them acquire an air of even bigger ambiguity. Alja and Žana claim that no rape attempt occurred, but, rather, that Simona simply walked away after the fair of her own free will with two young men. Žana's and Alja's own stories about the threatening "border guard," however, are in turn not believed by their local city acquaintances. When developed, the photographs that could prove either of the stories come out all white, increasing a lingering sense of uncertainty as to what actually took place in the forest far from the well-lit urban realms.

At the beginning of the rape scene, as the "border guard" and his two young helpers obscenely threaten the women from outside their tent, both Žana and Alja, usually rather assertive, end up on the defensive, silent and horrified, briefly attempting a defense with inadequate means (Žana's "I've got pictures!" which provokes an avalanche of scorn by the three men), or else sheepishly offering apologies for the offenses they had not committed (Alja's "OK, we're sorry!"). The two women are taken by surprise by this attack, have no means of defending themselves, and end up totally defeated. This ultimate defeat, furthermore, confirms and emphasizes the pattern of previous encounters with the "border guard": Žana and Alja, despite their repeated show of independence and toughness, have ended up pathetically helpless and conquered in every single confrontation with him, listening without a word to his raving about their "un-natural" looks and behavior earlier in the forest, obeying his orders to sit, be quiet, or get into his car, and eventually being defenseless against his and his men's real or imagined rape. The only way they can deal with this man and all that he represents, it seems, is through escaping from him and his territory altogether.

This ultimate defeat provides a perspective from which the irony towards nationalism, as sported, for instance, by Žana and Alja, is seen as ultimately flat and impotent. This irony dismisses nationalistic discourses and ideology, as well as national/istic territorial and identity borders (the girls' illegal crossing of the border into Croatia, their forging of a relationship with a Croatian actor), but it does so only with regard to the private space. Such displacing irony is clearly limited itself within the borders of the private realm: it neither wants nor is able to engage the wider public space, where both nationalist speech and exclusionary and non-liberal policies stay and grow alive and well.

Second, Alja and Žana leave Simona to her own destiny, presumably to be raped by the "border guard" and his helpers. The two are powerless to protect her, they are not too eager to do so either, and they let her get out of the tent. They can be left in peace and then pursue their own interests only by turning their back on Simona and her predicament: there is no solidarity with or sympathy for her, but instead they later blame her. Thus two radically different interpretations of rape emerge. Alja and Žana emphasize Simona's own choice, claiming that she left with the young men of her own free will. Simona asserts instead their abandonment and betrayal, insisting that she was raped in place of them, and that her volunteering to be raped saved them from the same fate.

The fact that the film shows Simona's version of the story seems to give primacy to her interpretation of what happened. In other words, Simona may be sexually attracted to the "border guard" and his demand for a woman's submission, and she may indeed have merely fantasized that her encounter with him took place, given the fantastic elements in the sequence following her getting out of the tent. However, the film does not feature a scene in which Simona goes with the two young men after the fair of her own free will, as Alja and Žana claim, but rather a thoroughly realistic scene in which the three men threaten the girls in the tent, and the two other women allow Simona to get out instead of them, and be used by the men at their will. It thus seems that *Border Guard* articulates a situation where, regardless of what "really" happened in the forest at night, it is primarily the complete abandonment of Simona by the other two women, the presumably emancipated ones, that allow her to become subjected both to the "border guard's" drive to possess her and her own vulnerability responding to this.

Defeat and betrayal end up characterizing Alja's and Žana's trip into the unknown, the pursuit of their potential sexualities and intimate pleasures; defeat when confronted with the "border guard," and betrayal of women who are not of immediate interest to them. The concerns of the two women are private and self-centered, and thus atomizing, not building any commonalities or communities with women who are not directly involved in these personal pursuits. Those women are abandoned to their own loneliness and vulnerability. Thus, the attraction of the domineering "border guard" increases for Simona in proportion to the growing rejection of her two travel companions. On the other hand, Alja and Žana are themselves doomed to impotence and defeat in any encounter with organized patriarchal forces on account of both their lack of interest in (and inability to see and know) the wider contexts in which they find themselves, and their lack of connection with other women. Any feminist solidarity, and indeed even basic feminist attitude, seeing gender as a place of commonality of at least somewhat shared destiny and interests, appears completely absent not only in the case of the traditional Simona, but also in the case of the non-conventional Alja and Žana.

Floating Down the River

The motif of the young women traveling down the river, or being taken by the river, acquires metaphorical overtones when seen in connection with the curious absence of clarity of direction or goals of any kind—private, professional, political, or any other. The three women seem to be generally "floating down the river" more than choosing some path, and seem to have no strong desires, wishes, or direction. Simona studies economy and languages, yet she shows more gratification when being approved by the people they meet (as studying pragmatically wise subjects) than she ever shows any interest in or passion for her studies. Žana, while pursuing a sexual encounter with Alja, also does not look like someone for whom her sexuality, or anything else for that matter, is a dearly paid subjective discovery that provides a source of energy and direction. And Alja does not seem to really want anything all that much, professionally or privately, although she sometimes mentions that she would like to be writing novels; she stumbles into the relationship with Žana and then stumbles out of it at the spur of the moment. Overall, she defines herself more by negations, by what she refuses to do, than by what she does: at the beginning of the trip she refuses to make love with Medo, and at the end of the trip she refuses to be with Žana.

This "floating" existence seems enabled by, among other things, the situation of comfort and privilege that does not appear to prompt—let alone force—the three women into engaging their environment as well as their own lives in a more active manner. They are shown as materially provided for, not wealthy but secure, never mentioning things such as money or the unpleasant jobs they may have to do while studying in order to support themselves. From the American perspective, the three women look unmistakably "European" in their lack of worries about how to pay for college, living expenses, or possible healthcare-related costs, living as they do in a place that combines universal healthcare and still largely free higher education with some not so unpleasant aspects of a more traditional society, such as mothers making food for and pampering their college-age daughters regardless of how ungratefully these daughters may behave. Such a materially privileged existence allows a lack of engagement in as well as a complete disconnect from the wider social context. It may be harder to become interested in or feel much concern for the situation of Slovenian workers, or global workers for that matter (those Chinese people trying to enter Slovenia), if one inhabits a vastly different position oneself, and it may be equally hard to feel the commonality with and concern for other women if one has not had to fight for things such as available family planning or abortion rights.[8]

---

[8]There was a major attempt to curb abortion rights in Slovenia right after the proclamation of independence, and a major fight against it that succeeded in

Thus, while the Slovenian political, social, and cultural realms have shifted greatly, the response by young, well-educated, urban women, the response as intimated in *Border Guard*, seems to be no response at all. Alja and Žana are temporarily disturbed by what they saw and experienced in the forested border region, and are trying to communicate to and impress upon their city acquaintances the presence and the utmost "insanity," in their view, of the "border guard" and his adherents. But they do not seem likely to keep this awareness, nor to use it for the possible mapping of their present and especially of their future environment, in which the "border guard" may well emerge from the real and symbolic forest and claim a more central place in the wider national areas where they themselves live. Such mapping of space and time is not done, and it seems that the young women's movement into the future will be just some more "floating down the river" rather than choosing this or that path, let alone forging new ones. The possible feminist project concerned with justice and gender solidarity is non-existent, and replaced with the fully private and rather distracted "floating down the river" and changing into the personae one stumbles onto, from a more traditional heterosexual partner to an exploratory traveler, from perhaps a writer to a one-night lesbian lover, to not being either at the end, in the moment of change into the next persona.

Walter Benjamin's classical insight into fascism (which is "giving ... masses not their right, but instead a chance to express themselves"), can be applied here to a historically very different situation.[9] Alja and Žana do not—and seem like they would not—pursue any political activity, but they do claim, though without much passion, their individual self-expression, partly through their own sexual involvement. Much of their self-expression, however, is defined by the market society, and allowed merely as the consumer's choice among available commodities symbolizing the pseudo-individual lifestyles.[10] Thus, possessing leather jackets or

---

keeping abortion rights intact, culminating on 11 December 1991 with a demonstration in front of the parliament building. It all happened, thus, while the young women of *Border Guard* were still only children.

[9] Walter Benjamin, *Illuminations: Essays and Reflections* (1989), 241.

[10] This situation can also be described, using Rayna Rapp's words, as the "reduction of feminist *social* goals to individual 'life-styles'." (Quoted in R.

Fig 10.2 Alja, *The Border Guard* (2002)

fashionable sun-glasses or new cameras, and sporting bare midriffs, like Alja and Žana, takes the place of doing something, and serves as the identity self-labeling. The photographs taken by Žana end up destroyed, developing into rolls of blank negatives, and Alja is never seen actually writing something, emphasizing in both cases the two women's impotence when it comes to doing something. The main thing—literally a thing—that comforts Žana after her solitary tantrum following Alja's refusal to kiss her, is her nose ring: she touches it by accident, remembers that she has it, and feels good about herself again. Feeling better about herself, however, does not lead to any practice other than that of self-expression: Alja and Žana end up dancing into the night, the two of them alone on the dancefloor but not together, with their backs turned to each other. This is the last image we see of them.

The "border guard's" official position—he is a government official and a prominent local politician running for the office of regional representative—indicates the relative institutionalization of his attitude, the attitude that has indeed gained a significant foothold in Slovenia's post-independence culture, largely due to the organized efforts of conservative factions and a weaker response

---

Dubrovsky, "Ally McBeal as Post-Feminist Icon: The Aestheticizing and Fetishizing of the Independent Working Woman," *Communication Review* 5 (2002), 278 (emphasis in original).

by the liberal parts of the society and by women themselves.[11] A stark contrast is evident between this patriarchal stance and the relatively recent official policies and ideology of socialism during the Yugoslav era, which included strong reproductive rights and support of work-related gender equality. *Border Guard* thus also acts as a clear reminder, at least for the older generations of Slovenian viewers, of the fact that post-Yugoslav and post-socialist Slovenia experienced a substantial reduction of much of the gender equality and women's rights that were taken for granted in the latter Yugoslav era.[12] The film was released in 2002; the year 2004

---

[11] The main characteristics of the women's nongovernmental organizations (NGOs) are problematic ... Having an anti-political orientation and being more interested in solving social problems, they tend to be autarchic and do not receive enough publicity. Above all, they act in an unstable climate of competitiveness instead of one of solidarity which is the result of inadequate funding ...

The main problem that I want to emphasize is that the influence of these groups is, in general, very small. There exist almost no continual, organized political efforts for the improvement of the position of women ... the total lack of political influence of women in Slovenia in comparison with countries which would be expected to have much worse opportunities.

The political participation of women did not become a constitutive part of the political agenda. Among the main parties, there dominated a viewpoint that men could represent women as well (if not better) that they could represent themselves ...

Liberal-democratic institution- and elite-building, along with economic reforms, were the main activities ... of the so-called transitional period to democracy ... the new institutions automatically produced gender-hierarchic structures.
(Vlasta Jalušič (1999), 127–9)

[12] Sabrina Ramet notes that "[i]n communist times, women filled 22 percent of elective posts in Slovenia (in 1986). But after the multiparty elections of 1990, only 10 percent of those elected to the Slovenian Assembly were women. After the 1996 elections, women made up only 8 percent of deputies in the Assembly ... Women's initiatives in almost all fields lack support and have difficulty attracting public recognition ... [O]ther factors [than war] have been at work ... the profound reaction against everything associated with socialism (hence, all talk of women's equality) ... the dedication with which the Christian Churches, now freed of the constraints imposed by the Communist parties, set about dismantling some of the prerogatives enjoyed by women (most especially access to abortion) and affirming the "naturalness" of what is rather self-servingly called the traditional role of women. Sabrina Ramet, *Balkan Babel: the Disintegration of Yugoslavia from the Death of Tito to the Fall of Milošević* (2002), 262–3.

Vlasta Jalušič writes that "[a]fter the breakdown of Yugoslavia and the end of the socialist system, women in Slovenia lost many of the social benefits they had in the saw the establishment of a right-wing government in Slovenia. And while some observers of contemporary Slovenia notice a clear diminishing of women's rights across the board, as well as the sharp worsening of women's overall situation in a transitional economy,[13] others see a more contradictory picture, including, in the words of one researcher, three simultaneous trends: the changes in the direction of the traditionalization of gender relations in some areas; the liberalization of gender relations in other areas of life (some of it promoted by Slovenia's 2004 entry into the EU); as well as the continuity, from the socialist period, of certain gender equality values (e.g., girls' and women's education as a strongly pursued value, positive attitudes towards women's employment outside of home and towards gender equality in general).[14]

While the situation in Slovenia is certainly changing with the passage of time, and is different for different people and in different localities of the country, *Border Guard* still delivers a poignant and important message about the threat posed to all internal "foreigners" in Slovenia by the aggressive patriarchal "border guards," who have managed to largely conflagrate the national, gender, and sexuality borders, portraying the defense of traditional gender and sexual policies and behavior as the defense of Slovenia. These border guards may be coming in and out of power, being stronger at one time and weaker at another, but they are clearly not leaving and not giving up, supported by and akin to their main conservative ally, the Catholic Church—whose crosses, as the film amply shows, are spread all over the border guard's territory. And while the Slovenian women's NGOs may be doing some important work, *Border Guard* paints a picture in which young educated women seem both unable to and uninterested in seeing their wider environments, a picture of these women's radical abandonment of privately uninteresting women and an absence of gender solidarity, carried out to the point of almost irrational animosity towards

---

last period of socialism ... (These social benefits were in many regards similar to the benefits in some Middle European and Scandinavian welfare states. The difference was a lower standard, but [regardless of that] it was still probably the highest among the East European states.)" Vlasta Jalušič (1999), 123.

[13] See Vlasta Jalušič (1999).

[14] I am paraphrasing here the main point made in Milica G. Antić's "Gender Equality in Slovenia" (2006), 215–32.

women who are different from oneself (as in Žana's gut-level reaction to Simona: "No, I don't like you!"). *Border Guard*'s vision includes a repeated defeat of such women when confronted with organized patriarchal forces, brought about by women's atomizing, not collective-building attitude, and the displacement of the potential political practice with (only) self-expression. Instead of potential feminist mapping and related practice or movement, *Border Guard* articulates the aimless "going down the river" and the trying-on of the multiplicity of personae as the young women's current way of life.

Dance, Lingering, and Community

The film's final scene of Žana and Alja dancing leads to interesting insights when seen together with the other dance scenes from *Border Guard*, as well as from a few other contemporary Slovenian films.[15] When the three girls emerge from the forest into the fair, they come upon a people's folk dance, performed as a traditional *kolo*, a circle of people holding hands and moving around in the same dance step. Later that night, Simona sees a similar *kolo* dancing by the fire in a surreal scene, close to the place where she has her real or imagined sexual encounter with the "border guard." A repeated visual contrast is created between a large homogenous group that does one thing and moves "in one step," and the individualizing and non-homogenizing trio of the three young women. The people's group is made to look like a desirable and self-induced community, and is coveted by lonely individuals such as Simona, who transfer the desirability of the community onto the aggressive individuals identifying themselves as its representatives, guardians, and spokesmen. The community, however, is shown as being false, not self-organizing but rather manipulated by the various "border guards," who use the non-critical atmosphere of the people's traditional gatherings (e.g., a fair), to turn the socializing and merrymaking of the community into a nationalist event. After the

---

[15] The motif of dance may also be an allusion to *Dance in the Rain* [*Ples v dežju*, 1961], Boštjan Hladnik's film considered by a number of critics to be the best Slovenian film ever.

"border guard's" speech, the folk songs turn into national(istic) ones, and singing the "Slovenia" song assumes ominous overtones after the "border guard's" repeated shouting of the slogan "Slovenia for the Slovenians!" The people's folk dance and gathering does not end up creating a community, but rather activating an energy that can be manipulated for nationalist and aggressive purposes. Alja's and Žana's dancing at the end of the film, in a local club, can be seen as opposite to the *kolo* dance: not only is it not carried out in a wider group, but it also portrays a failure of the two women to keep together as a couple. Their dance shows a complete mutual alienation of women, and becomes a symbol of their current existential situation.

This dance, placed at the rhetorically most significant point of the film, the very end, also articulates something else, namely the women's curious lingering in the present moment, not wanting to go on or not knowing where or how to go on. The comparison of *Border Guard* with other recent films from Slovenia shows the telling concurrence in this motive of lingering, of wanting to prolong the moment between the past and future, the moment which is a decisive one but in which a person does not quite know how to proceed or what to wish for or decide, and remains in a paralysis-like embrace of that precious time between the past and the future. This lingering is a dominant sentiment in *Murmurings* (*Šelestenje*, 2002), and in *Ljubljana* (2002), a film rhythmically organized by recurrent rave parties in which young people dance their nights away and show an unwillingness to proceed with their lives one way or another.[16]

The dance scenes in *Ljubljana* echo the atmosphere of loneliness,

---

[16] The recurrent rave scenes in *Ljubljana* organize the film and provide the main movement to both the film and its protagonists, as deafening music and rapid lightshows fill the close-ups and medium shots of young people frantically dancing through the night. There is a definite beauty and attraction in the quick motion of music, lights, and people, but as the morning light increasingly provides a better view of the scene, the misery of the space—a dilapidated industrial hall, ugly bare windows, garbage of all kinds—becomes obvious and is hard to ignore. The protagonists' refusal to deal with this unpleasant reality is articulated by the editing which melts the deserted dancehall into the sea and the sky, after which we see young dancers now dancing by the coast, in bright daylight and with shades on their eyes, and on the main city squares, in thousands and seemingly forever. The motif of not seeing and not wanting to see, present in *Border Guard*, is here repeated in the

lingering in the present, and the lack of direction and desire present in Alja's and Žana's final dance. In *Ljubljana*, shots of lone silent young people, immobile in their rooms, alternate with shots of these people frantically dancing in a mass. The lonely ones seek genuine community, but the community they find—that of rave dancers in *Ljubljana*, or of the "people" in the folk dances of *Border Guard*—is a false one. Group dances in both films indicate a potential and desirable community, but the real communities created by these dances end up being manipulated by nationalist goals in *Border Guard*, or by crass material motives in *Ljubljana* (rave parties as the prime distribution centers for drugs). And there is again a lack of strong desire to do or become anything: the dance, with its movement in always the same place, gives only the illusion of moving and doing something. The young women in *Ljubljana*, like those in *Border Guard*, stay alone and alienated, vulnerable before an uncertain future and unwilling to go into that future, with the never-ending dances being the means both of self-expression and of lingering in the eternal present.

The above-mentioned dance scenes articulate a number of aspects. They confirm the absence of gender (or any other) solidarity, and the absence of public politics *per se*, as well as the replacement of such solidarity and politics with self-expression, individual lifestyles, and a search—though often a rather vague, distracted, and languid search—for individual identity. Dancing

---

images of young people closing their eyes, wearing shades or sleeping in through the days.

In *Ljubljana*, dance scenes—in which the central female character passes time in movement, music and drugs—are also visually contrasted with the scenes of women sitting on their beds. In one sequence, a young woman from the rave parties sits on her bed and talks to her mother on the phone, unsuccessfully trying to talk her into sending some money; in the following sequence, another young woman, a student of medicine, sits on her bed and talks in person to her mother, telling her that she will not continue her studies because of the grim employment prospects, and that she will be fine anyhow. Both young women are successively shown as imprisoned in a space where they cannot move or progress in any meaningful way, but are literally glued to their beds. Evoked by their being framed by their beds, their sexuality will be their one tool of some change: a young rave woman will get together with a drug dealer, and a medicine student will become involved with a successful but, to her, unattractive bachelor businessman, become pregnant, and presumably end up as a stay-at-home wife and mother.

in these films also articulates the state or stasis of lingering. And thirdly, it also indicates the unfulfilled yet compelling need for community and belonging, as well as for joy in an activity that connects one with others. In all these ways, dance scenes can be seen as the metaphors of transitional and post-socialist identity, with its lingering and stepping back from the future, its loss of community and collective belonging and a need for such belonging (a vague sentiment often manipulated by nationalist or religious institutions for their own very clear agendas), and its not too passionate search for individual identity. These dance scenes mark the landscape where aspects of personal identity, gender, sexuality, nationalism, isolation, collectivity, and so on, intersect with the processes of transition, are themselves put into accelerated motion, and "where feminist intervention could be most valuable, not 'only' for women but as a broad intervention against the trends towards becoming a more xenophobic and racist society, present in Slovenia today."[17]

These scenes seem to indicate the need for the creation of a wider, "long shot" spatial and temporal mapping of the current situation of women,[18] a mapping which would include a reclaiming of the past[19] and tracing of possible futures, as well as the (self)-positioning of Slovenian women within global processes. Also needed is the creation of the community that is both playful and organized. Broader and collective, a newly-pursued feminist perception and practice could potentially trace past, present, and

---

[17] I am paraphrasing here a comment made by Ksenija Vidmar Horvat.
[18] This mapping should include the aggressive debunking of the bad reputation that the very names and concepts of feminism and feminists have in Slovenia, the bad reputation which originated in socialist Yugoslavia (with feminists being often seen as Western-influenced bourgeois intellectuals without much connection to the real life of the majority of women in Yugoslavia), and then carried on, though with very different connotations, into the independent Slovenia, where feminists are now supposed to be the remnants of the "un-natural" socialism that promoted women's work out of home, full support of family planning, etc.
[19] As Ksenija Vidmar Horvat astutely points out, Slovenian young women's perception of socialist past is "puzzling" in its discrepancy from the unquestionable facts of this rather recent era, and shows that it is dominantly formed by the present patriarchal recasting of history which, by doing so, deprives Slovenian women of their past and its many lessons. See Ksenija Vidmar Horvat, "The globalization of gender" (2005), 239–55.

possible futures, those that are wanted and those that should be fought against, and that clarity of collective vision could hopefully provide, in its turn, an impetus for moving out of the lingering present and into those futures.

One should also stress that, in addition to clearly articulating issues relevant for contemporary Slovenia, Maja Weiss's *Border Guard* has much to offer international audiences. With its exploration of the attractions and dangers of the exclusiveness of the close-up vision, its foregrounding of the paralysing effects of the stasis of lingering, and its engaging road movie story set in a stunning natural environment, the film speaks well to the many who may find themselves on a journey down the river similar to the one taken by the three girls on the Kolpa.

11

Foundations III
Success vs. Logic:
Miroslav Krleža's *On the Edge of Reason*

It is true: I was rather alone, but loneliness is still not a proof of not being right.[1]

A Rift

Logos/word/truth unites in itself conceptual abstraction or generality with a communal acceptance or communal agreement. In "this is a *pen*," for instance, the word or idea of the "pen" unites within itself, on one hand, a logical abstract that gives a common concept and name to all the millions of pens in the world (so that all of them are a "pen," an abstract notion applied to a particular thing), with, on the other hand, a communal acceptance or communal agreement: *we all agree* that this is, indeed, a pen. But what if there is a terrible rupture, and the two sides break apart? What if, quite suddenly, only I say that this is a pen, and you the reader, and all

---

[1]Miroslav Krleža, *On the Edge of Reason*, trans. Zora Depolo (1995), 54. I have slightly altered Depolo's translation in this and a few other places to achieve a more literal rendition of the original. Also, given that this edition omits a large part of the novel, where noted the citations are my own translations of the 1960 edition of Krleža's novel.

a rose

the rest of the people, claim that this is actually a rose, not a pen, and that I, holding onto my truth about the pen, have obviously gone mad? What happens then, and why is that, what happens, important for us?

This rift between *logos* or truthfulness as rational certainty, or as something logical, and truthfulness as a communal agreement, as something social, is at the heart of Miroslav Krleža's 1938 novel *On the Edge of Reason* (*Na rubu pameti*). A dinner party is taking place in the vineyard of Mr. Domaćinski, a wealthy and influential businessman. In one moment, reacting to Domaćinski's cheerful telling of "a gay anecdote of how, in 1918, he had shot four men there like four dogs,"[2] men who tried to rob his wine cellar, the unnamed main character and the first-person narrator, a well-off attorney and employee of Domaćinski, "absorbed in thought, completely calm, without any undertone betraying irritation, more to [him]self than to anybody else, as if absent-mindedly ... said that 'it [bragging about this act] was all a crime, a bloody thing, morally sick.'"[3] Later on, "fascinated by the naiveté of my

---

[2] Krleža (1995), 32.
[3] Krleža (1995), 34.

little truth,"⁴ upheld only and exclusively by him, he refuses to retract, apologize, plead guilty or insanity, and is as a consequence deserted by all his former colleagues and associates, his wife and children, is sued, torn apart by the papers and the city's gossip, imprisoned, and released only to face an avalanche of further law suits, probable future imprisonments, and certain ruin. The fissure between his certainty and that of the others reaches Orwellian proportions, where Domaćinski, a man expelled from the Austro-Hungarian state administration on account of his embezzlement, as the documents of the time show, is proclaimed by all others as having been fired on account of his courageous patriotism against Austro-Hungary and for what will become Yugoslavia, where the same man, who was also a police spy helping send patriots to the gallows, is again praised as a defender of the people's interests, and, eventually, where the vineyard scene's witnesses claim "that the cigarette case glittering in my hand was a revolver and that the revolver in Domaćinski's hand was indeed a cigarette case," recalling the final scene of the evening in the vineyard, when Domaćinski pulled out his revolver and yelled that "he would shoot [the narrator] like a dog."⁵

In the midst of it all, as the narrator puts it:

> One thing, however, became clear to me: one should remain logical, because, happen what may, logic is never an unreliable guide. It is true: I was rather alone, but loneliness is still not a proof of not being right.⁶

Logical but alone, in truthfulness in one way but not in another, he is, indeed, both in and out of *logos* or reason, within and without at the same time, or, as the novel's title accurately puts it, he is "on the edge" of reason.

---

⁴Krleža (1995), 37.
⁵Krleža (1995), 136, 38.
⁶Krleža (1995), 54.

The Repulsive Appearance of the Logical

What, then, to ask a rather simple initial question, does this logical but lonely truth look like? With this question, we should first remind ourselves that truth indeed has a certain look and body to it. We tend to think about it— *the truth*—as being a pure thought or a disembodied idea, but ideas, not having a body themselves, need bodies to be communicated and articulated or expressed. Ideas require the sensual materiality of spoken or written words, of pages on which they are written or technical tools through which they are shaped and communicated, of voices that tell them, or of people who look this or that way, and who are connected with these ideas. The sensual aspect is important in our appreciation of the truth because we are not only, or perhaps even primarily, cerebral beings, but are also sensual ones as well. Art, for example, as well as politics to the extent to which it works through aesthetical, sensual forms, as "aestheticized" politics, does not reach us through our rational minds, but through our senses, and though it can affect us as much or much more than the rational argument can, it does not work its impact through rational channels but through sensual and sensory ones, such as our eyes and our ears. Statements and words claiming "rational" truth, however, also have to employ bodily and sensual channels, and these sensual forms determine to a large extent whether that which is communicated by them is perceived as truth, largely according to the specific social conventions of what the truth is supposed to look like.

In *On the Edge of Reason*, we meet the look of the truth that is logical but lonely, and see that its appearance is rather disheveled and often unappealing and even repulsive, that of "an overstrained man with undermined nerves,"[7] or of a "decrepit old man with pouches under his eyes and bad teeth," and with "the sad features of a bold, fat, dull, lazy man."[8] This man's/the truth's speech has an underlying logical structure but does not have the sensual, bodily form of calmness or self-assurance assumed to accompany a truthful speech; instead, it is nervous, agitated, and often with a heightened tone. It is the speech of, at its most tranquil

---

[7] Krleža (1995), 152.
[8] Krleža (1995), 19.

state, "nervous restlessness, or rather neurasthenic fussing."⁹ The truth's behavior is increasingly decomposed, exalted, impatient, and eventually appears nothing less than insane. The effect of insanity is heightened because, looking from any position other than that of the narrator, looking from the outside, one is bound to notice only the visible and mad-looking conclusions of a certain situation or scene, and not the preceding causes. One thus sees the main character slapping someone across the face, or pushing a whole tea table in a café onto the man sitting on the other side of it; but one does not see or hear the persistent verbal abuses, threats, or physical aggression that preceded these actions. The narrator appears, at best, as a delusional Don Quixote, attacking the air or else basically innocent, normal, "ordinary" people.

In other words, the rupture between the conceptual and communal aspects of the truth is complemented—to go back to Plato's correspondence between truth, beauty, and goodness, where truthful is also beautiful—with a rupture between truth and beauty, because truthfulness starts to look ugly, worn out, unpleasantly disturbed, insane, and thus, in short, non-truthful.

The Attractive Social Truth

This logical but lonely and deranged-looking truth is put in opposition to the attractively draped truth that is not logical but is, instead, a pragmatic deduction. One looks good and one speaks well that which is opportune for one's survival and advancement; such people "have never known how, nor wanted to either, to think along the lines of any logic that does not bring about some kind of profit."¹⁰ This pragmatic and profit logic is no logic at all. Rather, this polished and convincingly looking "truth" is a part of the world where the only important thing, the goal that builds everything under it and towards it, is, of course, success.

> Generally, everything in life is a matter of success, and success in itself signifies sleeping: a pleasant sleep with hot and cold

---

⁹Krleža (1995), 15.
¹⁰Krleža (1995), 35.

running water, a sleep without a toothache or any special soporifics, a calm, sound sleep when conscience is at rest, when the brain is not at work, when one travels in a sleeping car and smokes the finest tobacco. Success is an end in itself, and success is for the sake of success, and everything is for the sake of success: big and trifling lies, dinners and tea parties, circles of people, friendships, deceptions, hatreds, wars, and careers. To secure success, roles are being played, masks worn; everybody is afraid of failure, everybody dreams of success. Ideas are confused, and success is the only criterion: you kill people; you wear elegant, pointed shoes, well-ironed trousers; you put polish on your nails; you travel; you deal in trade; you have houses built; you conduct wars; you write books; you make paintings; you are on a lighted stage, in an office, on a newspaper editorial board, and you are not thinking, that life actually should not be that, what it is thought to be in offices, on the stage, or in the press."[11]

Success names things: a woman who gained "a bracelet, a villa, a car, horses, servants, ships, summer resorts, jewelry, securities" and so on, is a "distinguished lady," whereas Jadviga Jasenska, the narrator's temporary companion, who "earned no villas," was "on that ground alone ... considered a loose woman. If she had lived in her own villa, she would have been a distinguished lady."[12] Success, and primarily financial success, shapes pragmatic truth, morality, and taste: it is the Director-General Domaćinski, as a boss, donor, and employer, who "lectures the boards, the rectors, the universities, the press, charitable societies, delegations, political parties, painters, public opinion, one whole society."[13] Success thus orders the work of the intellectual realms, which self-represent themselves as arbiters of truth and morality, acting independence, but actually working according to guidance from above.

---

[11] Krleža (1995), 46–7.
[12] Krleža (1995), 86–7.
[13] Krleža (1995), 29.

Cataloguing

The resulting pragmatic truth is related to legality and not to ethics. At the time of watching one war—the Spanish Civil War—and preparing to become engaged in another—World War Two—this pragmatic truthfulness, untouched by any ethical considerations, derives itself from the success of the premises that poison gas attacks are a necessary part of war, that wars themselves are "the way things are," and that there are large groups of people, in this case the poor and destitute of European cities, who are in fact "our human trash" that should be disposed of. Thus, such pragmatic truthfulness coolly writes, for instance,

> ... an article by an expert about poison gas attacks on European cities and about the socially selective advantages of such attacks. The author of the article correctly assumed that it was chiefly the overpopulated sections of a large city that would be victimized in the event of a well-planned attack with poison gas—that is, the sections inhabited by the demoralized city dregs. Since today, with our high degree of technology and mechanized production, unskilled manpower is, in the main, absolutely superfluous, a poison-gas attack on a large industrial city would, among other things, have the virtue of getting rid of our human trash. [14]

Pragmatic truthfulness is deduced and not self-thought or self-developed: "truth [is] that ... which we tend to believe (because this is profitable for us ...)."[15] Deduced truth is related to deduced or made people, manufactured and thus lifeless and doll-like. The sameness and the proliferation of such "pragmatic truth" people is articulated through the making of the catalogues of such people, associating and being connected with the catalogues of manufactured commodities:

> These beggars, intellectual good-for-nothings, blue blooded fools ... scribblers abounding in unhealthy ambitions, imitators

---

[14] Krleža (1995), 158.
[15] Miroslav Krleža, *Na rubu pameti* (1960), 258. Trans. by Gordana P. Crnković. This part is absent from the New Directions edition.

of other people's stupidities, dignitaries, orators, lecturers, insane people who chew on their own sorry careers as if they were pralines ... Jewelers, dentists, better-off salesmen, technical section chiefs, Romance linguists, cellists, shoe dealers, freethinkers, Lamarckians, pediatricians, wholesalers and private employees, cosmeticians and specialists in skin diseases, barons, landlords, master tailors who tailor books with their pens on schedule and according to measure, hired agitators ... bankrupt bankers, state finance administrators ... wax statues ... the number of lavatories, canals, shipbuilding, rails, rifles and machines in general are on the increase.[16]

Logical, Non-Communal

Being "on the edge of reason" means rejecting a well-heeled, attractive and successful pragmatic truth, and holding onto the truth which is logical, but not communal.

Not being communal, it is, in the main, considered to be "some sort of derangement of [one's] brain":

> ... that that same impersonal individual [the narrator] could have his own opinion, especially an opinion which is in no way coinciding with their own, was beyond the capacity of their fancy. They were unexpectedly confused thereby, and it could account for their ... in the main, general agreement that I was suffering some sort of derangement of my brain. Certainly, since I had stopped thinking along the lines of their logic, I might very well have seemed mad. Their "logic" was a kind of conventional social game played according to fixed rules. The rules read: the world is as is, one should not be fixing it. The game of dominoes is played to win, and everything else is sheer "philosophizing."[17]

This non-communal truthfulness, however, is logical, because it asks for the recognition of basic logical reasoning that seems rather self-evident, but to which people willfully "blind" themselves

---

[16] Krleža (1995), 42–5.
[17] Krleža (1995), 47-8.

because of the opposition of this logical reasoning to the convenient, pragmatic truthfulness.

If a person were to prove, with decisive logic, that he is not drunk but is only thinking logically, if he were to elaborate the theme, that our peasants, these "rebellious swine of outlaws," had in reality been no bandits, that at the time the walls of a dungeon, of a centuries-long unjust state of affairs, were breaking apart, that it was in reality an international catastrophe, elemental and, as it were, primeval, that our man was no "mad dog" in those days, but on the contrary, a human being from whom a dignity of a humiliated slave spoke out, the gentlemen around this table would not understand it, because the gentlemen around this table lacked even the most minute prerequisites to comprehend such logical thinking.

The "mad dogs" wanted to rob his cellar, to empty his costly barrels of wine, and he fired at them to defend his wine, which was undoubtedly his own property. However, when those other "mad dogs"—the emperor's and king's dogs—bottled and poured that same wine of his within the framework of requisition (and even other people's blood, which was likewise somebody's property), he did not, of course, fire at representatives of the imperial and royal authorities, since it was lawful requisition of the wine, in compliance with the positive laws on requisition. At that time, the Director-General did not, of course, fight on the battlefield, but made money as a meat- and fat- and brandy-supplier amid the massacre that was not, by any means, any kind of "criminal massacre" but a "just war," exclusively conducted for that purpose, i.e., that such and similar idiots could earn money as patriots and decent people. And, at any rate: what are these "positive laws" whose only basis is an unlawful violence, and why did Director-General not open fire against the unlawful requisition of wine in wartime but against "mad dogs" who barked at that unlawfulness of the war situation in general, and who, in their fight against this unlawfulness, had been the only guarantor of lawfulness, in a higher, ethical sense.[18]

---

[18] Krleža (1995), 33-4.

When the powers-that-be took Domaćinski's wine, that was fine, but when four hungry peasants allegedly tried to do the same, that was a crime deserving execution on the spot. According to the "positive laws" of the time, the same action, done by the emperor, is a lawful requisition, and done by the hungry peasants, is a crime. Logic, however, sees things differently, as it asks for the same terms and same logical reasoning when judging various events and various agents, regardless of their place in the social hierarchy. If World War One was indeed a "criminal massacre," a pragmatic endeavor conducted for profit and cynically named a "just war," then the government or governments supporting this "war machine" are, logically, themselves criminal. The outlaws, those fighting the unlawfulness of the war, may, on the contrary, end up being the "guarantor(s) of lawfulness in a higher, ethical sense." And if the "positive laws" are indeed based only on unlawful violence, then they, too, are unlawful. Viewed logically, the established and successful realms and people may end up being seen in ways quite different from the established ones, with Domaćinski himself, this "pride of the whole nation, a benefactor, a model Christian" (as his attorney Hugo-Hugo states in court), being found out to be, in fact, "obviously and logically nobody else but ... a murderer"[19] and a "criminal type of man,"[20] as the narrator summarizes it.

Detaching and Re-Attaching

On the Edge of Reason characterizes logic in three main ways. First, logic detaches and then re-attaches: it detaches socially accepted names from the realities named by them, and then re-names those same realities following its own consistency. If the war was a "criminal massacre" of millions, then those who supported the perpetuation of such a war were not patriots and "the pride of the whole nation," but instead criminals, evil-doers and murderers. Such logic is applied not only to the late 1930s' pragmatic and success-oriented capitalist society of European higher circles, with many of whom the narrator is confronted

---

[19] Krleža (1995), 32.
[20] ibid.

with having undisguised sympathies for the rising fascism, but also to its proclaimed opposite, Soviet communism of the time. In the chapter "Moonlight Can be a World View as Well," the narrator calls the violence done in the name of a "higher social order," again, "criminal butchering and killing."[21] Talking with his cellmate, nicknamed *Sinek* (an engineer, thus connoting Stalin's famous phrase about "engineers of human souls;" the word *sinek* ["a little son"] also implies the father, Stalin), the narrator asks: "Pray tell me ... will there, in the frame of your 'higher social order,' which will comply with all the demands of a modern world-view, will one again criminally butcher and kill, in the same way in which one criminally butchers and kills within the frame of this non-modern world-view, embodied in Domaćinski?"[22]

Detaching in one way, and re-attaching in another, logic throws one outside of community circles, both that of the pragmatic bourgeois realm and that of the established Soviet-style communist opposition. There is no collective any more, only an individual and his individual, logical truth. An affinity towards the silenced and the victimized slowly appears, however, and with it a certain non-self-conscious and parched community of those trying to acknowledge and hold on to their own logical truths, and attracting the kindred spirits in that quest. A fellow prison inmate, Valent Žganec— "Vudriga," an uneducated and gentle, wise man, whose last name connotes the common people's fare *žganci* (polenta)—was "a bit in love with me ... he got convinced that there are human beings among the suits too, and that very insight ... gave him hope that not all is lost."[23]

The Question of Morals as a Matter of Taste

Second, logic proceeds from certain grounding judgments, which the narrator calls "humanely logical" (*ljudski logično*), and which are themselves not derived but foundational. Such judgments

---

[21] This chapter is absent from the 1995 New Directions edition.
[22] Krleža (1960), 174. Trans. by Gordana P. Crnković. This part is absent from the 1995 edition.
[23] Krleža (1995), 143-4.

include, for instance, the narrator's assertion that bragging about the quadruple murder of unarmed people attempting to flee is "morally sick," or the one that sees the "positive laws" of the time as enforcing unlawful violence. The important aspect of these "humanely logical," beginning judgments, is that, by virtue of their not being derived from something prior to them, they are "immune" to the attempted primacy or dominance of any previously set notions or rules, any helpful and all-explaining "view of the world."

> If any unclear question shows up, a human being has his own metaphysical matches next to himself on his night table and can light the candle at any second if necessary. The "world view" puts asleep mind and conscience and heart, the "world view" improves potency, lengthens life, makes one younger. Every fear of earthquake or any other unexpected catastrophe is unfounded, while a citizen has on his night table a few boxes of his patented "world view," which helps a digestion of his intelligence, stops the belching of his conscience, clears the mind, guarantees life's success ...
> [What remains to us] is [n]ot "nothing", but also not, decisively, any "world view" which takes a monopoly for itself! ...
> I am not saying: it should stay the way it is, because it is good this way! But I am also not saying, that it is evil only because the "economic" is the way it is ...[24]

Not related to the overarching worldviews, the "humanely logical" judgments are related to, as it were, an aesthetic principle—one of taste and measure.

As the narrator puts it to one of his bemused interlocutors:

> To avoid all misunderstanding: I have never been a moralist and on no condition do I intend to become one. Just the opposite—I have my own bizarre notion of the world of moral values: to my mind, the question of morals is a matter of taste. The only measure of wisdom, it seems to me today,

---

[24] Krleža (1960), 161, 167, 171. Trans. by Gordana P. Crnković. This part is absent from the 1995 edition.

is the measure of form. Today, as far as the individual is concerned, there is nothing in the world that has not been disfigured. A lack of taste is a lack of wisdom, because something, that is intelligent, that is full of life, that is determined by nature, cannot be anything but harmonious and tasteful.[25]

"The question of morals is a matter of taste": it is as if Kant's aesthetic judgment, whereby something is confidently judged as beautiful without having the spelled-out verbalized notion or definition of beauty from which this judgment is deduced, is here applied to the ethical realm, so that something can be sensed as being good or ethical without having the notion or definition of goodness. One does not deduce that something is right or wrong, one senses it in a given situation, and this way of judging rejects the grounding of ethics on the pre-existing ideas or the "worldviews" that have their grounding outside of the act of the ethical judgment itself. People willfully close their eyes to the sheer and obvious deformity, disfiguration, or dreadfulness of mass carnage, or of a social system that creates people who exist on the level of "human trash" and those who publically regard them in that way, or of the violence enforced by "positive laws," or of butchering supposedly necessary for the creation of the "higher social order." If this deformity or wrongness of a certain state of affairs is acknowledged, it becomes a "human logic" basis for the further logical—rather than pragmatic—reasoning, and, in some cases, for the "logical" practice as well.

The Outcome

Third, regarding the fate of this non-social, logical, aesthetically related truth, one could ask: what is its destiny? In short, it is a resounding defeat: things go from bad to worse for the lonely speaker of truth. He has lost all the battles, is put in prison, will be finished up systematically, effectively, and quite horribly upon his release, has had one friend named Matko destroyed

---

[25] Krleža (1995), 77.

and Jadviga Jasenska, his one intimate support, is dead by her own hand. In the end, the one who chose the path of logic but not society ends up with the sole desire to "fall asleep. Certainly and forever. Not to be."[26] The solitary one cannot win, cannot even survive; in order to win or merely survive one needs a strong collective—but then, the stronger that collective gets, the more it destroys of that most precarious solitary truth of existence, the one that is seen as nothing other than the "poem":

> To you my poem is not political! It does not matter to me, what the name of this poem is; it is dear to me, and I think it is honest and should be sung on![27]

And yet ... yet ... the defeat is now and here, but perhaps, in time, that very defeat may become the seed of future victories. Maybe, if the dimension of time is taken in, this defeat may turn into something else.

> One day a young artillery officer ... having arrived via Budapest directly from the Ukrainian border ... had brought Dr. Werner a project based on the wartime experience of an intellectual titled "Give Us a Thousand Men." ...
> [A] young artillery officer sought a thousand souls ... because, unless that thousand found its way to the masses, unless it discovered a way of digging the foundations of a new universal humanistic structure here, on our own land, everything would remain unchanged, as it was in the past, with the sole difference that, instead of the Counts Khuen or Tisza or Franz Josef I, some new faces would rule ... Surrounded by a confused, uneducated, petty, short-sighted, narrow-minded, cunning quasi-intelligentsia, we should have at least a thousand people who were worried about the moral trap they were in—who saw that one day they themselves might be trapped by their own

---

[26] Krleža (1995), 182.
[27] Krleža (1960), 170. Trans. by Gordana P. Crnković. This part is absent from the 1995 edition.

contradictions or by some social success that would eventually amount to a negation of everything that now seemed to them the ideal.[28]

So, maybe, the narrator can be seen as the first, or one, of this thousand, and his "innocent little truth," his "honest song," may yet be the beginning of change?

The late Susan Sontag wrote in the 1990s that "*On the Edge of Reason* is one of the great European novels of the first half of the twentieth century ... [and] could hardly be more relevant to the century's end."[29] With its reminder of what success stands for and asks for, or that the genuine truth may not be social but only mine, that it may lead to a defeat, but that this defeat may perhaps be worth it if the world is to survive, Krleža's novel—with its innocent little truth that "loneliness is still not a proof of not being right"—seems even more relevant to us in these precarious beginnings of the twenty-first century.

---

[28] Krleža (1995), 75–6.
[29] Susan Sontag, back cover endorsement, in Krleža (1995).

12

Anarchists Today

The Lazarus Project
by Aleksandar Hemon

Then cometh the end, when he shall have put down all rule and all authority and power. Mere anarchy is loosed upon the world.

NORMAN O. BROWN, *LOVE'S BODY*[1]

All the lives he could have lived.

THE LAZARUS PROJECT[2]

The Lazarus Project, the 2008 novel by Bosnian-American writer Aleksandar Hemon, is built on two related stories. One is set in the present time, the first-person narrative of Vladimir Brik. A young Sarajevan, Brik came to the US as a tourist before the war in Bosnia and Herzegovina and ended up staying in America during the war and after. A former ESL teacher and now a newspaper columnist married

---

[1] Norman O. Brown, *Love's Body* (1966), 243. Brown here puts together the Bible's verse (I Cor. 15.24) with his own text.
[2] Aleksandar Hemon, *The Lazarus Project* (2009), 91. All future references to this volume will be marked by the page number in the body of the text.

to neurosurgeon Mary Fields, he gets a grant to do research for a book he wants to write, about one Lazarus Averbuch. A real person, Lazarus Averbuch was a young Jewish man who as a child survived the 1903 pogrom in Kishinev, part of the Russian Empire (now Moldova), and emigrated with his sister Olga to the US and Chicago, where Vladimir Brik now lives. Averbuch was killed at the age of 19, on 2 March 1908, in the house of Chicago Police Chief George Shippy. Brik's narrative revolves around his trip to the Ukraine and Moldova, places in Averbuch's life before emigration and also places related to Brik himself (given his own Ukrainian heritage), a trip that ends in Brik's home town of Sarajevo. He is accompanied on this voyage by Rora, a Sarajevan whom Brik has known since high-school, who also lives in Chicago, and who has been taking photographs since Brik has known him. The two end their travels as planned in Sarajevo, where they meet Rora's sister, the surgeon Azra, and where Rora is killed by a young man, high on drugs, who shoots Rora many times and then steals his camera.

The novel's second story is set in 1908. It starts with the killing of Lazarus Averbuch and relates the police and the media's handling of this affair and the treatment of Lazarus's sister Olga, and focuses on Olga's experience of it. In the novel's version of the Averbuch story, Lazarus came to Police Chief Shippy to deliver a confidential message, yet Shippy, already on guard against a man who was obviously "a Sicilian or a Jew" (7) killed the man in a fit of panic, thinking him an anarchist who had come to assassinate him.

The two stories alternate with each other. The first chapter starts the story of Lazarus Averbuch, told as a third-person narrative in the present tense ("March 2, 1908, Chicago ... Early in the morning, a scrawny young man rings the bell at 31 Lincoln Place, the residence of George Shippy ..." (1)), the second chapter starts the story of Aleksandar Brik ("I am a reasonably loyal citizen of a couple of countries. In America—that somber land—I waste my vote, pay taxes grudgingly, share my life with a native wife, and try hard not to wish painful death to the idiot president. But I also have a Bosnian passport ..." (11)), and then successive chapters alternate the two stories, with every odd chapter relating Lazarus's story and every even chapter Brik's, which in itself has many references to Lazarus given Brik's own preoccupation with the young man's life and destiny. The novel also includes a set of black-and-white photographs by Velibor Božović and from the Chicago Historical Society, with one photograph placed before every chapter.

The two stories echo and comment on each other, with emigrants from Eastern Europe, Lazarus and Brik, at their center, each with related causes of their leaving their native lands (violence of pogrom or the war), related causes of that violence (including media's hate mongering), and its shared characteristics (violence or war as a profit-making enterprise). America's response to anarchism then echoes its response to terrorism now: "The war against anarchism was much like the current war on terror—funny how old habits never die." (42) Characters with the same names appear in both stories and often embody the same roles and have a similar character, e.g. Miller the journalist or Brik the English teacher then and now (though the Schuettlers of today do not have an apparent likeliness to the assistant chief of police Schuettler of 1908). Many other components of the text—existential situations, character traits and thoughts, language phrases, and so on—are shared by both stories as well. Rora's older sister Azra "somehow ... reminded [Brik] of Olga Averbuch" (279); the two older sisters are thus related to each other, and Azra, about whom we learned little, instantly takes on many of Olga's characteristics (courage, great love for her younger brother, strength and beauty), and then the two also become related to another woman to whom the novel is dedicated, Hemon's own sister Kristina. Lazarus "used to be afraid of sparrows" (89) and Brik's wife Mary "was spooked by sparrows" too (283), for example, and Olga states to herself her own situation—"Isador [Lazarus's friend who is hiding from the police] is in the outhouse; policemen are everywhere ... Lazarus is dead; I stink of shit and sorrow; there is an endless storm outside; I am lost in a foreign country. Overall, not a bad lot" (95)—with a black humor and syntax shared by Sarajevans Brik and Rora in March of 1992: "things around us were getting rapidly worse; the weather was bad, the future uncertain, the war certain; other than that, everything as usual." (21) In his imaginary letter to his wife Mary, Brik echoes Olga's "Lord, why did you leave me in these dark woods?" (94) with his: "Why did you leave me in these woods?" (287) And Lazarus's insight—"home is where somebody notices when you are no longer there" (3)—is shared by Brik too, as he experiences how "nobody seemed to remember" him upon his return to Sarajevo: "Home is where somebody notices your absence." (278)

Bodies

The dreamer awakes not from a body but to a body. Not an ascent from body to spirit, but the descent of spirit into body: incarnation not sublimation. Hence to find the true meaning of history is to find the bodily meaning ... All fulfillment is carnal, carnaliter adimpleri.[3]

The Lazarus Project is a complex novel with many intriguing aspects. One of these aspects is a conspicuous foregrounding of bodies and their parts throughout the novel in both of its stories, faintly echoing the autopsy report of Lazarus's body in which a body is split into its constituent parts such as the cranium, the hair, the hands, the teeth and so on. (87–8) Getting into the focus of the narrative, the parts of a body seem to have a life of their own. They can become dislocated from the original body, travel to other places. Kidneys and spleen are taken out of a corpse, or else a kidney is detached while a man is still alive, and "shuttle[es] between different areas of his body" (172). It is not a woman who emerges from a car but instead a collection of body parts mixed with things: a pair of legs, high heels, flashing groin, bejeweled hands, insufficient skirt, bulbous silicone protuberances, head, shampoo-commercial hair. (209) Hearts are pierced or shot at but closely missed, and keep beating with bullets lodged close to them, or are taken from a body, or still beat calmly and are listened to: "She hears the heart booming steadily, indifferent to their shared sobs, to Isaac gasping for life." (173) Faces are being made and remade in different ways, with some people featuring "a different face every day," (105) and with the "American face" sometimes flashing among the others ("the raised eyebrows and the curved mouth of perpetual worry and wonder" (106)). The glass eye of one man "slid[es] out of the socket and tumble[s] to the gory floor" (264), echoing another man's "glass eye that stayed unexcited" (243). A man's head is being held upright by someone else, not the man himself, (57) and curly hair alone brings prosecution and possible death: "Indeed, the police cast a wide net in their hunt for the curly-haired man." (58) Hands, "well formed, indicating

---

[3] Brown (1966), 222.

manual labor," (87) work so hard that one man "do[es] not feel anything in [his] fingertips after work" and "cannot hold the pen" any more (96);or else are "deft hands" that can "saw open a skull, cut through bone and brains," and get "up to their wrists in somebody else's mind" (278). Or they come into focus as they are getting broken in the past and in the present: "I kept punching until ... my hand was finally and thoroughly broken;" (264) "[h]e stopped [punching] only after he hurt his hand." (244) This broken hand gets "doughier until it felt like it belonged to someone else" and then becomes "shades of indigo and swollen, as though it belonged to a corpse." (277) And the novel closes with Azra's words to Vladimir Brik: "Let's take care of your hand now. You will need it for writing." (292)

The focus on the body and the foregrounding of the parts and organs of the body create an environment in which these independent body parts seem to be, so to speak, "up for grabs," available to be made, like pieces of Lego, into a number of new bodies and new lives, and used in various ways. Exactly what new bodies and new lives are made is a subject of great struggle. On one hand, real or symbolic "old men" look for and violently appropriate a young body, or else take its youthful parts or organs—its kidneys, liver, and most importantly its heart and brain, leaving in place the personality set up (senses, thoughts, values), as well as the social structures of the old body. On the other hand, a new, young body searches for a viable life to grow into. It almost always needs something from the old bodies, most often the resources held almost exclusively by them, in exchange for which it gives parts or organs of its own young body—its hands, its heart, or its brain. A young body is thus forced to give its hands to work in an egg-packing or sewing factory (Lazarus and Olga), or its brain to work in the intellectual skills and knowledge-related industry. The struggle takes place between those who assert and embody the dominant and entrenched, thus the "old" ways of thinking, behaving, feeling, believing, and who look for and take a new—here, immigrant—young, healthy body to put into the specific places made by the old social forms, where a body or its parts becomes an instrument or a tool of these forms, on one hand, and the contested, unarticulated push of these new bodies, these young men and women, to create new, bigger lives for themselves, on the other. Lazarus's utterance "[a]ll the lives I could live" (2) expresses not just a choice among the presently available lives, but also a sense that new bodes and new lives should and could be attempted.

"But do let me know if some fresh bodies come in"

As mentioned above, the opening two chapters of the novel begin the two parallel stories, one taking place in 1908 and one in the present. Both chapters revolve around the contact of a young man, Lazarus Avebuch or Vladimir Brik, with an older couple or couples, a situation that invokes a potential parental relation but plays itself out quite differently.

After being turned away from the door of Chief Shippy and asked to come back later by Theresa, the maid, who "scan[ned] the young man from his soiled shoes up to his swarthy face, and smirk[ed]," (1) Lazarus Averbuch experiences more of a similar reception. When Lazarus, walking on a street, smiles at a young woman peeking from behind the curtain of her window, she quickly draws the curtains. In the store of Mr. and Mrs. Ludwig, a customer, Mr. Noth, "ignores the young man, who nods back at him" (4), and when Lazarus "bids good-bye to Mr. and Mrs. Ludwig ... they do not respond." (6) Coming back to the Shippy residence, Lazarus "nods at three women, as they pick up their pace passing him, ignoring him." (6) Aside from stressing the fact that the young man, incongruous in his poor clothes and his facial features ("*clearly a Sicilian or a Jew*" (7)) in the affluent neighborhood, is generally ignored and snarled at, the opening of the novel emphasizes that Lazarus is, most importantly, a *young man*. This phrase appears no less than 16 times in the first five pages, making the text resonate with itself: "the young man requests," "the young man descends," "the young man marches," "the young man stomps," "the young man smiles," "the young man says nothing."

This young man, then, interacts with the two old couples, the first couple being Mr. and Mrs. Ludwig. After coming into the grocery store, Ludwig's Supplies, Lazarus greets Mr. Ludwig, is haltingly greeted by Mrs. Ludwig, lingers in the store to avoid the cold of the early March Chicago morning, excessively felt by a hungry (his stomach is audibly growling, and Mr. Ludwig clearly "hears the howl" (6)) and poorly clad body, buys some lozenges and eventually leaves, bidding goodbye to the couple, to which they do not respond. A possible parental relation between the older couple and a younger man may be intimated by Mrs. Ludwig's maternal gesture: "she carries a gnarled loaf of bread ... as though it were a child." (4) It is not, however, a parental or supportive (nourishing) attitude on the part of the well-to-do older couple towards the apparently parentless young man that comes into being, but instead, lightly underscored by its absence, a different relationship between an old and a young man.

A customer named Mr. Noth (associative of nothing, or on the way to becoming fully nothing) enters the store; "the man is old" and his voice is "hoarse, tired." (4)

> Mr. Noth's walking stick is crooked. His tie is silk but stained; the young man can smell his breath—something is rotting inside him. I will never be like him, thinks the young man. He leaves the cozy small talk ...
> "I could use some camphor," Mr. Noth says. "And a new, young body."
> "We're out of bodies," Mr. Ludwig says. "But we do have camphor."
> "Worry not," Mrs. Ludwig says, cackling, "This body will serve you well for a long time."
> "Why, thank you, Mrs. Ludwig," Mr. Noth says. "But do let me know if some fresh bodies come in." (4–5)

On his way out, Mr. Noth is helped by Lazarus who holds the door for him while the old man says "Why, thank you," with his "stick poking the young man in his groin," (5) as if pointing to a particular part of the young body that he wants, in the way that Lazarus will tap the jar of white lozenges with his finger to show which ones he wants to buy from Mr. Ludwig only a moment later. Lazarus goes back to Police Chief Shippy's residence and encounters the second older couple, Police Chief Shippy and his wife, whom Shippy calls "Mother" (thus again invoking a possible parental relation between an older couple and a young man which has perverted itself, with the wife becoming a mother to her husband). When Lazarus is shot and killed by Shippy, prompted by his wife who cries "I think he [Lazarus] has a pistol" (8), it is as if Mr. Noth's order has been heard and is delivered:

Lazarus's "fresh body" is now available, the new young body Mr. Noth needed. While the narrative repeatedly returns to Lazarus's life before his emigration to the US, the main story starts with this killing of Lazarus and concerns his dead body, what happens to it and what is done with it. This body will be used and abused in numerous ways, made to fit its pre-made slot and serve its pre-defined functions in the "old men's" political, criminal, media, medical, symbolic (and so on) edifices. It will be desecrated by a policeman's taking off his pants to assert his being Jewish, meticulously seized in the official coronary description, made to sit as a mannequin on a chair with the victorious men holding it and posing around it, and photographed numerous times, with the photos made public. One of these photographs will be put on the front page of the newspaper with numbers around Lazarus's face and a legend accompanying these numbers: "1. low forehead; 2. large mouth; 3. receding chin ..." (143) This body will be secretly buried, then stolen from the grave and dismembered for the harvesting of some of its organs—spleen, kidneys, heart—and then reburied in a staged ceremony marking the pinnacle of institutional hypocrisy and cruelty.

"All the lives I could live" and Other Un-Needed Things

The plot of the 1908 story revolves around the literally or symbolically old men (the Ludwigs, the Shippys, men of the established network of journalists and the police), in their handling of Lazarus's body and their treatment of his sister Olga, while the narrative brings up some of the other things that constituted Lazarus and that were not needed by the "old men" before, when Lazarus was a worker employed in an egg-packing facility, and are not needed now when he is a corpse, and that have thus been superfluous and suppressed. These other parts include his tender and horrible memories, his sense of beauty, his talent for love, his knowledge of languages (English, Yiddish, German, Russian, French, Polish), his writing and his imagination, his sense of justice. A tension appears between the "old men" pushing a person into becoming only a "young body"—a fully instrumentalized, most efficiently working body that is turned into a means and a tool of production, or else a body used in other ways—and a person's trying to "push out" of this reduction and into a bigger life, as Lazarus puts it when he says "I imagine my life to be big, so big that I cannot see the end of it. " (288–9)

This second movement, the one of a young person looking for its own big life, is already intimated in the first chapter as well. After seeing and smiling at a young woman behind her curtain, Lazarus thinks: "All the lives I could live, all the people I will never know, never will be, they are everywhere. That is all that the world is." (2) The possible and plausible lives to live and people to become are many and everywhere. Yet, upon seeing and catching a smell of the "old man," Mr. Noth—"his tie is silk but stained; the young man can smell his breath—something is rotting inside him," the "young man" Lazarus thinks: "I will never be like him." (4) This is of course a prophetic statement, as Lazarus will indeed never be old and thus never like Mr. Noth; but it is also a proclamation of a choice not to become just another such "old man."

The old couples and old men need young, new bodies: "Do let me know if some fresh bodies come in," says Mr. Noth. A member of Chicago's Jewish establishment, Herr Taube, whose "cheeks are radiating consumption" making it visible that he is "going to die" (246), pushes his imminent death away—"'I don't wish to learn about death,'" he says (246)—by accomplishing a job of pressuring and molding a young woman's (Olga's) body into the performance of a dignified funeral for her brother Lazarus, "another job well done" as Taube sees it. The father of Brik's wife Mary, George ("Mary's Dead" as Brik once calls him), whose sick prostate has just been taken out, claims his daughter Mary in a number of ways and literally inhabits her: "I hated George in her," notes Brik. All the "old men" of the Lazarus story, Assistant Chief of Police Schuettler and journalist Miller, the intermediary Taube, alongside the "many distinguished Jews of Chicago," join in the use of Lazarus's body for the performance of a funeral that would preserve "the dominion of law and order," (270–1) and in which Lazarus is buried without his heart and other organs, or in which, as Olga puts it, "parts of my brother [are buried] as my brother." (223)

The need of old men for young, fresh bodies functions as a metonym of a system of personal and social construction that is established and thus tenacious but also old, a system that needs a continuous supply of young bodies and their living and working (or else dead) parts or organs to keep maintaining itself. These young bodies and their parts are needed in order to be plugged into the system and keep it working. Thus, Olga's and Lazarus's hands are put into the egg-packing industry and a sewing sweatshop, and Lazarus's organs are taken; Miller the journalist puts Lazarus and Olga into his pre-made story, verbally killing all of what they are to make them fit the scheme of dangerous anarchists and their exotic indomitable women. (Gentle, shy, and youthful Lazarus is described as having a "cruel, straight mouth" and a "pair of gray eyes ... cold and fierce" (7), and Olga, shunned by her "co-religionists," is written as regarding "offers of help ... with utmost disdain." (200)) A photographer working with Miller treats Olga like an inanimate object, coming into her home without the slightest hesitation, and moving her from place to place for a good picture ("'Excuse me, Mr. Miller ... Could she move closer to the window?'" (200)), and the two detectives, Fitzgerald and Fitzpatrick, claim Olga's body too, with a repeated "hand on her shoulder... fingers... pressing into her flesh," echoing Schuettler's "hand heavy on her knee." (62–3) The whole police and media machinery is revved up to find and capture another young man, Isador Maron, marked by his curly hair, and the neighbor of Lazarus and Olga, Isaac Lubel, is reduced by police to a body bag, his wife accurately stating (given the utter lack of rational need for such treatment): "I think they simply like beating him." (172) The individual body's organs are claimed too. These can become detached while a man is still alive, as in the case of beaten Isaac Lubel's kidney "shuttling between different areas of his body," (172) or are taken from a young man's corpse, as Herr Taube informs Olga:

"Unfortunately, it [Lazarus's body] is not complete."
"Not complete? What do you mean it is not complete?"
"Some organs are missing ..."
"What organs? Are you mad?"
"The spleen. The kidneys. The heart. And it appears they could not be retrieved." (220)

The story set in the present time starts with the first-person narrator, Bosnian Vladimir Brik now living in Chicago, as he tries to ingratiate himself with the elderly couple of Susie and Bill Schuettler during the celebration of Bosnian independence in one of Chicago's hotels. The Schuettlers are on the board of the Glory Foundation whose individual grant, a "brand-new heart" (16) as Brik calls it, he hopes to get in exchange for "laying down before" Susie Shuettler his own heart, or his own "writerly heart," and making her "feel young again." (17) The ensuing story again includes a number of situations in which old or established bodies use young ones to perpetuate and maintain themselves. A present-day journalist, Miller, pays young boys in besieged Sarajevo to run back and forth between cover despite heavy sniper fire, in order to get a perfect picture of them for his article. Young women, coming mostly from the Ukraine and Moldova, are consumed by select Sarajevo criminals tied to the government and distinguished foreign journalists and diplomats in a Sarajevo war-time brothel affectionately called "Duran-Duran." Another young women, Elena, is trafficked skillfully and under the threat of violence from rural Moldova into Romania to provide the fresh "new, young body" Mr. Noth was asking for. Young dead bodies are put into trading schemes and used for profit too, with enemy men's corpses found in Sarajevo sold to their families across the battle lines for burial. And the established and now elderly Sarajevo criminal boss, Rambo, who moves drugs across Sarajevo with the help of his government pals, claims the body of a young man who will be "high as a balloon" (291) on drugs and will kill Rora to get his camera.

The Opposite Thrust

The opposite direction concerns itself with patching up the bodies, assisting them and helping them live. Brik's parents "worried about the preservation of [his] body far more than that of [his] soul," having no qualms, though "agnostic-cum-Communist," (39) in making him go to church with his devout Ukrainian grandparents when he was a child, rather than stay alone in their village house with all the dangerous agricultural tools, matches and suchlike around him. Love is primarily taking care, as best as possible, of someone's body: Brik records how "Rora touched my cheek and turned my head slightly to assess the damage" (67) when he was hit by a truck's side mirror in Lviv, Ukraine; Rora's sister Azra patches Brik's hand and Mary sews broken heads; Lazarus washes his mother's feet, worries about her varicose legs, and saves up to buy her good shoes. In this thrust, people want and need other people to be alive and "big," as Lazarus puts it, not reduced to a tool or a body part. They want and help other people's hearts to be strong and calm, and their own life is tied to the strength of these other people and their hearts. Lazarus writes home to his mother to not be "oversad, for [she] must take care of [her] heart." "Olga and I need your heart. I want to rest my head on your chest and hear your heart beating." (74) Lazarus's sister Olga composes herself by embracing a neighbor woman, Pinya (whose husband, Isaac, was repeatedly beaten by the police and is about to die), and by listening to Pinya's heart:

> Olga embraces her. But Pinya is even taller now, so Olga has to press her cheek against her chest. She hears the heart booming steadily, indifferent to their shared sobs, to Isaac gasping for life. (173)

This moment echoes Lazarus's wish to rest his head on his mother's chest and hear her heart beating, as well as Vladimir Brik's calming himself down by resting his head against his wife Mary. "I put my head on her bosom; I could hear her heart beating, steadily, calmly..." (68)

A Big Life

Resisting the circumstances and people who push a person into becoming only a young body, reduced to its mechanical ability to work or to its bodily, non-individuated matter, or even just to a bag of parts and organs, a person attempts to grow into his/her own bigger life. "The day before his bar mitzvah ... the last day of his childhood," (269) Lazarus told Olga:

> I imagine my life to be big, so big that I cannot see the end of it. Big enough for everyone to fit into it. You will be in it, Mother and Father will be in it, people I have never met or known will be in it. I will be in it. I can see it. I have a picture of it in my

head. It's a field of blossom so deep you can swim in it. I can see it now, and I cannot see its end. (288–9)

What the old men and the established system need and take from Lazarus is his hands and then his whole body, and finally his corpse and its organs. All else that Lazarus is, his thoughts, memories, senses, ways of perceiving and thinking and knowing, his imagination, are superfluous and un-needed and suppressed. Lazarus, who wants to write a book, works so hard at packing eggs that he cannot hold a pen any longer: "Do you know, Olga, that I do not feel anything in my fingertips after work? When I write, I cannot hold the pen. Whatever I touch feels like an egg." (96) All the unclaimed aspects of Lazarus are practically all that he is, and they are beautiful. He thinks, for example, of his mother and remembers how she giggled like a schoolgirl when he washed her feet. He says, repeating someone else's words but also knowing them himself: "What is life without beauty, love, and justice?" (73) He hears the news, "Pat Garrett, the Lawman Who Shot Billy the Kid, Dies in a Gunfight," and then thinks how Billy is "a nice name, a name for a fretful, yet happy, dog. Pat is weighty, serious, like a rusted hammer." (6–7) He smiles a lot: he thanks, "smiling," Shippy's stern and unpleasant maid Theresa, he "smiles at" a young woman at the window, and at Mrs. Ludwig. He is courageous, fighting as a young boy the men who broke into their home and attacked his sister. He speaks all the languages his older sister Olga speaks—Russian, German, English, Yiddish—plus French and Polish, and is a good, conscientious student of English. His imagination is wide and can grasp a desired life that is big, full of people, and imbued with love, beauty, and justice not just in the most private realm, but also in the wider world that it is a part of.

Lazarus's "big life," of course, would nourish and make memories, loves, beauty, justice, compassion. These would not only live in his head, gradually more vague, with the fingers that were supposed to write increasingly unable to hold the pen and losing any feeling, but would instead live in his material, bodily life. His reduction to a pair of working hands or a set of body parts can also be seen as a metonym for the present-day reduction of a person into her or his work function, into an often insignificant, replaceable screw in a global space.

Being Complete

As opposed to the situation that reduces a person to his or her young body, "plugged" into the system of old men, a system perpetuating itself through a steady supply of fresh young bodies, that "pushes" onto a person from the outside in, molding a body or even breaking it into its constituent parts and organs, a different push is done from the inside out, attempting to make a person into what she or he wants to become. Thus Olga's curse, "May they never become who they want to be," (171) and Brik's defeat in failing "to be the person I wanted to be." (106)

> Mary could see no deep face of mine, because she did not know what my life in Bosnia had been like, what made me, what I had come from; she could see only my American face, acquired through failing to be the person I wanted to be. (106)

Brik fails in becoming who he wanted to be, but he finds himself "wanting to be him"—Rora—again.

> But then I saw him coming down the street, tall and skinny, his dark hair impeccably curly, in a leather jacket new and shiny, his sunglasses reflective and cool. He stuck out in the morning Andersonville crowd embarking upon their day's work of achieving perfection. I recognized him then; that is, I finally comprehended what I had known but have never been able to formulate: he had always been complete. He had finished the work of becoming himself, long before any of us could even imagine such a feat was possible. Needless to say, I envied him. (30)

Rora had always been complete, had finished the work of becoming himself. This does not mean that he is impervious to change, but rather that he makes and changes himself from the inside out: "each life, however imaginary, could be validated by its rightful, sovereign owner, from the inside." (20) He is always physically complete: with the exception of his curly hair that connects him to all the young Jewish suspects of Lazarus's time ("'He has Jewish hair'" (158)), the narrative never isolates any separate parts of his body until the very end. He is whole—tall, thin, "a handsome man," as someone comments. Wearing a new and shiny leather jacket, with reflective sunglasses, he is enclosed, with no cracks or blemishes: the light bounces off of his perfect surface. Rora is not even "opened" by sleep ("whenever I woke up he was always already awake" (210)), or by a personal conversation ("inability to communicate emotion," as Brik puts it (210)). His behavior is rounded too, with swift and assured making of decisions and prompt acting on them ("Rora made his decisions quickly, without hesitation" (44)), and his speech is whole as well: "his statements were completed, his sentences did not spill into each other." (250) This calm and persistent completeness, Rora's not being shaped or torn asunder by the outside-in thrust but instead maintaining and making himself "from the inside," seems so impossible to achieve and believe in that it becomes fantastic: he "was steadily unreal." (19)

Silence, Stories, Camera

I don't think I should go, I said. I had plenty more research to do in the libraries, many more books to read ... there was no rush; nobody was waiting for my book to arrive. The world would be exactly the same with my book as it was without it. Rora did not argue; I drove him home. The Lake Shore high-rises cast long, mawkish shadows into the oncoming waves; he said nothing.

He produced a particular kind of silence: it was not heavy, not accusing, not demanding. I imagined that was the same kind of silence as when he waited for a picture to appear on the photographic paper sunk in emulsion. I was learning that I liked such silence, as I liked his sounds and stories ... and I understood that not only did I have to find a way to go to Kishinev as soon as possible, but that Rora had to come along. It seemed to me that if he didn't come along I would never see him again, and I needed him around, for his silence, for his stories, for his camera. (47–8)

Rora's making of himself "inside out," rather than being made the other way around, is enabled by a few chance circumstances given to him, such as his material independence (he comes from a wealthy merchant family), his being an orphan from an early age and raising himself practically by himself, his many travels and school absences for which "inexplicably, [he] never [got] reprimanded." (19) But his making of his own "big life" also includes his silences, his story-telling, and his picture-taking. His silence, for instance, allows the existence and growth of another body, it is giving and nurturing in its withholding from a ceaseless activity characterizing the environment where Brik and Rora now live, and in its creating a space of separate time for that other being to go someplace, do something, simply happen as "a picture ... appear[ing] on the photographic paper sunk in emulsion." On the other hand, his story-telling lifts his language out of the oppressive enslavement within the literal and referential.

A "recently acquired habit of American reasonability" (31) and lack of a conducive environment destroys Vladimir Brik's own story-telling confidence and practice. He had once, for instance, told a story about the Berlin Wall rabbits, in which "at mating time, the hormone-crazy rabbits would smell a partner on the other side, and they would go crazy, producing the pining-rabbit sound, trying desperately to find a hole in the Wall;" they would "drive the guards out of their minds," and "everybody in Berlin knew that the rabbit-mating season was the worst time to attempt to escape across the Wall, because the rabbits made the guards very trigger-happy." (103) Brik knows, of course, that the story is "outrageous," but that only works in its favor. The story is "funny and poignant" with its seizing of and playing with the "unnaturalness of the Cold War, the love that knew no boundaries," and so on (103). It "required no effort for [him] to suspend [his] disbelief and admire" the story and the story-teller's "narrative embroidery." (103-4) But his Wisconsin listeners are perplexed, and his wife Mary states, speaking for all of them, "I find that hard to believe," with another listener asking, "Why didn't the rabbits find a mate on their own side of the Wall?" (104) Brik is deflated. How to explain non-literal language in referential, literal terms? How to explain its ways of working, its charm, wit, and wisdom? Once it is "explained," it disappears, like a photographic negative exposed to light.

Rora himself has presumably lived in a similar literal-minded environment, but has lost none of his story-telling ability. Dry pieces of information from Brik are taken by Rora and turned into stories.

Brik notes a mentally sick man on the Chicago streets, and Rora tells a story about another crazy man, this one in besieged Sarajevo, who used to run all the time with a plastic lemon in his mouth, and had eventually run all the way to the plane across the tarmac at Sarajevo airport. While snipers shot at the crowd, he got way ahead of them thanks to his great physical shape, and saved himself. Or Brik mentions that his wife Mary's family is Irish American, upon which Rora tells a story about an Irishman who was trying to get the Pope to come to besieged Sarajevo. The Pope actually said he would, but under one condition. Or Brik says that something is a miracle (31), and Rora takes this one word, "miracle," and tells a story about how it came to be that the best seafood in town is obtainable in the hardware store next to the Miracle Video. Most of the stories have a moral and a deeper wisdom, if one bothers to look for it: not everything is crazy that looks that way, the judges of the morals are themselves callous (the Pope allegedly says he would come to besieged Sarajevo if "they stopped fighting"), a miracle is not in the pre-manufactured spectacle (films, videos), but in the everyday life and seemingly "drab and disciplined" world that allows and hides "exquisite aberrations."

Rora's stories tell a lot about life in besieged Sarajevo, however non-factual they may be on the literal level. (Rora thus ends up being revealed as the unreliable narrator, with his main suspense story about gangster Rambo eventually killing American journalist Miller apparently proven to be fictional, though with some factual truth in all that he was saying too: "something is always true," as his sister Azra puts it. (291)) But the telling of these stories is also and most importantly a goal in itself. They are not told for the purpose of extracting some moral substance or factual information from them, but for the pleasure of being told, as the Sarajevans of Brik's memory did. "You listened, rapt, ready to laugh, indifferent to doubt or implausibility ... Disbelief was permanently suspended, for nobody expected truth or information, just the pleasure of being in the story." (102–3) And Rora is a consummate story-teller, "good with the audience, as judged by [Brik's] unflagging, unquestioning, decades-long interest in his stories." (104)

Rora is still able to do "free speech; free associations, random thoughts; spontaneous movements,"[4] and "wisdom [that] is in

---

[4]Brown (1966), 243.

wit, in fooling, most excellent fooling; in play, and not in heavy puritanical seriousness. In levity, not gravity."[5] He responds to the Ukrainian cab driver Andriy's words which imply that Muslims and homosexuals are to blame for the world's dangers, by playing with him with such "fooling":

> I am Muslim, I heard Rora say to him, in Bosnian. I have seven veiled wives, forty-three children ... Rora's right hand flew into his left hand straight up like a tower, he produced a roaring-engine sound, then collapsed his left hand, slapping his thigh.
> That was me, Rora said, and Andriy laughed even louder ...
> Mujahedeen, Rora said and pointed at himself. Homosexual, he pointed at me, laughing in concert with now hysterical Andriy, slapping him on the back.
> Stop it, I said.
> We are the problems, Rora said. Big problems. (110–11)

Rora's picture-taking—Brik remembers Rora taking pictures since he was a high-school student, always showing them to the other pupils—is also a goal in itself. "Why did you take that picture?" Brik once asks him. "That's a stupid question, Rora said. I take pictures" (75), and "I take pictures because I like to look at the pictures I take." (76) But Rora's picture-taking is also his way of perceiving and experiencing his environment, his way of relating to it. Brik and Rora sit in a Chisinau McDonald's alongside a few locals—a father with two daughters having Cokes, a couple, a middle-aged professorial looking woman—and then a "businessman" (most probably some kind of a criminal) comes in with his girlfriend and his bodyguard, exuding arrogance and power. Customers are drawn into their orbit, with the "little girls star[ing]" at the woman. But Rora takes a picture not of the gangster, but of the two girls drinking their Cokes. The gangster's power that seems to electrify everyone in the small circle does not touch him at all. He "bares a device," so to speak, of a persona construction of this "goon," who is the same as all the others: "These people, these gangsters, Rora said" once before, "they are the same wherever you go—the same smirk, the same cell phone, the same goon," (131); the same, as

---

[5]Brown (1966), 245.

Brik put it, "throwing his shoulders and jerking his neck, pursing his lips, the mouth half open to show that he was halfway to being very pissed," (131) as if "they must have all been made in the same factory." (209) Rora is not attracted to power, and does not want it himself. He shirks from "consuming" a young Moldovan prostitute handed to him, and while she sleeps in Sarajevo's war-time brothel, he takes her picture and thinks: "How did she end up here? ... She had family somewhere, a mother or a brother. Everybody comes from somewhere." (153)

Rora makes his "big life" and achieves his bodily "completeness" by not allowing the utilitarian reduction of himself; a reduction into a functional young body or its functional parts, a reduction of his potentially poetic, philosophical, absurd, or nonsensical language into a sensible, reasonable language serving the goal of clear reference and quick information; or of his life and things he does in life into solely purposeful, goal-oriented activities. Rora can do whatever and be wherever he likes, because his every action or non-action makes sense, is worth it, can be lived through and photographed. Just like "every face is a landscape," as he puts it to Brik, (35) every moment and place is a universe in itself, if they are not subsumed into a means to reaching some infinitely postponed goal. Being complete, Rora stands out from the crowd that has to work, forever, on "achieving perfection," and he is different from Brik who has to continually prove his own successful transformation into an instrumentalized body, into someone who lives in order to achieve something. Brik turned his moments of life into tools of getting something else: "I'm making a lot of mental notes" (72), as he dutifully characterizes his trip to Mary.

Non-instrumentalizing himself and not reducing himself into functional body parts, Rora builds his own complete body and "big life" that includes a need for the lives related to his to be complete and big as well. Thus he needs his city whole, or, as Brik puts it, "Back then Rora believed in a Bosnia in which everybody lived together; he loved Sarajevo and wanted to defend it" (66) so he joins one of the few units defending the city. He now fights a cab driver Seryozha in order to release a young Moldovan girl Elena whom he just met a few hours ago and whom Seryozha is trafficking probably for sex work. Rora acts against the symbolic old men (old power relations with their old profit-making from young bodies), and their "body snatching." Steadily unreal, he is not slowly becoming one of the "old men," not turning other people into instrumentialized or commodified bodies, not becoming anyone other than himself. He is also not molded into being one of the ultimately dismembered young men as he pushes back with his life, and makes at least one of "all the lives [Lazarus] could have lived" (91) with his big, complete life lived through his stories and live language, through quick decisions and actions, and through his camera, his way of perceiving and feeling the world. His ultimate demise and dismembering in Sarajevo at the hands of a "buff young man" (284) who shot Rora with so many bullets that "his nose was blasted away, he had brains in his curls, there were no eyes to be seen, the ocean of blood expanding," (285) would intimate an impossibility of such a "steadily unreal" human being to survive in a world held by the old men and their successful reproduction through the bodies of the young. Vladimir Brik's writing and Hemon's novel bring the bodies of Rora—and Lazarus—back again, and make them whole and alive in a text. A needed anarchy of making these bodies possible in reality in which the dominion of old bodies over the young is abolished thus is realized, again and at least, in a novel.

BIBLIOGRAPHY

Books

Albahari, David. *Götz and Meyer*. Trans. Ellen Elias-Bursać. Orlando: Harcourt, Inc., 1998.
Alexander, Ronelle. *Bosnian, Croatian, Serbian, a Grammar: with Sociolinguistic Commentary*. Madison, WI: University of Wisconsin Press, 2006.
—"Bosnian, Croatian, Serbian: One Language or Three?" Available online at http://www.irex.org/sites/default/files/alexander.pdf (accessed 7 November 2011).
Ali, Rabia and Lawrence Lifschultz (eds), *Why Bosnia? Writings on the Balkan War*. Stony Creek: The Pamphleteer's Press, Inc., 1993.
Anderson, Benedict. *Imagined Communities*. London: Verso, 1983.
Andonovski, Venko. "Semiološkata fobija od tugoto: semiotikata na sličnostite i semiotikata na razlikite vo filmot *Pred doždot* na Milčo Mančevski," *Kinopis* 12(7), 1995.
Andrić, Ivo. *Ex Ponto. Nemiri* [*Unrest*]. Sarajevo: Svjetlost, 1975.
—*The Bridge on the Drina* [*Na Drini ćuprija*]. Trans. Lovett F. Edwards. Chicago: University of Chicago Press, 1977.
—*Bosnian Chronicle* [*Travnička hronika*]. Trans. Joseph Hitrec. New York: Arcade Publishing, 1993.
Antić, Milica G. "Gender equality in Slovenia." In Sabrina P. Ramet and Danica Fink-Hafner (eds), *Democratic Transition in Slovenia: Value Transformation, Education, and Media*. College Station: Texas A & M University Press, 2006.
Arsenijević, Vladimir. *In the Hold*. Trans. Celia Hawkesworth. London: The Harvill Press, 1996.
—*Anđela*. Beograd: Stubovi Kulture, 1998.
—*U potpalublju* [*In The Hold*]. Zagreb: Arkzin, 1998.
—*Mexico: ratni dnevnik* [*Mexico: A War Diary*]. Beograd: Rende, 2000.
Auerbach, Erich. *Mimesis: The Representation of Reality in Western Literature*. Trans. Willard R. Trask. Princeton: Princeton University Press, 1974.

Auty, Phyllis. "Yugoslavia's international relations (1945–1965)." In Wayne S. Vucinich ed. *Contemporary Yugoslavia: Twenty Years of Socialist Experiment*. Berkeley and Los Angeles: University of California Press, 1969.
Bakhtin, Mikhail. *Rabelais and His World*. Trans. Helene Iswolsky. Bloomington: Indiana University Press, 1984.
Banac, Ivo. "The fearful asymmetry of war: the causes and consequences of Yugoslavia's demise." *Daedalus*, 121(2), 1992.
—*Protiv Straha [Against Fear]*. Zagreb: Slon, 1992.
Bazdulj, Muharem. *Travničko trojstvo [The Travnik Trinity]*. Zagreb: Durieux; Sarajevo: Buybook; Cetinje: Otvoreni kulturni forum, 2002.
Benjamin, Walter. *Illuminations: Essays and Reflections*. Ed. Hannah Arendt, trans. Harry Zohn. New York: Schocken Books, 1989.
Berger, John. *Ways of Seeing*. London: British Broadcasting Corporation and Penguin Books, 1972.
Berman, Russell A. *Enlightenment or Empire: Colonial Discourse in German Culture*. Lincoln, NE, and London: University of Nebraska Press, 1998.
—*Fiction Sets You Free: Literature, Liberty, and Western Culture*. Iowa City: University of Iowa Press, 2007.
Bois, Yve-Alain and Rosalind E. Krauss. *Formless: A User's Guide*. New York: Zone Books, 1997.
Brown, Keith. "An interview with Milcho Manchevski," *World Literature Today*, 82(1): 12–15, January–February 2008.
Brown, Norman O. *Love's Body*. Berkeley: University of California Press, 1966.
Bruns, Gerald L. *Heidegger's Estrangements: Language, Truth and Poetry in the Later Writings*. New Haven: Yale University Press, 1989.
Buturović, Amila. *Stone Speaker: Medieval Tombs, Landscape, and Bosnian Identity in the Poetry of Mak Dizdar*. New York: Palgrave, 2002.
Čadež, Tomislav. "Visković: 'Sanader nas je spasio of hrvatskog slučaja Pamuk'; intervju s Velimirom Viskovićem, predsjednikom Hrvatskog društva književnika" [An Interview with Velimir Visković, the President of the Croatian Writers' Association], *Jutarnji list* (Zagreb), 12 November 2005.
Čengić, Enes. *Krleža*. Zagreb: Mladost; Sarajevo: Oslobođenje, 1982.
Clausen, Christopher. *Moral Imagination: Essays on Literature and Ethics*. Iowa City: University of Iowa Press, 1986.
Corradi Fiumara, Gemma. *The Other Side of Language: A Philosophy of Listening*. Trans. Charles Lambert. London and New York: Routledge, 1990.

Crnković, Gordana P. *Imagined Dialogues: Eastern European Literature in Conversation with American and English Literature.* Northwestern University Press: Evanston, 2000.

—"From the eye to the hand: the victim's double vision in the cinema of Roman Polanski," *Kinoeye: New Perspectives on European Film* 4, no. 5 (29 November 2004). Available online at http://www.kinoeye.org/04/05/crnkovic05.php (accessed 8 November 2011).

Crnogorski književni list [Montenegrin Literary Magazine]. Podgorica: DUKS-Izdavačko, 2001.

Dizdar, Mak. "Roads." Trans. Francis R. Jones. In Rabia Ali and Lawrence Lifschultz (eds), *Why Bosnia? Writings on the Balkan War.* Stony Creek: The Pamphleteer's Press, Inc., 1993.

Dizdarević, Zlatko. *Sarajevo: A War Journal.* New York: Fromm International, 1992.

Donia, Robert J. and John V. A. Fine, Jr. *Bosnia and Hercegovina: A Tradition Betrayed.* New York: Columbia University Press, 1994.

Đurić, Dubravka and Miško Šuvaković (eds), *Impossible Histories: Historical Avant-gardes, Neo-avant-gardes, and Post-avant-gardes in Yugoslavia, 1918–1991.* Cambridge, MA: MIT Press, 2003.

Eagle, Herbert. "Yugoslav Marxist humanism and the films of Dušan Makavejev." In David W. Paul ed. *Politics, Art, and Commitment in the East European Cinema.* New York: St. Martin's, 1983.

Eagleton, Terry. *The Ideology of the Aesthetic.* Oxford: Basil Blackwell, 1990.

—*After Theory.* New York: Basic Books, 2003.

Friedman, Victor A. "Fable as history: the Macedonian context," *Rethinking History* 4(2), July 2000.

Gadamer, Hans-Georg. *Truth and Method.* Trans. W. Glen-Doepel, John Cumming, and Garrett Barden. London: Sheed and Ward, 1979.

Gagnon Jr., V. P. *The Myth of Ethnic War: Serbia and Croatia in the 1990s.* Ithaca and London: Cornell University Press, 2004.

Glaurdić, Josip. *The Hour of Europe: Western Powers and the Breakup of Yugoslavia.* New Haven: Yale University Press, 2011.

Goldstein, Albert ed. *Sinovi: pogled u suvremenu crnogorsku prozu [Sons: A View into Contemporary Montenegrin Prose].* Pula, Ulcinj, Zagreb: kod Tomasa, 2006.

Goldstein, Slavko. *1941. Godina koja se vraća [1941. The Year that Keeps Returning]*, 2nd edition. Zagreb: Novi Liber, 2007.

Gombrowicz, Witold. *Diary, Volume 1.* Trans. Lillian Vallee. Evanston, IL: Northwestern University Press, 1988.

Goulding, Daniel ed. *Post New Wave Cinema in the Soviet Union and Eastern Europe.* Bloomington: Indiana University Press, 1989.

—ed. *Five Filmmakers*. Bloomington: Indiana University Press, 1994.
—*Liberated Cinema: The Yugoslav Experience (1945–2001)*. Bloomington: Indiana University Press, 1985; revised and expanded 2nd edition, 2002.
Grayling, A.C. *Meditations for the Humanist: Ethics for a Secular Age*. Oxford: Oxford University Press, 2002.
Hawkesworth, Celia. *Ivo Andrić: Bridge between East and West*. London: Athlone Press, 1984.
Heidegger, Martin. *Poetry, Language, Thought*. Trans. Alfred Hofstadter. New York: Harper and Rowe, 1971.
—*Early Greek Thinking*. Trans. David Farrell Krell and Frank A. Capuzzi. New York: Harper and Rowe, 1975.
Helms, Elissa. "East and West kiss: gender, orientalism, and balkanism in Muslim-majority Bosnia-Herzegovina," *Slavic Review* 67(1), Spring 2008.
Hemon, Aleksandar. *The Lazarus Project*. New York: Riverhead Books, 2008.
Hempton, Gordon and John Grossman. *One Square Inch of Silence: One Man's Search for Natural Silence in a Noisy World*. New York: Free Press, 2009.
Hoffman, George W. and Fred Warner Neal. *Yugoslavia and the New Communism*. New York: Twentieth Century Fund, 1962.
Horvat, Branko, Mihailo Marković, and Rudi Supek (eds). *Self-Governing Socialism: A Reader*. Vol.1. *Historical Development—Social and Political Philosophy*. White Plains, NY: International Arts and Sciences Press, 1975.
Horvat, Ksenija Vidmar. "The globalization of gender," *European Journal of Cultural Studies* 8(2), 2005; 239–55.
Horton, Andrew ed. *Kinoeye: New Perspectives on European Film*. Available online at http://www.kinoeye.org/archive/articles.php (accessed 8 November 2011).
—ed. *The celluloid tinderbox: Yugoslav screen reflections of a turbulent decade*. Telford: Central European Review Ltd, 2000. Available online at http://www.kinoeye.org/03/10/celluloidtinderbox.pdf (accessed 8 November 2011).
Huizinga, Johan. *Homo Ludens: A Study of the Play Element in Culture*. Boston: The Beacon Press, 1955.
Ibrahimović, Nedžad. "Između naracije i kreacije (Bosanskohercegovački igrani film, 1995–2008)" ["Between narration and creation (the feature films of Bosnia and Herzegovina, 1995–2008)"]. In Velimir Visković ed. *Sarajevske sveske*, 19/20, 2008.
Imamović, Jasmin. *Besmrtni jeleni* [*Immortal Deers*]. Celovec: Bosanska biblioteka, 1996.

Iordanova, Dina. "Introduction." In Andrew James Horton ed. *The Celluloid Tinderbox: Yugoslav Screen Reflections of a Turbulent Decade*. Telford: Central European Review Ltd, 2000. Available online at http://www.kinoeye.org/03/10/celluloidtinderbox.pdf (accessed 8 November 2011).
—*Cinema of Flames: Balkan Film, Culture and the Media*. London: British Film Institute, 2001.
Jakovljević, Branislav. *Daniil Kharms: Writing and the Event*. Evanston, IL: Northwestern University Press, 2009.
Jalušič, Vlasta. "Women in post-socialist Slovenia." In Sabrina P. Ramet ed. *Gender Politics in the Western Balkans: Women and Society in Yugoslavia and the Yugoslav Successor States*. University Park: Pennsylvania State University Press, 1999.
Johnson, Vida (guest ed.). *KinoKultura* Special Issue 8: *Serbian Cinema*, August 2009. Available online at http://www.kinokultura.com/specials/8/serbian.shtml (accessed 8 November 2011).
Judah, Tim. *Kosovo: War and Revenge*. 2nd edition. New Haven: Yale University Press, 2002.
Juzbašić, Živko. *Srpsko pitanje i hrvatska politika: Svjedočanstva i dokumenti 1990–2000* [*The Serbian Question and Croatian Politics: Testimonies and Documents 1990–2000*]. Zagreb: Prometej, 2009.
Karahasan, Dževad. *Sarajevo, Exodus of a City*. New York, Tokyo, London: Kodansha International, 1994.
Kiš, Danilo. *Garden, Ashes*. New York: Harcourt Brace Jovanovich, 1975.
—*Čas anatomije* [*The Anatomy Lesson*]. Beograd: Nolit, 1978.
—*Tomb for Boris Davidovich*. Trans. Duška Mikić-Mitchell. New York: Penguin, 1980.
—*The Encyclopedia of the Dead*. Trans. Michael Henry Heim. New York: Penguin, 1991.
—*Varia*. Mirjana Miočinović ed. Beograd: BIGZ, 1995.
Klaić, Dragan. "'Danilo Kiš': the theatrical connection," *The Review of Contemporary Fiction*, 14(1), Spring 1994.
Krasztev, Péter. "Who will take the blame? How to make an audience grateful for a family massacre." In Andrew James Horton ed. *The Celluloid Tinderbox: Yugoslav Screen Reflections of a Turbulent Decade*. Telford: Central European Review Ltd, 2000. Available online at http://www.kinoeye.org/03/10/celluloidtinderbox.pdf (accessed 8 November 2011).
Krleža, Miroslav. *Deset krvavih godina i drugi eseji*. [*Ten Bloody Years and Other Essays*]. Beograd: Nolit, 1960.
—*Izlet u Rusiju 1925* [*Trip to Russia 1925*]. Zagreb: Zora, 1960.
—*Na rubu pameti* [*On The Edge of Reason*]. Zagreb: Zora, 1960.

—*Hrvatski bog mars*. [*The Croatian God Mars*]. Zagreb: Zora, 1965.
—*Povratak Filipa Latinovicza*. Zagreb: Zora, 1969.
—*The Cricket Beneath the Waterfall and Other Stories*, ed. Branko Lenski. New York: The Vanguard Press, Inc., 1972.
—*Dnevnik* [*Diary*]. Sarajevo: Oslobođenje, 1977.
—*On the Edge of Reason*. Trans. Zora Depolo. New York, New Directions, 1995.
—*The Banquet in Blitva*. Trans. Edward Dennis Goy and Jasna Levinger-Goy. Evanton, IL: Northwestern University Press, 2004.
—*Mnogopoštovanoj gospodi mravima* [*To Much Esteemed Gentlemen Ants*], Conversations with Miloš Jevtić. Zagreb: Naklada Ljevak, 2009.
Kundera, Milan. *Testaments Betrayed: An Essay in Nine Parts*. Trans. Linda Asher. New York: HarperCollins, 1996.
Kurelec, Tomislav. *Filmska kronika: zapisi o hrvatskom filmu* [*The Film Chronicle: Writings on Croatian Film*]. Zagreb: AGM, Hrvatsko društvo filmskih kritičara, 2004.
Laclau, Ernesto and Chantal Mouffe. *Hegemony and Socialist Strategy*. London: Verso, 1985.
Lagumdžija, Razija ed. *Kritičari o Meši Selimoviću, sa autobiografijom* [*Critics on Meša Selimović, with Autobiography*]. Sarajevo: Svjetlost, 1973.
Lazić, Zoran. *Ljeto u gradu* [*Summer in the City*]. Zagreb: AGM, 2004.
Levi, Pavle. *Disintegration in Frames: Aesthetics and Ideology in Yugoslav and Post-Yugoslav Film*. Stanford: Stanford University Press, 2007.
Lovrenović, Ivan. *Liber memorabilium*. Zagreb: Durieux, 1994.
Luthar, Breda and Maruša Pušnik. *Remembering Utopia: The Culture of Everyday Life in Socialist Yugoslavia*. Washington DC: New Academia Publishing, 2010.
Manchevski, Milcho. "Rainmaking and Personal Truth," *Rethinking History* 4(2), July 2000.
—*Before the Rain/Pred doždot*. Skopje: Slovo, 2002.
Matanović, Julijana. *Zašto sam vam lagala* [*Why Did I Lie To You*]. 7th edition. Zagreb: Mozaik knjiga, 2002.
Matvejević, Predrag. *Razgovori s Krležom* [*Conversations with Krleža*]. 7th edition. Zagreb: Prometej, 2001.
Mehmedinović, Semezdin. *Sarajevo Blues*. Trans. Ammiel Alcalay. San Francisco: City Light Books, 1998.
Mirković, Alenka. *91.6 MHz: Glasom protiv topova* [*91.6 MHz: With the Voice Against the Guns*]. Zagreb: Algoritam, 1997.
Montiglio, Silvia. *Silence in the Land of Logos*. Princeton: Princeton University Press, 2000.

Morson, Gary Saul. *Narrative and Freedom: The Shadows of Time.* New Haven and London: Yale University Press, 1994.
Mortimer, Lorraine. *Terror and Joy: The Films of Dušan Makavejev.* Minneapolis: University of Minnesota Press, 2009.
Neher, André. *The Exile of the Word: From the Silence of the Bible to the Silence of Auschwitz.* Trans. David Maisel. Philadelphia: The Jewish Publication Society of America, 1981.
Nussbaum, Martha Craven. *The Fragility of Goodness.* 21st printing. Cambridge and New York: Cambridge University Press, 2007.
—*Love's Knowledge.* New York: Oxford University Press, 1990.
Okey, Robin. *Eastern Europe 1740–1985: Feudalism to Communism.* Minneapolis: University of Minnesota Press, 1986.
Orwell, George. *The Collected Essays, Journalism and Letters,* Volume 3, *As I Please, 1943–1945,* Sonia Orwell and Ian Angus (eds). Boston: Nonpareil Books and David R. Godine, 2000.
Owen, Wilfred. "Dulce Et Decorum Est." In C. Day Lewis ed. *The Collected Poems of Wilfred Owen.* New York: New Directions Books, 1963.
Pavičić, Jurica. *Ovce od gipsa* [*Plaster Sheep*]. 2nd edition. Zagreb: Konzor, 1998.
—"Moving into the frame: Croatian film in the 1990s," *Central Europe Review*, 2(19), 15 May 2000. Available online at http://www.ce-review.org/00/19/kinoeye19_pavicic.html (accessed 8 November 2011).
—*Split by Night.* Split–Zagreb: Ex Libris, 2004.
Pavličić, Pavao. *Dunav. P.S. Vukovarske razglednice* [*The Danube. P.S. Postcards from Vukovar*]. Zagreb: Znanje, 1992.
Perica, Vjekoslav. "The Catholic Church and Croatian statehood." In Vjeran Pavlaković ed. *Nationalism, culture, and religion in Croatia since 1990.* Donald W. Treadgold Papers in Russian, East European, and Central Asian Studies, no. 32. Seattle, WA: Henry M. Jackson School of International Studies, 2001.
Quart, Barbara Koenig. *Women Directors: The Emergence of a New Cinema.* New York: Praeger, 1988.
Ramet, Sabrina ed. *Gender Politics in Western Balkans: Women, Society, and Politics in Yugoslavia and the Yugoslav Successor States.* University Park: Pennsylvania State University Press, 1998.
—*Balkan Babel: The Disintegration of Yugoslavia from the Death of Tito to the Fall of Milošević.* 4th edition. Boulder, CT: Westview Press, 2002.
—*Thinking About Yugoslavia: Scholarly Debates About the Yugoslav Breakup and the Wars in Bosnia and Kosovo.* Cambridge University Press, 2005.

—Serbia, Croatia and Slovenia at Peace and at War: Selected Writings, 1983-2007. Wien, Berlin: Lit Verlag, 2008.
—ed. Nezavisna država Hrvatska [The Independent State of Croatia]. Zagreb: Alinea, 2009.
Ramet, Sabrina, Konrad Clewing and Reneo Lukić (eds), Croatia Since Independence: War, Politics, Society, Foreign Relations. Munich: R. Oldenbourg Verlag, 2008.
Ramet, Sabrina and Danica Fink-Hafner (eds), Democratic Transition in Slovenia: Value Transformation, Education, and Media. College Station: Texas A & M University Press, 2006.
Ramet, Sabrina and Davorka Matić (eds), Democratic transition in Croatia: value transformation, education & media. College Station: Texas A & M University Press, 2007.
Ramet, Sabrina and Vjeran Pavlaković (eds), Serbia Since 1989: Politics and Society Under Milošević and After. Seattle: University of Washington Press, 2005.
Revija slobodne misli. 10(43–4), January–June. Sarajevo: Krug 99, 2004.
Rizvić, Muhsin. Bosanskohercegovačke književne studije [Bosnian-Herzegovinian Literary Studies]. Sarajevo: Veselin Masleša, 1980.
Rorty, Richard. Contingency, Irony, and Solidarity. Cambridge: Cambridge University Press, 1989.
Rusinow, Dennison. The Yugoslav Experiment: 1948–1974. Berkeley: University of California Press, 1977.
Selimović, Meša. Derviš i smrt [Dervish and Death]. Sarajevo: Svjetlost, 1970.
—Death and the Dervish [Derviš i smrt]. Trans. Bogdan Rakić and Stephen M. Dickey. Evanston, IL: Northwestern University Press, 1996.
—The Fortress [Tvrđava]. Trans. E. D. Goy and Jasna Levinger. Evanston, IL: Northwestern University Press, 1999.
Šerbedžija, Rade. Do posljednjeg daha: Autobiografski zapisi i refleksije [To the Last Breath: Autobiographical Notes and Reflections]. Zagreb: Profil International, 2004.
Silber, Laura and Allan Little. Yugoslavia, Death of a Nation. New York: TV Books (distributed by Penguin USA), 1996.
Simmon, Cynthia. "Women engaged/engaged art in postwar Bosnia: Reconciliation, recovery, and civil society." The Carl Beck Papers in Russian and East European Studies, Number 2005, June 2010.
Singleton, Fred. Twentieth Century Yugoslavia. New York: Columbia University Press, 1976.
Solar, Milivoj. Predavanja o lošem ukusu [Lectures on Bad Taste]. Zagreb: Politička kultura, 2004.

—Uvod u filozofiju književnosti [Introduction to the Philosophy of Literature]. Zagreb: Golden Marketing–Tehnička knjiga, 2004.
—Smrt Sancha Panze i drugi eseji [The Death of Sancho Panza and other essays]. Zagreb: Golden Marketing–Tehnička knjiga, 2006.
Spahić, Ognjen. Hansenova djeca [Hansen's Children]. Zagreb: Durieux, 2004.
Stiglmayer, Alexandra ed. Mass Rape: The War Against Women in Bosnia-Herzegovina. Lincoln, NE, and London: University of Nebraska Press, 1994.
Tängerstad, Erik. "Before the Rain—After the War?" Rethinking History 4(2), July 2000; 175–81.
Tomić, Ante. Zaboravio sam gdje sam parkirao i druge priče [I Forgot Where I Parked and Other Stories]. Zagreb: Hena Com, 2001.
—Što je muškarac bez brkova [What is a Man Without a Moustache]. Zagreb: Hena Com, 2002.
—Ništa nas ne smije iznenaditi [Nothing Should Surprise Us]. Zagreb: Fraktura, 2003.
Ugrešić, Dubravka. The Culture of Lies. University Park: Pennsylvania State University Press, 1998. (Croatian edition 1996.)
Uzunović, Damir. Kesten [The Chestnut]. Sarajevo: Soros Foundation, 1996.
Veličković, Nenad. Đavo u Sarajevu [The Devil in Sarajevo]. Split: Feral Tribune, 1998.
—Sahib: Impresije iz depresije [Sahib: Impressions from Depressions]. Split: Feral Tribune, 2002.
Velikonja, Mitja. Titostalgia: A Study of Nostalgia for Josip Broz. Ljubljana: Peace Institute, 2009.
Vidan, Aida and Gordana P. Crnković (guest eds). In Contrast: Croatian Film Today. KinoKultura Special Issue 11: Croatian Cinema, May 2011. Available online at http://www.kinokultura.com/specials/11/croatian.shtml (accessed 8 November 2011).
—"A conversation with Vinko Brešan: No aesthetics without ethics." In In Contrast: Croatian Film Today. KinoKultura Special Issue 11: Croatian Cinema, May 2011. Available online at http://www.kinokultura.com/specials/11/croatian.shtml (accessed 8 November 2011).
Vucinich, Wayne S. ed. Contemporary Yugoslavia: Twenty Years of Socialist Experiment. University of California Press: Berkeley and Los Angeles, 1969.
—ed. Ivo Andrić Revisited: The Bridge Still Stands. Berkeley: University of California, Berkeley, International and Area Studies, 1996.
Wachtel, Andrew Baruch. Making a Nation, Breaking a Nation:

Literature and Cultural Politics in Yugoslavia. Stanford: Stanford University Press, 1998.
Weil, Simone. *The Need for Roots: Prelude to a Declaration of Duties Toward Mankind.* Trans. Arthur Wills. New York: Putnam, 1952.
—*Simone Weil: An Anthology.* Sian Miles (ed). London: Virago Press, 1986.
Weschler, Lawrence. *Vermeer in Bosnia: Selected Writings.* New York: Vintage Books, 2005.
Westling, Louise. "Literature, the environment, and the question of the posthuman." In Catrin Gersdorf and Sylvia Mayer (eds), *Nature in Literary and Cultural Studies: Transatlantic Conversations on Ecocriticism.* Amsterdam: Rodopi, 2006.
Wittgenstein, Ludwig. *Culture and Value.* Trans. Peter Winch, ed. G. H. von Wright in collaboration with Heikki Nyman. Chicago: University of Chicago Press, 1984.
Zaninovich, M. George. "The Yugoslav Variation on Marx." In Wayne S. Vucinich ed. *Contemporary Yugoslavia: Twenty Years of Socialist Experiment.* Berkeley: University of California Press, 1969.
Žižek, Slavoj. "Multiculturalism, or the cultural logic of multinational capitalism," *New Left Review* 225, September–October 1995.
Zlatar, Andrea. *Tekst, Tijelo, Trauma: Ogledi o suvremenoj ženskoj književnosti [Text, Body, Trauma: Essays on Contemporary Women's Literature].* Zagreb: Naklada Ljevak, 2004.

Films

Armin (2007). Directed by Ognjen Sviličić. Berlin: Absolut Medien, 2009. DVD.
Čovek nije tica [Man Is Not a Bird] (1965). Directed by Dušan Makavejev. Irvington, NY: The Criterion Collection, 2009. DVD.
Gori vatra [Fuse] (2003). Directed by Pjer Žalica. New York: First Run Features, 2006. DVD.
Grbavica: The Land of My Dreams (2006). Directed by Jasmila Žbanić. United States: Strand Releasing Home Video, 2007. DVD.
Kajmak in marmelada [Cheese and Jam] (2003). Directed by Branko Đurić Đuro. Ljubljana: ATA Produkcija, 2004. DVD.
Kako je počeo rat na mom otoku [How the War Began on My Island] (1996). Directed by Vinko Brešan. Zagreb: "Orfej" HRT, 1997. VHS.
Kod amidže Idriza [At Uncle Idriz's] (2004). Directed by Pjer Žalica. Sarajevo: Refresh Production, 2005. DVD.
Ljeto u zlatnoj dolini [Summer in the Golden Valley] (2003). Directed by Srđan Vuletić. Sarajevo: Refresh Production, 2005. DVD.

Loves of a Blond (1965). Directed by Miloš Forman. Irvington, NY: Criterion Collection, 2002. DVD.

Maršal [*Marshal Tito's Spirit*] (1999). Directed by Vinko Brešan. Zagreb: HRT, Interfilm, 1999. Film.

Nije kraj [*Will Not End Here*] (2008). Directed by Vinko Brešan. Zagreb: Interfilm, 2008. Film.

Ples v dežju [*Dance in the Rain*] (1961). Directed by Boštjan Hladnik. Ljubljana: Filmski sklad Republike Slovenije: Andromeda d.o.o. [distributor], 2005. DVD.

Pred doždot [*Before The Rain*] (1994). Directed by Milcho Manchevski. Irvington, NY: Criterion Collection, 2008. DVD.

Rane [*Wounds*] (1998). Directed by Srđan Dragojević. New York: First Run Features, 2000. DVD.

Rondo (1966). Directed by Zvonimir Berković. Zagreb: Jadran Film, 1966. Film.

Savršeni krug [*Perfect Circle*] (1997). Directed by Ademir Kenović. Sarajevo: Refresh Production, 2006. DVD.

Šelestenje [Murmurings] (2002). Directed by Janez Lapajne. Ljubljana: Filmski sklad Republike Slovenije: Andromeda d.o.o. [distributor], 2005. DVD.

Snijeg [*Snow*] (2008). Directed by Aida Begić. Sarajevo: mamafilm, distrib. by Tropik i Film Video, 2008. DVD.

Surogat [*Ersatz*] (1961). Directed by Dušan Vukotić. On *The Best of Zagreb Film: Be Careful What You Wish For and the Classic Collection*. Chatsworth, CA: Rembrandt Films, 2000. DVD.

Sve džaba [*All For Free*] (2006). Directed by Antonio Nuić. Zenica: Tropik Film & Video, 2008. DVD.

Svjedoci [*Witnesses*] (2003). Directed by Vinko Brešan. New York: Film Movement, 2007. DVD.

Varuh meje [*The Border Guard*] (2002). Directed by Maja Weiss. Distributed under the title "Guardian of the Frontier." Ljubljana: Filmski sklad Republike Slovenije: Andromeda d.o.o., 2005. DVD.

INDEX

An "n." after a page number indicates a footnote; page number in italics indicates a figure.

91.6 MHz
   as archive 42
   community 44–5, 48–9, 50, 56–7
   ethnicity 42–4, 49n. 9, 51–2
   everyday life 45–8
   immediacy 41–2
   language 49n. 9, 49–52, 56–7, 58–60, 61–2
   as novel 41
   as personal record 41–2
   playfulness 58–61
   storyline 42–4, 46–7

abortion rights 235–6n. 8
   curtailed 228n. 6
Agamemnon 1–2
Alexander, Ronelle 171n. 27
alienation 29–30
All for Free 130n. 4, *146*
   disempowerment 147
   freedom 145–6
   past in 131, 147
   storyline 145
   structure 145–6
   unpredictability 145–8
anarchy 260, 262, 278–9
Anatomy Lesson, The 202
Andrić, Ivo 107–8, 108n. 4, 125–6
   pathways 35, 35–6n. 27

Armin 130n. 4, *134*
   hyperreal settings 134–5
   past in 132–4
   systemic settings 135
At Uncle Idriz's 140–1, *141*
   community 141–3
   light and dark 141
   past in 131
   scope 142
   storyline 141–2
aura 74–5, 76, 77, 78
   disparities 75
Auty, Phyllis 28

Bakhtin, Mikhail 75n. 7
Balašević, Đorđe 204–6, 208–9, 211, 212n. 4
   on anti-nationalism 218–20, 220n. 11
   on ethnicity 218–20
   on language 211–12, 221
beauty 16–17
   happiness and 124
   individual life and 123, 124
   shame and 13, 16
Before the Rain 79, 79–80n. 1, 84, 87
   children 94n. 20, 97–103, 99n. 29, 101n. 31, 104–5
   coexistence 96–7
   disparities 90
   ethnicity 80
   fairy-tale settings 99
   language 83–4, 89–90, 91–2,

91n. 15, 92n. 16, 92–3n.
  17, 97
 laying down 96
 listening 82, 83–4, 85–7, 88–9,
  92–3n. 17, 92–5, 99, 99n.
  29, 103–4, 105–6
 natural world 97–9, 98n. 27,
  101–2
 pathways 31–2, 80
 religion 87–8, 88n. 13
 scope 82, 82n. 4
 seeing 81, 81–2n. 4, 82
 storyline 80, 89–90
 structure 80–1
Belgrade 67–8n. 3
Benjamin, Walter
 on aura 74–5
 on self-expression 236
Berger, John 127n. 2
Berman, Russell A. 225–6n. 4
bodies 64–6, 67, 68, 69–70,
  263–9, 270–1, 272–4, 275,
  278–9
Border Guard, The 224, 225, 237
 characters 224–5
 community 240–1, 242, 243
 dance 240, 241–3
 disempowerment 232–4,
  237–8, 239–40
 ethnicity 226–8, 229, 231, 239
 fairy-tale settings 232
 gender issues 224–5, 227,
  228–30, 231–8, 239–40,
  241, 242, 243–4
 goals 234
 insularity 231, 234, 235
 natural world 228
 past in 241, 243–4
 pathways 33–4
 privilege 235–6
 scope 225–6, 228, 231, 244
 seeing 230–1
 self-expression 231, 236–7

 sexual issues 227, 228–30,
  231–4, 235
 storyline 224–5, 231–2
 unreal settings 231–3
Bosnia and Herzegovina 5–6 *see
  also individual terms*
Bosnian Chronicle 108
 community 112–13
 scope 113
Brešan, Vinko 175–6, 199–201
 on ethics 199
 on freedom 197
Bridge on the Drina, The 108
 art 110–11
 community 110–12
 scope 111–12, 113
Brown, Norman O. 263

Čadež, Tomislav 157n. 7
Cage, John 8
carnival themes 179–81, 184
Cassese, Antonio 136
Čengić, Enes 17n. 8
censorship 57
Cheese and Jam 34
children
 adults and 94n. 20, 101, 102,
  103
 fairy-tale settings 99
 as game masters 100–1, 101n.
  31, 102
 language 97
 natural world 97–9
 silence 100, 102–3, 104–5
Clausen, Christopher 60
comedy 19, 20, 176, 183–4
 scope 176–7, 180–1, 181n. 9
community 141–2
 breaking point 56, 69, 70, 164
 disparities 26–7, 56–7, 137–8,
  139, 150, 152, 166–7,
  187–8, 190, 198, 240–1,
  242, 243

ethnicity and 42–3, 44–5
home and 181–2, 195
individual life and 21–2,
  110–13, 200, 240, 241–2,
  243, 255
language 49, 50, 56–7
logic, truth, and 255
scope 60, 138–40, 142–3, 169,
  177, 184, 197–8, 199n. 21
self-awareness and 48n. 8,
  48–9
conformism 172–4
corporate concerns 137–8, 140n.
  14
Corradi Fiumara, Gemma
  on language 96
  on listening 84, 85–6, 94, 94n.
  20, 94n. 21 94n. 22, 104n.
  32, 105
Croatia 5–6 *see also individual
  terms*

dance 240n. 15
  disparities 240, 241n. 16,
  241–3, 242n. 16
Dance in the Rain 240n. 15
Death and the Dervish 11, 12,
  22–3, 79
  beauty 13, 16
  community 26–7
  eternity 25–6
  fear 27
  goals 23, 26–7
  instruction 23–5
  knowledge 26
  pathways 31–2, 80
  scope 26
disempowerment 151, 277–8
  disparities 232–4, 237–9, 238n.
  11, 238n. 12, 239–40, 242,
  242n. 16
  unpredictability and 143–5,
  147

Dizdar, Mak 153
Dnevnik 17, 17n. 8
Đurić Đuro, Branko 223, 223n. 1
  pathways 34

eco-criticism 99n. 29
Eighth Representative, The 34
Erceg, Heni 213–16, 216n. 9
Ersatz 12, 12n. 2, *13*
eternity 25–6
  individual life and 119–20,
  121–2, 124
  religion and 121
ethics 23–6, 199
  disparities 194–7, 198, 276
  instinct and 144–5
  limitations 73–4
  logic, truth, and 255–7
ethnicity 170
  breaking point 43–4, 49n. 9,
  53–4, 54–5n. 16, 80, 136,
  161n. 11, 194–5, 262
  community and 42–3, 44–5
  disparities 20–1, 32–4, 146–7,
  226–8, 229, 231, 239
  invisibility 49–50n. 9
  language and 91, 91n. 15
  lies and 155n. 5, 156n. 6, 158,
  164–5
  religion and 20n. 13, 87–8,
  88n. 13
  rumor and 51–6, 55n. 17
  scope 35–6n. 27, 49n. 9, 156n.
  6, 199, 218–20
everyday life 45, 221
  breaking point 46–7
  playfulness 47–8
  scope 45–6
Ex Ponto 107, 108
  art 115, 116
  eternity 119–20
  fragmentation 114–16, 118–19
  religion 116–17, 118

scope 113, 114–15
structure 113–14
victimization 114–20, 125

fairy-tale settings 85n. 9, 145, 232
natural world and 99
fear 27
formlessness 64–6, 67–70, 68–9n. 4
freedom 76, 77–8, 197
unpredictability and 143, 145–6
Friedman, Victor A.
on clothing 90n. 14
on language 91n. 15
on seeing 81–2n. 4
Fuse 128f.
past in 127–9, 131, 132
seeing 127–9
storyline 127–8
unreal settings 127–9

Gadamer, Hans-Georg 83
Gagnon Jr., V. P.
on ethnicity 55 n. 16, 156n. 6
on protest 66n. 2
Garden, Ashes 17–18
gender issues 14 n. 5, 235–6n. 8
disparities *see individual terms*
limitations 234–7, 236–7n. 10, 239–40, 241, 242
scope 243–4
Glavašević, Siniša 57, 58
goals 23, 249–50, 276, 277, 278
disparities 30
limitations 26–7, 234–5
Gojanović, Vladimir 199n. 21
Grbavica: the Land of My Dreams 149
community 150, 152
disempowerment 151
gender issues 148–51
past in 148–9, 150–2, 152n. 16

religion 152, 152n. 16
sexual issues 148–50, 151
storyline 148
structure 149–50
victimization 148–9, 150–1
grotesque realism 75–6, 75–6n. 7

happiness, beauty and 124
Hawkesworth, Celia 108n. 4
Heidegger, Martin
on language 95–6
on listening 83, 84–5
history 5, 7, 8–9, 9n. 14, 18, 39, 40, 41, 46–7, 53–4, 125, 185, 188–9, 188n. 17, 188-9n. 18
scope 27–8, 177–8, 177–8n. 3, 178n. 4, 178n. 5, 179
as stream of consciousness 12–16, 13–14n. 5, 30–1
unknowable 10, 11–12
see also individual terms
home 262
community and 181–2, 195
nation and 181–2
Horvat, Ksenija Vidmar 243n. 19
Hotel Zagorje 130
How the War Began on My Island 179
carnival themes 179–81
characters 178–9
comedy 176–7, 180–1, 181n. 9
community 177, 181–2
scope 177, 178, 182
storyline 177, 178–9
unpredictability 178–9
Huizinga, Johannes 47–8, 47–8n. 6
hunting 101
natural world and 98–9

I Forgot Where I Parked and Other Stories

ethnicity 158
lies 157, 158
scope 157–8
In the Hold 63
  aura 74–5, 76, 77, 78
  characters 71–5, 76–8
  community 69, 70
  freedom 76, 77–8
  grotesque realism 75–6, 75–6n. 7
  language 76, 77
  storyline 63–4
  structure 71–2
  uncontrolled settings 64–6, 67–71
  unreal settings 64–6, 67–71, 76–7
  wakefulness in 70–1
individual life
  anti-nationalism and 218–20
  beauty and 123, 124
  community and 21–2, 110–13, 200, 240, 241–2, 243, 255
  disparities 23–5
  eternity and 119–20, 121–2, 124
  religion and 123–4
  scope 177, 180–1, 181n. 9, 182
  victimization and 115–17, 118–20, 121–3, 124–6
insanity 276
  logic, truth, and 249, 252, 253
instruction 23–5
  on knowledge 3–4
  limitations 24, 25
insularity 231, 234, 235
intensity of life 13, 15, 45
Iordanova, Dina 80n. 1
"It is Glorious to Die for One's Homeland" 215

Jakovljević, Branislav 69n. 4
Jalušič, Vlasta 228n. 6, 238n. 11, 238–9n. 12
Karanović, Mirjana 34
Kardov, Kruno 49–50n. 9
Kiš, Danilo 17–18, 207, 216n. 9
  on anti-nationalism 213, 215, 216n. 9
  pathways 35, 36
knowledge
  arts and 1, 3–5
  disparities 15, 15n. 6, 26
  limitations 1–3
  scope 4–5, 35–6
Koran 23, 24, 26
Kosovo 5–6 *see also individual terms*
Kovačević, Dušan 207
Krleža, Miroslav 17, 17n. 8
  on history 38–9
  on language 17n. 8
  pathways 35, 36–9
  on science 38
  on socialism 37
  on technology 37–8
Kurelec, Tomislav 175n. 2
  on comedy 181n. 9

language 17n. 8, 76, 77, 97, 202
  breaking point 56, 204
  death-affirming 92–3n. 17
  disparities 50, 211, 211–12n. 3
  ethnicity and 91, 91n. 15
  immediacy 41–2
  life-affirming 92n. 17
  listening and 83–4, 92–3n. 17
  as personal record 41–2
  playfulness 58–60
  rumor 50–6
  scope 50, 56–7, 61–2, 95–6, 170–1n. 27, 170–2, 195–6, 206–7, 211–12, 221
  silence and 89–90, 91–2, 92n.

16, 92-3n. 17, 95, 165–6, 167
spoken and unspoken 49, 49 n.9
Lazarus Project, The
  anarchy 260, 262, 278–9
  bodies 263–9, 270–1, 272–4, 275, 278–9
  ethnicity 262
  goals 276, 277, 278
  knowledge 3
  lives and completeness 268, 271–9
  past in 260–2
  storyline 260–1, 265–7, 269–70
  structure 260–2, 265
  unreal settings 263–5, 266–9, 270–1, 272–3, 275, 278–9
  young and old characters 261, 264, 265–70, 273, 278–9
Levi, Pavle 19
lies 166
  ethnicity and 155n. 5, 156n. 6, 158, 164–5
  history and 66, 66n. 2, 67, 67–8n. 3, 185–7
  religion and 155n. 5
  scope 155–7, 161–2, 163, 164–5, 167–8, 172, 185–6n. 13
  see also rumor; truth
lifestyles 236–7, 236–7n. 10
Lipavsky, Leonid 69n. 4
listening
  inner self and 105–6
  language and 83–4, 92–3n. 17
  limitations 83
  natural world and 99
  scope 82–3, 84–5, 94n. 21, 94n. 22, 94–5
  seeing and 95n. 23

silence and 85–7, 88–9, 92–4, 95, 99–100n. 29, 103–4, 104n. 32, 105, 106
Little, Allan
  on ethnicity 49n. 9, 54n. 16, 55n. 17
  on lies 67–8n. 3
Ljubljana
  community 242, 243
  dance 241n. 16, 241–3, 242n. 16
  disempowerment 242, 242n. 16
  gender issues 242, 242n. 16, 243–4
  past in 241–2, 243–4
  seeing 241–2n. 16
  sexual issues 242n. 16
logic and truth
  attraction and 249–50
  breaking point 245–7, 246, 248–9, 257–8
  cataloguing 251–2
  community and 255
  disparities 247, 258
  ethics and 255–7
  insanity and 249, 252, 253
  as non-communal 252–4
  as pragmatic 251–2
  repulsion and 248–9
  scope 245, 247–8, 254–5, 258–9
  success and 249–50
  taste and 256–7
  worldview and 256
loneliness *see* logic and truth
Lovrić, Jelena 185
Lukić, Slavica 53–4, 161n. 11

Macedonia 5–6 *see also individual terms*
Magaš, Branka 14n. 5
Makarushka, Irena 88n. 13

Makavejev, Dušan 18n. 9
  on ethnicity 20–1
  Man is Not a Bird 12, 18–19, *19*,
    21
  comedy 19, 20
  community 21–2
  ethnicity 20
  storyline 19–20
Manchevski, Milcho
  on fairy-tale settings 85n. 9
  on natural world 98n. 27
Marshal Tito's Spirit 182, *183*
  carnival themes 184
  comedy 176, 183–4
  community 184, 187–8, 190
  past in 183–5, 187–91
  scope 191
  storyline 183–4, 190–1
Matanović, Julijana 158–9
materialism 235, 236–7, 250
media
  censorship 57
  community and 56–7, 60
  lies 67–8n. 3
  playfulness 58, 60
  rumor and 50, 51–2, 55n. 17,
    55–6
  scope 213–16
Merleau-Ponty, Maurice 99–100n.
  29
mimesis 132–3
  limitations 133–4
Mirković, Alenka 40–1, 46–8
  on language 49n. 9, 50
  on playfulness 58–9, 60–1
  on rumor 53
Montenegro 5–6 *see also*
  individual terms
Muslims 20n. 13

nationalism 54, 196, 231,
  239
  anti-nationalism 179–80,
    213–16, 216n. 9, 218–20,
    220n. 11
  breaking point 203
  disparities 217–18, 226n. 5,
    226–8, 229–30, 233,
    240–1
  individual life and 177, 180–1,
    181n. 9, 182
  lies and 164–5
  listening and 88
  rumor and 52
  scope 177–8, 225–6
natural world 98n. 27, 101–2
  disparities 228
  fairy-tale settings and 99
  hunting and 98–9
  listening and 99
  silence and 97–8, 99
Neher, André 92n. 16
neo-avant-garde 27
No Man's Land 129–30
non-alignment 27–8
Nothing Should Surprise Us
  159–60, 169
  characters 169–71, 173–4
  community 169
  conformism 172–4
  ethnicity 170
  language 170–2
  lies 172
  pathways 34, 173–4
  storyline 169–70
Nussbaum, Martha Craven 1–2,
  3, 4

Okey, Robin 186
On the Edge of Reason 1, 245
  community 255
  goals 249–50
  logic, truth, and 246–7,
    248–50, 251–9
  storyline 246–7
  victimization 251

298 INDEX

Orwell, George 154
  on lies 155

past into present 127–9, 131, 132, 151–2, 188–9, 200, 260–2
  betrayal 131–2
  disempowerment 151
  disparities 137, 148–9, 185–8, 190, 243n. 19
  everyday life and 221
  future and 150–1, 241–2, 243–4
  lies and 185–6n. 13, 185–7
  limitations 148
  mimesis from 132–4
  performance 183–5, 189–91
  religion 152n. 16
  scope 138–40, 158–9, 192–3, 194–5
  unpredictability 147
pathways 31–9, 35–6n. 27, 80, 173–4, 197–8, 200
Pavičić, Jurica 161
peace 136–7n. 12
  war and 136–7
Perica, Vjekoslav 185–6n. 13
photography 275, 277
  scope 277–8
Plaster Sheep 159–60
  community 164, 166–7
  ethnicity 161n. 11, 164–5
  language 165–6, 167
  lies 161–2, 163, 164–5, 166, 167–8
  oppressed city 160, 162–3, 166, 167, 168
  pathways 197–8
  storyline 160–1, 162, 167–8
  uncontrolled settings 163–4, 166
  see also Witnesses
playfulness 58–61, 277
  death and 60

everyday life 47–8
Pride and Prejudice 2
privatization 190
privilege 235–6
protest 65–7, 66n. 2, 67–8n. 3

Rabelais, François 75, 75–6n. 7, 179–80
Ramet, Sabrina P.
  on gender issues 14n. 5, 238n. 12
  on lies 155n. 5
  on war 31n. 25
Reid, Paul 9n.1 4
religion 116–17, 118, 121, 152n. 16
  disparities 152
  eternity and 121
  ethnicity and 20n. 13, 87–8, 88n. 13
  individual life and 123–4
  lies and 155n. 5
  peace and 136–7, 136–7n. 12
  scope 138, 139
  war and 69
Roads 127
rumor
  ethnicity and 51–6, 55n. 17
  spread 50–6
  see also lies; truth
Rusinow, Dennison 15n. 6

Sarajevo 276
science 38
Scusa Signora 12
seeing 81, 81–2n. 4, 82
  disparities 230–1
  limitations 241–2n. 16
  listening and 95n. 23
  scope 127–9
self-awareness 48n. 8
  limitations 48–9, 72–3
self-expression

limitations 231, 236–7
see also language; silence; talking
Selimović, Meša 16–17, 17n. 7
Šerbedžija, Rade 18, 32–3, 33n. 26
  ethnicity 32–3
  pathways 32–3
Serbia 5–6 *see also individual terms*
Serbian culture in Croatia 202–3
  Balašević 204–6, 209, 211–12, 220–1
  breaking point 203, 204, 210–11
  disparities 210, 217–18
  Kiš 207, 213, 215
  Kovačević 207
  language 204, 206–7, 211–12, 221
  past in 221
  scope 203, 204, 207–8, 209–10, 221–2
  The Wounds 206–7, 216–17
sexual issues
  breaking point 148–50, 151
  disparities 227, 228–30, 231–4, 242n. 16
  limitations 235
shame, beauty and 13, 16
Silber, Laura
  on ethnicity 49 n. 9, 54–5n. 16, 55n. 17
  on lies 67–8n. 3
silence 274, 275
  language and 89–90, 91–2, 92 n. 16, 92n. 17, 95, 165–6, 167
  listening and 85–7, 88–9, 92–4, 95, 99–100n. 29, 103–4, 104n. 32, 105, 106
  natural world and 97–8, 99

talking and 100–1, 102–3, 104–5
Singleton, Fred 22
sleep, wakefulness and 70–1
Slovenia 5–6 *see also individual terms*
Snow 137, *138*
  community 137–40
  corporate concerns 137–8, 140n.1 4
  past in 132, 137, 138–40
  religion in 138, 139
  storyline 137–8
socialism 37
  disparities 238, 243nn. 18–19
  performance 183–5
socio-economic issues 18–19
  disparities 29, 30, 31, 187–8, 190
  scope 29–30, 184
socio-political issues 17, 18–19, 37
  conformism and 172–3
  disparities 15, 15n. 6, 16, 19–20, 22, 29, 30–1, 157n. 7
  fear in 27
  lies and 172
  performance in 183–5
  scope 27–8, 29–30
  see also ethnicity
Sontag, Susan 259
Split 160–1, 161n. 11, 162–3
Star is Born, A 2–3
Stipetić, Zorica 188n. 17, 188–9nn. 17–18
story-telling 275–7
  limitations 275
  logic, truth, and 249–50
Summer in the Golden Valley 144
  disempowerment 143–5

fairy-tale settings 145
freedom 143
storyline 143
unpredictability 143–5

talking
  scope 142
  silence and 100–1, 102–3, 104–5
Tanović, Danis 129–30
taste, logic, truth, and 256–7
technology 37–8
Tito, Josip Broz 28, 182–3, 184, 188–9, 188n. 17, 188–9n. 18, 190–1
Tomić, Ante
  on lies 157, 158
  pathways 34
Top List of Surrealists 34
Travnik 112–13
truth 127, 153
  history and 9–10, 49
  scope 157, 157n. 7
  victimization and 117
  see also lies; logic and truth; rumor

unpredictability 74, 76–8, 101–2, 143–4, 145, 146–7, 178–9, 192, 194, 195–6
  disempowerment and 143–5, 147
  freedom and 143, 145–6
  instinct and 144–5, 147–8
Unrest 108
  beauty 123, 124
  eternity 121–2, 124
  fragmentation 121
  religion 121, 123–4
  scope 120
  structure 120–1
  victimization 109–10, 121–3, 125

van Beek, Martijn 156n. 6
victimization 108, 114–15, 148–9, 150–1
  disparities 117–18, 213–16
  individual life and 115–17, 118–20, 121–3, 124–6
  as pragmatic 251
  truth and 117
  victories and 109–10
Vidan, Aida 206n. 2
Visković, Velimir 157n. 7
Vukotić, Dušan 12
Vukovar 49–50n. 9, 72–3 *see also 91.6 MHz*
Vurušić, Vlado 186n. 13

wakefulness, sleep and 70–1
war 31, 31n. 25, 46–7, 53–4, 64, 72–3, 125
  scope 70, 153, 251, 253, 254, 262
  see also individual terms
Ways of Seeing 127n. 2
weapons 101–2
Weschler, Lawrence 136
West, the 35–6, 132–3
  limitations 132–3n. 5, 133–4, 135, 190
Westling, Louise 99–100n. 29
When the Pumpkins Blossomed 173–4
Why Did I Lie to You 158–9
Will Not End Here 199, 200
  ethnicity 199
Witnesses 193
  characters 197–8
  community 195, 197–8, 200
  distancing 193–4
  ethics 194–7, 198
  ethnicity 194–5
  language 195–6
  mixed reception 198–9n. 21
  past in 192–3, 194–5

pathways 197–8
storyline 192–3, 196–7, 198, 198n. 21
structure 192–3, 194–5
unpredictability 192, 194, 195–6
see also Plaster Sheep
Wittgenstein, Ludwig
  on history 178
  on knowledge 3–4
  work 45
worldview, logic, truth, and 256

Wounds, The 206n. 2, 216–17, 218
  disparities 217
  language 206–7
  scope 206
WR: Mysteries of the Organism 20–1

Zagreb 133–4, 161n. 11, 204–5
Zaninovich, M. George 29–30
Zlatar, Andrea 41
Žnidaršič, Jonas 226n. 5

www.ingramcontent.com/pod-product-compliance
Lightning Source LLC
Chambersburg PA
CBHW070017010526
44117CB00011B/1605